PUSH

Pray until something happens,

ACTS

A New Testament Commentary

Bob Yandian

Linda needs a gift of healing or gift of miracles

James - list ... prayer (realm of Spirit)

God will not do anything for you because He has already given you the power to do it.

To be healed you must get in the realm of the Spirit.

Fast for the realm of Spirit

My soul his to come with my Spirit.

Acts: A New Testament Commentary

ISBN: 978-1-68031-083-2
© 2016 by Bob Yandian
Bob Yandian Ministries
PO Box 55236
Tulsa, OK 74155
www.bobyandian.com

Published by Harrison House Publishers
Tulsa, OK 74155
www.harrisonhouse.com

19 18 17 16   10 9 8 7 6 5 4 3 2 1

Printed in the United States of America .

Table of Contents

ACTS

VERSE BY VERSE COMMENTARY

The personal study notes of BOB YANDIAN

Introduction

My heart echoes a statement Peter made in his last epistle:

For this reason I will not be negligent to remind you always of these things, though you know and are established in the present truth.

2 Peter 1:12

The "for this reason" was to build on his previous statement — Peter's desire for all believers not just to get to heaven, but to have an abundant entrance into heaven. A working knowledge and practice of the word of God is necessary for an abundant entrance, which is marked by rewards and rulership.

In order to establish that abundant entrance, Peter taught believers what they should know repeatedly, "though you know them." What was taught them was the present truth. The present truth is what was being written in the day of the apostles Peter, Paul, John, and James.

This present truth is what believers still need to be gloriously saved. The Old Testament is to be studied in the light of the New Testament epistles. The four gospels are to be studied in the light of the New Testament epistles. Not only should every Christian know the epistles, they should be established in them.

This is why I have written this series of books, verse-by-verse teachings on the epistles of Paul, Peter, John, and James. This is truly meat for our time period, our dispensation: the church age.

Bob Yandian
Author

11

Acts Overview

Writer: Luke

Time: 61–66 AD

Occasion: The book of Acts was written during the time Paul was writing the four prison epistles. This book continues where the book of Luke ends and could be entitled Second Luke. Acts begins with the end of the earthly ministry of Jesus and covers the formation and development of the church. In essence, it is the passing of the torch from Jesus to the church. The human subjects change in the book, but the message and the Holy Spirit's anointing remain the same.

Theme: The central theme is the diminishing of the Jew and the increasing of the Gentiles. This theme is found in Acts 1:8, in Jesus' command to preach the gospel in "Jerusalem, and in all Judea and Samaria, and to the end of the earth." This is also the outline of Acts. The gospel begins in Jerusalem where the first church is established (chapters 1–7). Samaria will come next, with the ministry of Phillip (chapter 8). The book will end with the Gentile revivals in Antioch and Ephesus with Paul as the main minister (chapters 9–28).

Background: The day of Pentecost began a new dispensation, the "mystery," which was unknown to the Old Testament prophets. Another name for this new dispensation is the "church age" or "the dispensation of grace." The major difference between the Old and New Testaments is the new ministry of the Holy Spirit. The Holy Spirit was present in the Old Testament, but would only anoint specific individuals for specific purposes. The day of Pentecost introduced the new birth and the infilling of the Holy Spirit to empower believers to fulfill the great commission.

The Local Churches
- Chapters 2–10: Jerusalem
- Chapters 12–17: Antioch
- Chapters 18–20: Ephesus

The Predominate Characters
- Chapters 1–5: Peter
- Chapters 6–7: Stephen
- Chapters 8–12: Barnabas, Philip, and Saul of Tarsus
- Chapters 13–28: Saul as Paul

1:1–26 After the Cross

The Challenge of Chapter One

Like Jesus, one day all believers will receive an eternal, resurrection body. Until that time, we need the power of the Holy Spirit to be witnesses in the earth. No longer are we required to wait for the promised Holy Spirit as the disciples did on the day of Pentecost. Since that time, He is available to all who will receive Him.

Those first disciples wanted to know when Jesus would come to establish His kingdom on earth. Today, many Christians ask the same question. But Jesus' answer remains the same, "It is not for you to know the times or the seasons, which the Father hath put in his own power" (v. 7). Instead, Jesus points the attention of the disciples toward the promised Holy Spirit, which would enable them to be witnesses throughout the entire earth. We must be careful not to make the same mistake Peter did by making decisions according to the flesh and doing that which the Lord did not instruct him to do. It is easy to do things that seem good and right but are not according to God's perfect plan and purpose.

I. Waiting for the Promise (1–5)

Luke addresses the book of Acts to Theophilus, a born-again Roman dignitary. Luke recounts the events following the resurrection of Jesus, including the forty days He walked among the disciples and His command for them to wait for the promised Holy Spirit.

A. Opening Salutation

1:1 ¶ The former account I made, O Theophilus, of all that Jesus began both to do and teach,

Theophilus (meaning loved of God) is a born-again dignitary in Rome. Luke addressed the books of Luke and Acts to him (Luke 1:3). In Luke's gospel, Theophilus is called "most excellent," which is an address for his nobility. Luke, being a physician, was familiar with many wealthy and powerful people in the Roman Empire.

Luke is the only Gentile author in the New Testament. The gospel of Luke began the story of the works and teachings of Jesus. The book of Acts continues the story. Jesus not only taught the people, he also performed miracles and healings. The church in Acts was to follow this pattern of doing and teaching (Acts 8:6).

> **1:2 until the day in which He was taken up, after He through the Holy Spirit had given commandments to the apostles whom He had chosen,**

The book of Luke brings us to the day of the resurrection (Luke 24:51) but no further. Acts chapter one continues recording the events of the same day where the gospel of Luke ends. Jesus gave His disciples the commandment to wait for the Holy Spirit (Luke 24:49).

Jesus had been empowered by the Holy Spirit (Isaiah 11:2–3, 61:1–2) without measure (John 3:34). He began His public ministry when He was baptized by John the Baptist. This is when the Holy Spirit came upon Him for supernatural ministry. When Jesus became sin for us at the cross, the ministry of the Spirit temporarily ceased (Psalm 22:1, Matthew 27:46) but came upon Him again at the resurrection (Romans 8:11, 1 Peter 3:18). Then the Holy Spirit empowered Jesus in His resurrection body (Acts 1:2) as well as the eleven apostles who were chosen by the Lord Jesus.

B. The Resurrection Appearances of Jesus

> **1:3 to whom He also presented Himself alive after His suffering by many infallible proofs, being seen by them during forty days and speaking of the things pertaining to the kingdom of God.**

To whom (disciples) also he showed himself alive after his passion (suffering) by many infallible proofs, being seen of them forty days, and speaking of the things pertaining to the kingdom of God,

Pentecost is fifty days after Firstfruits, the day Jesus was raised from the dead. He walked among the disciples for forty days leaving ten days for the disciples to wait in Jerusalem in the upper room. These ten days are the subject of chapter one.

1. Before His ascension, Jesus made appearances to:

    a) Mary Magdalene and the other Mary (Matthew 28:1, 9–10)

    b) Peter (1 Corinthians 15:5)

    c) Two believers on the road to Emmaus (Mark 16:12; Luke 24:13)

    d) Ten of the disciples (Thomas was not present — John 20:19–25)

    e) The eleven disciples (John 26–29)

f) Seven disciples by the Sea of Galilee (John 21:1)

g) Five hundred believers at once, probably at the ascension (1 Corinthians 15:6, Acts 1:3–11)

h) His half-brother, James (1 Corinthians 15:7)

i) The eleven disciples on the mountain near Galilee (Matthew 28:16–17)

2. After the ascension, Jesus appeared to:

a) Stephen (Acts 7:56)

b) Paul on the road to Damascus (Acts 9:3–4)

c) John on Patmos (Revelation 1:12–13)

After the resurrection, Jesus had a different body than He had on earth; He had a resurrection body, so many did not recognize him right away.

C. The Command to Wait

1:4 ¶ And being assembled together with *them*, He commanded them not to depart from Jerusalem, but to wait for the Promise of the Father, "which," *He said*, "you have heard from Me;

The formation and development of the church begins in Jerusalem, the very place where Jesus was rejected, crucified, and became sin and sickness for mankind. The city of the curse now became the city of blessing to the rest of the world — Judea, Samaria, and the uttermost parts of the earth.

The promise of the Father includes both the new birth and the infilling of the Holy Spirit (John 14:12–17, 15:16, 16:7–15).

1:5 for John truly baptized with water, but you shall be baptized with the Holy Spirit not many days from now."

Matthew 3:11 records John's prophecy: "I indeed baptize you with water unto repentance: but he that cometh after me is mightier than I, whose shoes I am not worthy to bear: he shall baptize you with the Holy Ghost, and with fire." John compares his own water baptism of Jesus to the Spirit Jesus would send on the day of Pentecost.

II. Jesus' Ascension (6–11)

Jesus gives His final instructions to the disciples concerning the Holy Spirit, and they watch while He ascends into heaven. As the disciples stand gazing, two angels appear and speak to them of the second coming.

A. The Establishment of the Kingdom

1:6 Therefore, when they had come together, they asked Him, saying, "Lord, will You at this time restore the kingdom to Israel?"

This is a selfish request because they want Jesus to remove the Roman rulers and usher in the millennium. Jesus has just finished teaching about the baptism of the Spirit, which is an introduction to the church age. But the disciples are thinking in terms of the old covenant and desire the millennial kingdom to be established in the earth.

1:7 And He said to them, "It is not for you to know times or seasons which the Father has put in His own authority.

And he said unto them, It is not for you to know the times (*chronos*) or the seasons (*kairos*), which the Father hath put in his own power (*exousia*).

The Greek word *chronos*, translated time, refers to the successive time of chronological events and, more specifically, means each passing moment. This word is typically connected with history. From this point on, Israel's history is hidden from the disciples. They don't know their nation will be destroyed, the Jews dispersed and persecuted, and, after going through tribulation, eventually restored as a people and a nation.

The Greek word *kairos*, translated seasons, refers to a specific period of time such as a dispensation or section of time. The disciples also don't understand the church age is coming. They won't learn about the church age until after Pentecost when they are taught by the Holy Spirit. Jesus is telling them their questions are premature.

B. Power to Be Witnesses

1:8 But you shall receive power when the Holy Spirit has come upon you; and you shall be witnesses to Me in Jerusalem, and in all Judea and Samaria, and to the end of the earth."

But ye shall receive (*lambano*: seize, take hold of) power (*dunamis*: inherent power), after that the Holy Ghost is come upon you: and ye shall (future tense) be witnesses unto me both in Jerusalem, and in all Judaea, and in Samaria, and unto the uttermost part of the earth.

This is a play on words. The Father has authority over times and seasons, but they will receive authority to be witnesses in the dispensation. Believers have been given power to operate in the times and seasons which come under the Father's sovereignty. We need to be concerned with our dominion, and God will be ruler over His.

The ultimate use of the power of the Holy Spirit is witnessing. Whether the power is released through the gifts of the Spirit or through the words of the disciple's mouths, the final result is the winning of souls. No gift is given to enhance the user or build his reputation. God is interested in spiritual results.

Jesus is preparing the disciples for the mantle of power to witness. Their public ministry, like Jesus', begins after the Holy Spirit comes upon them.

In the new birth, the Holy Spirit comes to live *in* us. Following the new birth, we can receive power after the Holy Spirit comes *upon* us. This event will occur many times in the book of Acts (10:45, 19:6). The gospel will spread from Jerusalem (northern kingdom) and Judea (southern kingdom) to the Gentiles all over the world.

1:9 ¶ Now when He had spoken these things, while they watched, He was taken up, and a cloud received Him out of their sight.

And when he had spoken these things, while they beheld, he was taken up (passive voice); and a cloud (glory cloud) received him out of their sight.

Acts records man's view from earth as Jesus ascends into heaven. Hebrews 1:3 reveals the view from heaven as Jesus ascends: ". . . when he had by himself purged our sins, sat down on the right hand of the Majesty on high." Verse 13 continues, "But to which of the angels said he at any time, Sit on my right hand, until I make thine enemies thy footstool?"

1:10 And while they looked steadfastly toward heaven as He went up, behold, two men stood by them in white apparel,

The two men are angels who have already been with them but have suddenly materialized, appearing to the disciples. Jesus has already seen them, just as He had seen Moses and Elijah on the Mount of Transfiguration.

1:11 who also said, "Men of Galilee, why do you stand gazing up into heaven? This *same* Jesus, who was taken up from you

into heaven, will so come in like manner as you saw Him go
into heaven."

The angels are referring to the second advent, not the rapture of the church.
At the second advent, Jesus will descend through the heavens and touch
the Mount of Olives (Zechariah 14:4).

III. Man Chooses an Apostle (12–26)

As 120 disciples wait in the upper room, Peter addresses the selection of a
disciple to replace Judas.

**1:12 ¶ Then they returned to Jerusalem from the mount called
Olivet, which is near Jerusalem, a Sabbath day's journey away.**

A Sabbath day's journey is approximately three-fifths of a mile (John 11:18).

**1:13 And when they had entered, they went up into the upper
room where they were staying: Peter, James, John, and Andrew;
Philip and Thomas; Bartholomew and Matthew; James *the son*
of Alphaeus and Simon the Zealot; and Judas *the son* of James.**

This may be the same upper room used by Jesus and His disciples for the
last supper (Mark 14:15, Luke 22:11–12). Upper rooms were common
in the time in which Jesus lived, and were usually owned by people who
would rent them out for special occasions.

**1:14 These all continued with one accord in prayer and sup-
plication, with the women and Mary the mother of Jesus, and
with His brothers.**

Along with the eleven disciples are the women who followed Jesus and
ministered to Him (Matthew 27:55, 56, Luke 8:3) Also present are Jesus'
mother and two half-brothers, James and Joses (Joseph Jr.) (Matthew
13:55, Mark 6:3).

**1:15–16 ¶ And in those days Peter stood up in the midst of the
disciples (altogether the number of names was about a hundred
and twenty), and said, 16 "Men *and* brethren, this Scripture had
to be fulfilled, which the Holy Spirit spoke before by the mouth**

of David concerning Judas, who became a guide to those who arrested Jesus;

Peter's address of "men" is to all in the upper room. "Brethren" addresses the other ten disciples.

1:17–18 for he was numbered with us and obtained a part in this ministry." 18 ⸶ (Now this man purchased a field with the wages of iniquity; and falling headlong, he burst open in the middle and all his entrails gushed out.

After Judas had hung himself (Matthew 27:5), no one cut him down. The rope eventually rotted and broke, and Judas's decayed body burst apart and his inner parts gushed out.

1:19 And it became known to all those dwelling in Jerusalem; so that field is called in their own language, Akel Dama, that is, Field of Blood.)

And it was known unto all the dwellers at Jerusalem; insomuch as that field is called in their proper tongue, Aceldama, that is to say, The field of blood.

1:20 ⸶ "For it is written in the Book of Psalms:

'Let his dwelling place be desolate,
And let no one live in it'; and,
'Let another take his office.'

For it is written in the book of Psalms, Let his habitation be desolate, and let no man dwell therein: and his bishopric (oversight) let another take.

1:21–26 ⸶ "Therefore, of these men who have accompanied us all the time that the Lord Jesus went in and out among us, 22 beginning from the baptism of John to that day when He was taken up from us, one of these must become a witness with us of His resurrection." 23 ⸶ And they proposed two: Joseph called Barsabas, who was surnamed Justus, and Matthias. 24 And they prayed and said, "You, O Lord, who know the hearts of all, show which of these two You have chosen 25 to take part in this

ministry and apostleship from which Judas by transgression fell, that he might go to his own place." 26 And they cast their lots, and the lot fell on Matthias. And he was numbered with the eleven apostles.

Jesus did not instruct His followers to go to the upper room and choose an apostle. It was Peter who took it upon himself to lead the group into choosing an apostle to replace Judas.

In Galatians 1:1 Paul calls himself, "an apostle, not of men, neither by man, but by Jesus Christ, and God the Father, who raised him from the dead." The Greek says, "not from the source of men, neither by the source of man."

Apostleship cannot be conferred by a group of men or by an individual. An apostle also cannot be elected by casting lots or by natural birth. Apostleship is sovereignly given by God the Father and the Lord Jesus Christ.

Ephesians 1:1 says, "Paul, an apostle of Jesus Christ by the will of God, to the saints which are at Ephesus, and to the faithful in Christ Jesus." Paul was an apostle not based upon a vote or the selection of men, nor was he qualified because of natural qualifications. He was an apostle by the will of God.

2:1–47 The Outpouring of the Holy Spirit

The Challenge of Chapter Two

At salvation, every believer enters into the fruit of the Spirit. However, the gifts of the Holy Spirit operate in conjunction with the infilling. Since the day of Pentecost, the baptism in the Holy Spirit with the evidence of speaking in other tongues is still available to all believers who will receive. There is no age, gender, or racial distinction.

As Spirit-filled believers, we have the power to be witnesses before anyone who crosses our path. We may not preach to massive crowds as Peter did, but every day we can walk in the power and fullness of the Holy Spirit causing others to be drawn to the Lord Jesus Christ. As with the early church, the Word of God should be the number one priority in our lives. Prayer too, should be part of our daily walk with the Lord as well as fellowship with the saints. The supernatural power of the Holy Spirit flowing in and through our lives should draw people into the church and away from religion.

I. The Day of Pentecost (1–4)

The day of Pentecost marks the fullness of the Holy Spirit being poured out, giving every believer from then until now an opportunity to become like Jesus. The eyes of the disciples are opened to see tongues of fire manifested as evidence of the outpouring of the Holy Spirit. All 120 who are present in the upper room were filled with the Holy Spirit and begin to speak in tongues as the Spirit gives them utterance.

A. The First Advent of the Holy Spirit

2:1 ⁊ When the Day of Pentecost had fully come, they were all with one accord in one place.

And when the day of Pentecost was fully come (*sumpleroo*: completed), they were all with one accord in one place.

In the Old Testament, the ministry of the Holy Spirit was limited in both operation and persons. The church age, beginning on the day of Pentecost, brings the fullness of the Holy Spirit, allowing every believer to become like Jesus Himself.

After the day of Pentecost, every believer in the upper room had become:

1. A born-again child of God
2. A member of the church
3. A part of the body of Christ
4. A full-time minister
5. A part of the bride of Christ
6. Indwelled by the Holy Spirit
7. Filled with the Holy Spirit
8. A vessel for spiritual gifts
9. An ambassador for God

There are two advents of the Holy Spirit, just as there are two advents of the Lord Jesus. The first advent of the Holy Spirit is the subject of Acts 2. This occurred at the beginning of the church age. There are also prophecies that refer to the second advent which will begin the millennial kingdom.

In the Jewish tradition, Pentecost is an important feast day, which occurs fifty days after the Feast of Firstfruits (Leviticus 23:15–17). Pentecost always occurs on a Sunday. The Holy Spirit fulfills Pentecost, and Jesus Christ is our Firstfruits. First Corinthians 15:22–23 says, "For as in Adam all die, even so in Christ shall all be made alive. But every man in his own order: Christ the firstfruits; afterward they that are Christ's at his coming."

The 120 in the upper room were of one accord, one mind, and one purpose. They were in prayer, waiting for the outpouring of the Holy Spirit from the newly resurrected and ascended Lord Jesus.

B. A Sound from Heaven

2:2 And suddenly there came a sound from heaven, as of a rushing mighty wind, and it filled the whole house where they were sitting.

And suddenly there came a sound (*echos*: booming roar) from heaven as of a rushing mighty (violent) wind, and it (the sound, roar) filled all the house where they were sitting.

The work of the Holy Spirit is sometimes progressive in Christian growth, but when His work relates to the giving of a gift or calling, it is an instantaneous work (Acts 16:16–18). This is how the church age began and also how it will end (1 Corinthians 15:51–53, 1 Thessalonians 4:16).

The booming, echoing sound from heaven hit the atmosphere over Jerusalem and descended into the room where the disciples were sitting. Though they were sitting, the position of prayer is not important to the Lord. Prayer is heard whether we kneel or sit. While waiting a number of days for the promise of the Spirit, the disciples probably took on many postures including sitting.

Wind is a symbol of the Holy Spirit (John 3:8). The church began with a noise and it will end with one also — the sound of a shout and trumpet! The church swept in like a wind and it will be swept out like one also.

C. They Began to Speak in Other Tongues

2:3 Then there appeared to them divided tongues, as of fire, and *one* sat upon each of them.

The Holy Spirit and tongues of fire had already arrived, but the disciples could not see them with their physical eyes. Suddenly, what already existed manifested as tongues like fire and the disciples could actually see this manifestation. This is the same way the angels suddenly appeared to the disciples on the Mount of Olives (Acts 1:10), and they way Peter's eyes will later be opened to an angel while he is in prison (Acts 12:7).

The Holy Spirit is one person, but He divides to everyone (1 Corinthians 12:11). On this day, the disciples spoke many languages of men and angels (1 Corinthians 13:1), but all were given by the Holy Spirit. Each tongue over each head represented a language unique to that person. No two from the upper room went into the streets speaking the same language (Acts 2:8–11).

2:4 And they were all filled with the Holy Spirit and began to speak with other tongues, as the Spirit gave them utterance.

And they were all filled (*pletho*) with the Holy Ghost (*pneuma*), and began to speak with other tongues, as the Spirit gave them utterance (the words to speak).

Speaking in tongues began on the day of Pentecost and continued from that day on (Acts 4:31). But the personal experience of speaking in tongues is not one that continues on its own; we must choose to remain filled with the Holy Spirit (Ephesians 5:18). The speaking comes from man, the words we speak come from the Holy Spirit. The language we receive is supernatural, but the Holy Spirit uses our voice and will.

The Holy Spirit came on the first disciples the same way He comes upon us today. When the Holy Spirit comes upon us, He must be received (Acts 8:15), and His words are spoken through us as we are filled (*pletho*) to overflowing.

The disciples had an experience with the Holy Spirit when the tongues like fire sat upon them, but they spoke with tongues when they were filled. When believers now are filled, they also speak with tongues. This has never changed since the day the Holy Spirit was given. The evidence of being filled with the Holy Spirit is speaking in tongues. There may be no initial outward evidence of the Spirit's indwelling (which is the new birth), but the infilling, the coming on and equipping with power, does have a manifestation: speaking in other tongues.

Through the new birth (the indwelling), we enter into the fruit of the Spirit. Through the infilling, we enter into the gifts of the Spirit. The gifts are manifestations of the Holy Spirit (1 Corinthians 12:7) and the initial entering of this area has a manifestation also.

For the disciples, speaking with tongues was a fulfillment of Isaiah 28:9–13. It was also a sign of the coming church age, not only to the believer but also to the Jews concerning their coming destruction and dispersion. This manifestation of the Spirit was heard by the Jews first (Acts 2) and then carried to the rest of the world. Isaiah foretold tongues would be heard by the Jew first as an opportunity to receive the Lord or be destroyed in the upcoming Roman invasion. Tongues was one of three signs given to the Jews in the book of Isaiah.

D. Three Signs Given to the Jews in the Book of Isaiah

1. The Virgin Birth (Isaiah 7:14)
2. Tongues (Isaiah 28:9–13)
3. The Crucifixion (Isaiah 53)

II. The Crowd's Reaction (5–13)

Jews from all around the world are gathered in Jerusalem to celebrate the Feast of Pentecost. The crowds hear the 120 speaking in other tongues and are amazed because they hear the disciples speaking their different languages, and even specific dialects. The disciples are speaking praise and worship to God in tongues unknown to them, but understood by certain Jews who had gathered for the Feast of Pentecost. Some of those who hear accuse the disciples of being drunk because they cannot explain what they are hearing.

A. The Multitude Is Confounded

2:5 ¶ And there were dwelling in Jerusalem Jews, devout men, from every nation under heaven.

These Jews dwelling in Jerusalem are religious Jews from all over the known world. The Jews had gone into all the world to spread the Jewish law and religion (Matthew 23:15) and had returned to Jerusalem to celebrate this feast day.

God chose this day not only as a fulfillment of Pentecost but also for this crowd of religious Jews to hear and receive. These men are bilingual and tri-lingual and probably speak Hebrew and Greek in addition to the language of the nation they are evangelizing. Most of these men had not been born in Jerusalem, but in the nations in which they are presently living. Many of these Jews receive the Lord on this day and take the gospel back into their own countries.

2:6 And when this sound occurred, the multitude came together, and were confused, because everyone heard them speak in his own language.

The Greek for the first part of this verse says, "When this noise was heard abroad." The "sound" from verse 2 is heard all over the city of Jerusalem and brings the crowd together. When the devout, religious Jews come to-gether, they are shocked and speechless because they all hear these illit-erate men speaking in the dialects of the nations in which they are living!

2:7 Then they were all amazed and marveled, saying to one another, "Look, are not all these who speak Galileans?

And they were all amazed (shocked) and marveled (wondered), saying one to another, Behold, are not all these which speak Galileans?

Galileans were usually illiterate, poorly educated, and spoke only Aramaic.

2:8 And how *is it that* we hear, each in our own language in which we were born?

These Jews born in other countries are amazed because the disciples speak the languages as if they are natives. They even speak the dialects of the parts of the countries the Jews are from.

B. Praise to God in Every Tongue

2:9–10 Parthians and Medes and Elamites, those dwelling in Mesopotamia, Judea and Cappadocia, Pontus and Asia, 10 Phrygia and Pamphylia, Egypt and the parts of Libya adjoining Cyrene, visitors from Rome, both Jews and proselytes, 11 Cretans and Arabs—we hear them speaking in our own tongues the wonderful works of God."

. . . Cretes and Arabians, we do hear them speak in our tongues (*glossa*) the wonderful works of God.

Verses 9 through 11 list the countries the Jews are from and the languages they hear spoken. These Jews are from several different areas:

1. Parthia: The Parthians, now eastern Turkey
2. Media: Part of the Chaldean Empire, now Northeastern Iran
3. Judea: The southern kingdom of Israel
4. Cappadocia in Pontus: Part of Armenia

As the disciples speak in tongues, they are not preaching of the gospel, but praising and worshiping God (1 Corinthians 14:2, 17). On this day, no one receives Jesus as savior until Peter quits speaking with tongues and preaches the gospel in a language they can all understand.

God's purpose for the disciples speaking with tongues this day is to edify and build them up while grabbing the attention of those listening (1 Corinthians 14:22).

C. From Shock to Mocking

2:12 So they were all amazed and perplexed, saying to one another, "Whatever could this mean?"

And they were all amazed (shocked), and were in doubt, saying one to another, What meaneth this?

2:13 ⁋ Others mocking said, "They are full of new wine."

New wine was sweet wine, and it took a lot to make a person drunk. The resulting drunkenness was not a great intoxication, but a looseness and joy.

The crowds do not think those filled with the Holy Spirit are drunk because they are falling down or reeling around, but because they are speaking loudly and joyfully in other tongues.

III. Peter Preaches to the Crowd (14–40)

Peter, now filled with the Holy Spirit, preaches his first sermon by explaining what has just happened to the 120 in the upper room. He quotes what was spoken by the prophet Joel concerning the Holy Spirit. Peter then ministers about salvation and the day of wrath that will one day come on the earth. He also quotes a prophecy given by David which has been fulfilled through the death, burial, and resurrection of Jesus. As Peter preaches under the anointing of the Holy Spirit, many are convicted in their hearts.

A. Not Drunk as You Suppose

2:14 ¶ But Peter, standing up with the eleven, raised his voice and said to them, "Men of Judea and all who dwell in Jerusalem, let this be known to you, and heed my words.

But Peter, standing up with the eleven, lifted up his voice, and said unto them, Ye men of Judea (visitors), and all ye that dwell at Jerusalem (home town people), be this known unto you, and hearken to my words (*rhema*):

The preaching of the gospel begins after Peter quits speaking with tongues and begins preaching in the language the people understand. Again, tongues was not given to preach the gospel, but to magnify God and edify those speaking with tongues.

2:15 For these are not drunk, as you suppose, since it is *only* the third hour of the day.

In indignation against the work of the Holy Spirit, these religious men make a case against speaking with tongues. To say the disciples are drunk casts mockery and derision on the credibility of those who are obviously under the control of something supernatural. So Peter explains that these men and women are not drunk. It is only nine o'clock in the morning, and it would be difficult for such a large group to be drunk at this early hour.

2:16 But this is what was spoken by the prophet Joel:

Peter now quotes Joel 2:28 and 29. He turns the crowd's attention to something familiar, the Old Testament prophets. Although Joel was not necessarily prophesying about the coming church age, his prophecy is used by Peter to tell of a similar outpouring of the Holy Spirit at Pentecost (after the second advent of Jesus). This portrays the dual kingdom, the church and the millennium. There is a former and a latter rain spoken of by Joel before he brings out this prophecy of the millennium (Joel 2:23). The former rain was given at Pentecost, and the latter rain will occur at the beginning of the millennium.

B. In the Last Days

> **2:17 'And it shall come to pass in the last days, says God,**
> **That I will pour out of My Spirit on all flesh;**
> **Your sons and your daughters shall prophesy,**
> **Your young men shall see visions,**
> **Your old men shall dream dreams.**

And it shall come to pass (*eimi*: it shall be) in the last days, saith God, I will pour out of my Spirit upon all flesh: and your sons and your daughters shall prophesy, and your young men shall see visions, and your old men shall dream dreams.

The "last days" is a reference to the time period of Jesus' absence from the earth (Hebrews 1:2). The "last days" began at Pentecost and will continue through the rapture of the church and for the duration of the Tribulation.

The church age is God's spiritual preview of the millennial reign of Jesus. During the church age, Jesus rules only over His body, the church; during the millennium, He will rule over the entire earth for one thousand years. Many scriptures dealing with the millennium have a double meaning in the New Testament because they are also speaking of the church age.

The outpouring of the Spirit is for all believers, male and female, young and old. There is no gender or age distinction in the body of Christ (Galatians 3:29). Part of the ministry of the Holy Spirit is supernatural guidance. The Spirit's guidance is no longer confined to the inward voice. Dreams and visions are now available to all who trust in the Lord, young and old, male and female. In the Old Testament, this type of guidance was only given to those who held high spiritual offices. Now it is available to all.

2:18 *And on My menservants and on My maidservants*
I will pour out My Spirit in those days;
And they shall prophesy.

"Menservants" and "maidservants" refer to gender and social distinctions. The Holy Spirit not only cares equally for men and women, He makes no distinction in whether a person is rich or poor or of high- or low-class standing.

Prophecy does not mean everyone will operate as a prophet, but it does mean they will receive spiritual revelation and utter words of edification to other believers (1 Corinthians 14:4).

2:19 *I will show wonders in heaven above*
And signs in the earth beneath:
Blood and fire and vapor of smoke.

20 *The sun shall be turned into darkness,*
And the moon into blood,
Before the coming of the great and awesome day of the
Lord.

All these signs and wonders listed in verses 19 and 20 occur after the outpouring of the Holy Spirit in Acts 2. In Joel 2, these occurrences precede the second advent of the Lord (Matthew 24:29–30); the outpouring of the Holy Spirit will occur "afterward" (Joel 2:28).

2:21 *And it shall come to pass*
That whoever calls on the name of the Lord
Shall be saved.'

Peter uses the last verse of Joel 2 to begin his sermon on salvation from the day of wrath coming on the earth. The Jews listening to the sermon will not face that day but will face the great white throne judgment of the Lord Jesus.

C. Jesus Came to Die

2:22 ¶ **"Men of Israel, hear these words: Jesus of Nazareth, a Man attested by God to you by miracles, wonders, and signs which God did through Him in your midst, as you yourselves also know—**

Ye men of Israel, hear these words; Jesus of Nazareth (humanity), a man (double emphasis on His humanity) approved of God among you by (*dia*: through) miracles and wonders and signs, which God did by him in the midst of you, as ye yourselves also know:

Peter begins his sermon to the Jew first (Isaiah 28:11, Acts 1:8, Romans 1:16). As deity, Jesus did not have to be approved among men, but as humanity He did. Miracles, signs, and wonders are God's stamp of approval on a ministry (Hebrews 2:3–4). Peter tells these men of the signs and wonders Jesus did, but he also reminds them that they already have knowledge of these things.

2:23 Him, being delivered by the determined purpose and foreknowledge of God, you have taken by lawless hands, have crucified, and put to death;

Him, being delivered by the determinate counsel (fixed purpose) and foreknowledge (*prognosis*) of God, ye have taken, and by wicked hands have crucified and slain:

Jesus' primary purpose in coming to earth was not to heal or perform signs and wonders. He came into the earth to die (Hebrews 2:9, Revelation 13:8). This was the determined, fixed will of God from eternity past. Peter informs the Jews that it was not the Romans who crucified Jesus, but them, the religious Jews.

Religion has and always will be the greatest hindrance to the gospel and the greatest persecutor of the church and the believer.

2:24 whom God raised up, having loosed the pains of death, because it was not possible that He should be held by it.

Whom God hath raised up, having (already) loosed the pains (birth pangs) of death: because it was not possible that he should be holden of (held by) it.

God always turns cursing into blessing. This is also His plan for Jesus and for us. Men took the gift of God and crucified Him, but God raised Him up from the dead again. In resurrection, Jesus has greater power than He ever did in His earthly humanity. Through death, He had the right to give this power over to the church, which has just begun.

Here Peter compares the resurrection to a miscarriage. Jesus was in the heart of the earth suffering for our sins and was about to be "born" into death when God raised Him from the dead. Hell had a miscarriage and instead, Jesus was delivered out of the womb of spiritual death and eternal separation from God!

The following passage from verses 25 through 28 is a quote from Psalms 16:8 through 11. This is the second time Peter quotes the Old Testament to document what the Jews have seen.

2:25 For David says concerning Him:

'I foresaw the Lord always before my face,
For He is at my right hand, that I may not be shaken.

David foresaw the Lord being delivered from hell. David also foresaw the time when he would be in paradise observing this spectacle happening in the regions of the dead. (He wrote this passage one thousand years before the resurrection.)

2:26 Therefore my heart rejoiced, and my tongue was glad; Moreover my flesh also will rest in hope.

Therefore (as a result) did my heart rejoice (give glory), and my tongue was glad; moreover also my flesh shall rest in hope:

You can only rejoice and give glory when you are stable, unshaken in your faith and trust in the Lord. Our tongue is present with us in eternity and words of praise can be formed. David's tongue rejoiced because his heart was glad at what it saw. This caused his flesh to rest in the grave with a newfound hope. The hope was his future resurrection based on the resurrection of Jesus.

2:27 For You will not leave my soul in Hades, Nor will You allow Your Holy One to see corruption.

Because thou (God) wilt not leave my soul in hell (Hades), neither wilt thou suffer (allow) thine Holy One (Jesus) to see corruption.

David was in the region of the righteous dead, Abraham's bosom (Luke 16:22). He looked across the impassable gulf (Luke 16:26) and saw Jesus in the regions of the damned, suffering for the sins of all mankind.

He also saw Jesus finish the penalty and receive the power of God to raise Him from the dead. David's courage and stability came from seeing Jesus raised from the dead. The resurrection of Jesus gave David the assurance that he too would be raised up on the day of the great resurrection.

> 2:28 *You have made known to me the ways of life;*
>   *You will make me full of joy in Your presence.'*

D. David the "Seer"

2:29 ¶"Men *and* brethren, let *me* speak freely to you of the patriarch David, that he is both dead and buried, and his tomb is with us to this day.

Men and brethren, let me freely (boldly) speak unto you of the patriarch David, that he is both dead and buried, and his sepulcher is with us unto this day.

David was loved by all Israel. Next to Moses, he was the favorite of the people of God. David had lived in Jerusalem, and the site of his grave was known to the people Peter was preaching to.

2:30 Therefore, being a prophet, and knowing that God had sworn with an oath to him that of the fruit of his body, according to the flesh, He would raise up the Christ to sit on his throne,

Because David was a prophet, he was a seer. He could see future events and accurately record these events through revelation of the Holy Spirit. David saw Jesus, the one prophesied of who would come from his loins and who would be the future and Eternal King over Israel.

In 2 Samuel 7:12–16, God gave David an oath:

> And when thy days be fulfilled, and thou shalt sleep with thy fathers, I will set up thy seed after thee, which shall proceed out of thy bowels, and I will establish his kingdom.

> He shall build an house for my name, and I will stablish the throne of his kingdom for ever.

I will be his father, and he shall be my son. If he commit iniquity, I will chasten him with the rod of men, and with the stripes of the children of men:

But my mercy shall not depart away from him, as I took it from Saul, whom I put away before thee.

And thine house and thy kingdom shall be established for ever before thee: thy throne shall be established for ever.

David now sees how this prophecy will be manifested through the death, burial, and resurrection of Jesus. Jesus would be raised up to sit on David's throne.

2:31 he, foreseeing this, spoke concerning the resurrection of the Christ, that His soul was not left in Hades, nor did His flesh see corruption.

David saw this event centuries before it occurred. He knew Jesus' body and soul would not be left in the earth to see corruption or eternal separation from God.

E. Raised from the Dead

2:32 This Jesus God has raised up, of which we are all witnesses.

Peter is saying, "We have seen the fulfillment of David's prophecy before our very eyes. We are witnesses of the Word of God given through David. The scripture spoke of Jesus."

2:33 Therefore being exalted to the right hand of God, and having received from the Father the promise of the Holy Spirit, He poured out this which you now see and hear.

The humanity of Jesus was lifted up by the power of God the Father and the Holy Spirit (Romans 8:11). He sat down at the right hand of God in heaven. Once Jesus was seated, He gave the Holy Spirit. Jesus first received the promise of the Spirit at the Jordan River and has now given that promise to the church. The promise of the Holy Spirit is not the new birth but the infilling, "which ye now see and hear."

2:34 ¶ "For David did not ascend into the heavens, but he says himself:

> 'The Lord said to my Lord,
> "Sit at My right hand,

For David is not ascended into the heavens: but he saith himself (Psalm 110:1), The Lord said unto my Lord, Sit thou on my right hand,

The Father is called the Lord, and Jesus is called my Lord. Jesus is "my Lord" because He is our personal savior, our link to God, the Lord.

2:35 Till I make Your enemies Your footstool." '

Until I make thy foes (Satan and demons) thy footstool.

Jesus will be seated in heaven throughout the church age and the tribulation. At the end of the tribulation, He will leave His throne in heaven and take His throne on earth for the thousand-year reign, the millennium. During this time, Satan and the demons will be removed from earth and banished to the bottomless pit, awaiting the great white throne judgment.

2:36 ¶ "Therefore let all the house of Israel know assuredly that God has made this Jesus, whom you crucified, both Lord and Christ."

The first church sermon preached is about the resurrection of Jesus. Peter puts the blame for the crucifixion on the shoulders of the religious Jews. He puts the resurrection on the shoulders of God. God took the curse men had created and turned it into a blessing.

F. Holy Spirit Conviction

2:37 ¶ Now when they heard this, they were cut to the heart, and said to Peter and the rest of the apostles, "Men and brethren, what shall we do?"

Now when they heard this, they were pricked (cut, pierced — Hebrews 4:12) in their heart, and said unto Peter and to the rest of the apostles, Men and brethren, what shall we do?

The convicting ministry of the Holy Spirit comes with the preaching of the gospel, especially the resurrection of Jesus. Peter's life has greatly changed, and now the evidence is before him proving it. Religious Jews are asking him how to be saved.

2:38 ⸿ Then Peter said to them, "Repent, and let every one of you be baptized in the name of Jesus Christ for the remission of sins; and you shall receive the gift of the Holy Spirit.

Then Peter said unto them, Repent (*metanoeo*: to change the mind), and be baptized every one of you in the name of Jesus Christ for (*ei*: because of) the remission (pardoning) of sins, and ye shall receive the gift of the Holy Ghost.

Repenting is the other side of believing (Acts 16:31). To repent means to change the mind not about sin, but about Jesus. In the Greek, the word for "repent" is in the active voice, and "be baptized" is in the passive voice. We do not become baptized for the forgiveness of sins, but because of forgiveness. Once we have been saved, we show the outward act, the declaration of forgiveness by being water baptized. This is an outward act signifying a finished inward salvation. Then we are ready to receive the promise of the Father, the infilling of the Holy Spirit. This verse teaches the infilling of the Holy Spirit is received after the new birth — after the remission of sins — and water baptism is an act that follows repentance.

2:39 For the promise is to you and to your children, and to all who are afar off, as many as the Lord our God will call."

For the promise (of the Spirit—Acts 1:4, 2:33) is unto you, and to your children, and to all that are afar off, even as many as the Lord our God shall call (invite).

This verse tells us the infilling of the Holy Spirit is for the many future generations throughout the church age. The invitation from heaven is to repent, be forgiven, and receive the gift of the Holy Spirit.

2:40 ⸿ And with many other words he testified and exhorted them, saying, "Be saved from this perverse generation."

And with many other words (typical of Peter) did he testify and exhort, saying, Save yourselves from this untoward (crooked, perverted) generation.

Peter has done everything he can by preaching the gospel to those present. The Holy Spirit has done everything he can by "pricking" or convicting them of their sins. Now it is time for them to do something. There is only one decision that will save the people from the evil generation they belong to and eternal damnation after death. No one can force a person to be saved. The decision belongs to each person alone.

IV. The Church Is Born (41–47)

After Peter's sermon, approximately 3,000 are added to God's kingdom and the first local church begins. The Word, prayer, and fellowship are all established in the church. Many of the early believers will go on to voluntarily sell their possessions and goods to dispense as needed to various members of the newly formed church body. The Lord added to the church daily.

A. The Success of the Early Church

> **2:41 Then those who gladly received his word were baptized; and that day about three thousand souls were added *to them*.**

Then they that gladly received (*apodechomai*: welcomed) his word were baptized: and the same day there were added unto them about three thousand souls.

These people receive the gospel, are born again, baptized in water, and filled with the Holy Spirit. The first local church is formed around these three thousand who have been born again. The leadership from the 120 will form the first church government and disciple the new converts.

> **2:42 And they continued steadfastly in the apostles' doctrine and fellowship, in the breaking of bread, and in prayers.**

Four areas of successful discipleship are listed in this verse by order of importance. First, a commitment by the disciple to hear the Word of God taught in the local church by those anointed to minister. Notice the Word comes before the fellowship of saints, eating together, or praying together in the early church. Discipleship does not begin with one-on-one relationships but with that dedication to the Word.

Next, fellowship which begins with the Father is established among the individuals within the congregation (1 John 1:3). This fellowship is not necessarily times of prayer but is worship to God and spiritual communion with one another.

The third area mentioned is breaking of bread or covenant meals. In this early church, there are specific times the congregation meets for meals either as a large group or together as small groups of friends.

Finally, these new believers learn to pray individually and in groups (Acts 12:5). The word "prayers" is plural in this verse, and refers to different types of prayer.

2:43 Then fear came upon every soul, and many wonders and signs were done through the apostles.

And fear came upon every soul: and many wonders and signs were done by (*dia*: through) the apostles.

"Fear" describes great reverence for the Lord and the presence of the Holy Spirit. This is the setting for signs and wonders to be performed in the congregation. Miracles begin in the early church through the leadership and later move to the streets and operate through the congregational members.

B. All Things in Common

2:44 Now all who believed were together, and had all things in common,

New believers are now facing a time of catastrophic persecution and are united in helping one another. In no way does this verse promote communism or communal living. Because they are being threatened by the Romans and Jews, these new converts pool most of their possessions to protect them from being taken or destroyed if their lives are not spared by those who oppose them.

2:45 and sold their possessions and goods, and divided them among all, as anyone had need.

No one coerces these believers into selling their possessions and goods; they do so voluntarily, putting everything together to dispense as needed.

The verse does not say they sold all their possessions and goods. Funds were distributed from a "common pot." Chapter 6 deals with the selection of deacons to administer funds because of the inequalities that exist in the distribution.

2:46 ¶ So continuing daily with one accord in the temple, and breaking bread from house to house, they ate their food with gladness and simplicity of heart,

And they, continuing daily with one accord in the temple, and breaking bread from house to house, did eat their meat with gladness and singleness of heart.

Church is a daily activity; believers meet in the church to study the Word and to worship the Lord. They also meet in homes to eat together. They discuss scriptures and their new lives as children of God in the church age. Unity in the local church is the focus of this verse. The early believers are united both in the church and outside of it. Unity provides the power and refreshment of the Holy Spirit (Psalm 133:1–3).

2:47 praising God and having favor with all the people. And the Lord added to the church daily those who were being saved.

The church begins with great power, demonstrations of the Holy Spirit, and favor among the people of Jerusalem. This will change as the religious leaders plot to destroy and dismantle the church. Like the ministry of Jesus, this occurs as the supernatural pulls people into the church and away from religion.

3:1–26 A Call to Repentance

The Challenge of Chapter Three

The whole purpose of miracles, healings, signs and wonders is for people to come to the saving knowledge of Jesus Christ. Born-again, Spirit-filled believers are exhorted to "desire spiritual gifts" (1 Corinthians 14:1). But the operation of spiritual gifts is not intended to draw attention to individuals, rather to cause unbelievers to repent and receive Jesus Christ as their Lord and Savior.

We must never seek the gifts for our own glory. Our motive should always be to glorify the one who made salvation possible and sent the gift of the Holy Spirit to abide with us forever — Jesus Christ!

I. Lame Man Healed (1–11)

Some time after the day of Pentecost, Peter and John are headed to the temple, a lame man asks them for money. This man is well-known because he has asked for alms at the temple gate for many years. This day, however, would be different. Although Peter and John have no money to offer the lame man, Peter, operating in the working of miracles, offers him the healing power of Jesus Christ. When bystanders in the temple see the man walking, they give glory to God and stand amazed at his healing.

A. The Habit of Attending Church

3:1 ¶ Now Peter and John went up together to the temple at the hour of prayer, the ninth *hour*.

Now Peter and John went up (linear action, "continually went up") together into the temple at the hour of prayer, being the ninth hour (3:00 pm).

Going to the temple to pray is something Peter and John do daily. They have developed the habit of attending church (Hebrews 10:25). There is no record of the number of days after Pentecost this event occurs, but enough time has elapsed for Peter and John to establish the habit of attending church.

The day this miracle occurs is probably not the first day Peter and John have seen the lame man at the gate, but this will be a day of divine appointment for the lame man. He will have the faith to be healed, and the crowd is large enough to be affected by the miracle.

The primary purpose of miracles, signs, and wonders is for the salvation of the lost (Acts 1:8).

B. The Lame Man's Daily Routine

3:2 And a certain man lame from his mother's womb was carried, whom they laid daily at the gate of the temple which is called Beautiful, to ask alms from those who entered the temple;

Being laid at the temple gate has been the lame man's daily routine for many years. He is placed at the opening of the temple at the main gate, and all who enter the temple pass by him. If Peter and John had not seen the lame man on this particular day, he would have been seen on many days preceding it.

This man and his condition are well known outside of the temple. Religion has not helped him, but the power of Jesus stands in opposition to religion on this day even as it had during His earthly ministry.

As the man sits at the gate, many pass him on their way into the temple, especially at the hour of prayer when the gate gets very busy. As people pass, the man asks for a small portion of the money they are going to offer in the temple. Their alms are what keep him alive.

Outward problems, like this man's dependency on alms, always have a root cause, and this man does not fully realize that cause. It is not his lack of money, but his lameness. His financial situation is a *result* of his problem, not the problem itself. Peter and John minister to the root of his problem.

3:3 who, seeing Peter and John about to go into the temple, asked for alms.

This man asks to be rid of the symptoms, but Peter and John are going to remedy the cause.

3:4 And fixing his eyes on him, with John, Peter said, "Look at us."

While John and Peter are standing there, the lame man is probably looking beyond Peter and John and trying to catch the attention of others. The man has given them a glance after catching their attention and expects to receive money, but at the same time continues speaking to others. Peter now asks the man to put his attention on them. Faith always demands our full attention.

C. Faith Demands Attention

3:5 So he gave them his attention, expecting to receive something from them.

The lame man's faith is in operation, even if it was for money. Peter uses his attention and simply diverts it toward the Lord; the lame man expects to receive.

3:6 Then Peter said, "Silver and gold I do not have, but what I do have I give you: In the name of Jesus Christ of Nazareth, rise up and walk."

Then Peter said, Silver and gold have I none; but such as I have give I thee: In the name of Jesus Christ of Nazareth rise up and walk (start walking and keep on walking).

Peter does not speak until he has the lame man's attention. He has no money to offer since he had given it all into the common treasury (Acts 2:44–45), but Peter has more than money. He carries the healing authority of Jesus. Peter speaks to the man in the name of the humanity of Jesus Christ. He also commands the man to do what he normally cannot do.

Throughout the Word, healing commands are to be acted upon. Men are commanded to stretch out a withered hand or pick up a bed and walk. Faith demands simple action. Faith acts on the Word it has received, not on the manifestation.

D. A Miracle Performed

3:7 And he took him by the right hand and lifted *him* up, and immediately his feet and ankle bones received strength.

This is an operation of the working of miracles. It is a result of Peter being Spirit-filled. The writer Luke, being a physician, naturally describes the internal results of God's power being manifested in this man's body.

3:8 So he, leaping up, stood and walked and entered the temple with them—walking, leaping, and praising God.

Since the man is healed, he is led to church and willingly follows. The excitement of being healed causes the man to follow Peter and John into the temple. By the time the man enters the church, he has received Jesus as his lord and is on the path toward maturity and becoming a disciple of the Lord. The best time to take a person to church is immediately after they receive the Lord.

3:9–10 And all the people saw him walking and praising God. 10 Then they knew that it was he who sat begging alms at the Beautiful Gate of the temple; and they were filled with wonder and amazement at what had happened to him.

And they knew that it was he which sat for alms at the Beautiful gate of the temple: and they were filled with wonder (awe) and amazement (confusion) at that which had happened unto him.

Because this man is so well known, the miracle in his body is producing an attitude of wonder in the people. This is the purpose of miracles and wonders: to bring attention to the Lord and open hearts to the new birth. This is the time to preach the gospel, and Peter will soon know it.

3:11 ¶ Now as the lame man who was healed held on to Peter and John, all the people ran together to them in the porch which is called Solomon's, greatly amazed.

And as the lame man which was healed held Peter and John, all the people ran together unto them in the porch that is called Solomon's, greatly wondering (completely flabbergasted [Wuest]).

The man is holding on to Peter and John because he has never walked in his life. After the initial leaping and walking, he is still quite shaky and is learning to walk normally for the first time. The miracle has caused a crowd of people to gather under the covered terrace on the east side of the temple.

II. The God of Abraham, Isaac, and Jacob (12–17)

Now at the center of an amazed crowd, Peter directs their attention away from himself and toward God. He explains that the Messiah had already come, but they had rejected Him. He also informs them that the lame man's faith in God brought healing to his physical body.

A. The Crowd's Attention Turned Toward God

3:12 So when Peter saw *it*, he responded to the people: "Men of Israel, why do you marvel at this? Or why look so intently at us, as though by our own power or godliness we had made this man walk?

When Peter sees the amazement of the crowd, he answers the questions they are thinking. Peter begins by letting the people know that this healing has come from God's grace and is not from his works of righteousness. Grace and healing power both come from God.

B. The Messiah Denied

3:13 The God of Abraham, Isaac, and Jacob, the God of our fathers, glorified His Servant Jesus, whom you delivered up and denied in the presence of Pilate, when he was determined to let *Him* go.

Peter informs the crowd that the patriarchs were believers, and the Messiah they had believed in and waited for had already been sent. Jesus had already come, but they denied Him and delivered Him up to be killed. By reminding these religious Jews of Abraham, Isaac, and Jacob, Peter gets their spiritual attention. He then proclaims Jesus as the Messiah as evidenced by God glorifying Him and raising Him from the dead. Most likely these people in the temple are part of the same crowd who stood before Pilate and cried, "Crucify Him!"

3:14 But you denied the Holy One and the Just, and asked for a murderer to be granted to you,

Although Jesus was holy before God and just (innocent) before men, the people had asked for Barabas, a known gangster, to be released in Jesus' place. A guilty man (Barabas) released for the life of an innocent one (Jesus) was a type of what would happen for those in the crowd who will put their trust in Jesus.

3:15 and killed the Prince of life, whom God raised from the dead, of which we are witnesses.

Jesus is the Prince of eternal life (Hebrews 2:10). He was not only raised from the dead, but first born from the dead. The people present that day were witnesses to His death, and they now stood in the presence of witnesses to His resurrection.

C. Faith in the Name

3:16 And His name, through faith in His name, has made this man strong, whom you see and know. Yes, the faith which *comes* through Him has given him this perfect soundness in the presence of you all.

Peter is now giving them the method to receive any blessing from God, whether it be salvation, healing, or temporal needs. We receive by faith and even that faith is not of ourselves, it is the gift of God (Ephesians 2:8–9). Both the ability to receive and the gift come from God. This is grace.

Grace diverts attention away from Peter, John, and even the man who was healed. All attention is now focused on the Lord of their ancestors. Peter is giving them an opportunity to make Him their Lord too.

Peter explains to the crowd that the once lame man had received "perfect soundness." Whatever else might have been wrong with the man as a result of his lameness is made perfectly sound when he was healed.

3:17 ¶ "Yet now, brethren, I know that you did *it* in ignorance, as *did* also your rulers.

After hearing Peter's sermon, the crowd is no longer ignorant.

III. The Messiah Has Come (18–22)

Peter now exhorts the people to stop looking for the Messiah because He has already come. He then calls them to repentance and conversion which will open the doors to the infilling of the Holy Spirit and brings "times of refreshing." Peter encourages the crowd to take heed to what Moses had spoken concerning Jesus.

3:18 But those things which God foretold by the mouth of all His prophets, that the Christ would suffer, He has thus fulfilled.

All of the prophets spoke by the mouth of the Holy Spirit (2 Peter 1:21). Peter is exhorting them to stop looking for the Messiah. Peter is saying,

"The Messiah has come!" This crowd had been a witness to the fulfillment of a major portion of the Old Testament and now they would be held accountable.

A. A Call to Repentance

3:19 Repent therefore and be converted, that your sins may be blotted out, so that times of refreshing may come from the presence of the Lord,

Repent (*mataneo*) ye therefore (turn from something), and be converted (turn toward something), that (for) your sins may be blotted out, when (*opos*: so that) the times of refreshing shall come from the presence of the Lord;

The new birth — repentance, conversion and blotting out of sins — are the door to the infilling of the Holy Spirit. This also reveals that the new birth is not the infilling. The infilling of the Holy Spirit is called the "times of refreshing." This is also the description Isaiah gave (Isaiah 28:11–12). Times of refreshing and the blotting out of sins both come from the presence of the Father. This is the gift of the Father which was "shed forth" from His presence (2:33).

The new birth is also the guarantee of participating in the resurrection of the saints and being a part of the millennial kingdom which was prophesied to them (20–21).

3:20 and that He may send Jesus Christ, who was preached to you before,

This sending is at the second advent, which has been prophesied throughout the Old Testament. These people had heard the passages many times, but did not understand they had crucified and rejected the one who was the fulfillment of Old Testament prophecies concerning the second coming.

B. The Restoration of All Things

3:21 whom heaven must receive until the times of restoration of all things, which God has spoken by the mouth of all His holy prophets since the world began.

Whom the heaven must receive until the times of restitution (restoration) of all things, which God hath spoken by the mouth of all his holy prophets since the world began (from old).

The heavens received Jesus in Acts chapter 1. He will remain in heaven until the time for the restoration of all things: the second advent and millennial reign. Jesus will accomplish the restoration of all things, not the church. We are here and will have momentary and partial victories, but the complete victory will be accomplished by the Lord Jesus at Armageddon. The Alpha must also be the Omega; the beginning must also be the end. He that began a good work will also complete it.

> **3:22 For Moses truly said to the fathers, *'The Lord your God will raise up for you a Prophet like me from your brethren. Him you shall hear in all things, whatever He says to you.***

For Moses truly said unto the fathers, A prophet shall the Lord your God raise up unto you of your brethren, like unto me; him (Jesus) shall ye hear in all things whatsoever he (the Father) shall say unto you.

This quote is a compilation of Deuteronomy 18:15, 18, and 19. Stephen will also quote this later in Acts 7:37. The prophet spoken of in this verse is Jesus. He, like Moses, will be unique. Peter is telling them that their hero, Moses, was telling them to listen to Jesus even as he himself had.

IV. Foretold by the Prophets (23–26)

Peter brings the crowd to a place of decision. They must now choose whether to accept or reject Jesus Christ as their personal Lord and Savior. He highlights the fact that Jesus was given first to the Jew and all that have an opportunity to turn from sin to receive eternal life.

> **3:23 *And it shall be that every soul who will not hear that Prophet shall be utterly destroyed from among the people.'***

This is the end of Moses's word (Deuteronomy 18:19). The word applies to the crowd that stands before Peter. Their eternal life or damnation rests upon their acceptance or rejection of Jesus, the Prophet.

> **3:24 Yes, and all the prophets, from Samuel and those who follow, as many as have spoken, have also foretold these days.**

Yea, and all the prophets from Samuel and those that follow after, as many as have spoken (not all prophets wrote scripture), have likewise foretold of these days.

Samuel was the first prophet and began the school of the prophets. Everyone agrees with Moses, and this crowd now stands in a place of decision.

3:25 You are sons of the prophets, and of the covenant which God made with our fathers, saying to Abraham, 'And in your seed all the families of the earth shall be blessed.'

Ye are the children (descendants) of the prophets, and of the covenant which God made with our fathers, saying unto Abraham, And in thy seed shall all the kindreds of the earth be blessed (Genesis 12:3, 18:18, 22:18, 26:4, 28:4).

The "seed," which would bring blessing was not Abraham but the Lord Jesus, the "seed" of Abraham (Galatians 3:8). The only way to be blessed with the new birth or the infilling of the Holy Spirit is to be in the seed of Abraham.

3:26 To you first, God, having raised up His Servant Jesus, sent Him to bless you, in turning away every one *of you* from your iniquities."

The gospel is to the Jew first (John 1:11, Romans 1:16). However, Jesus came to make salvation possible so all would have an opportunity to turn from iniquities and receive eternal life.

4:1–37 Behold Their Threatenings

The Challenge of Chapter Four

The Word of God instructs us to obey those in authority over us, including government officials, as long as our obedience does not violate the Word of God. So although Peter and John are instructed to no longer preach the gospel, Jesus commanded them (and us) to go into all the world and preach the gospel.

Most of us will never experience the persecution the early disciples faced, but if we are ever in a situation similar to theirs, God will fill our mouths with an answer. God can accomplish much through the unity of believers. When we give willingly to the Lord and walk in unity, favor will be upon our lives and many will be supernaturally ministered to.

I. Peter, John, and the Religious Council (1–23)

Peter and John are brought before the religious council. They want to put a stop to the message Peter and John are preaching. Peter and John are held overnight to be questioned the next day.

Peter, under the anointing of the Holy Spirit preaches a salvation message to the council. Observing their boldness, the council recognizes that Peter and John had been with Jesus. Yet they cannot deny the miracle of the lame man, and they fear the people.

They finally release Peter and John threatening to punish them if they speak about Jesus, but these disciples respond by saying they must obey God. Upon their release, Peter and John go to the local church and report everything the chief priests had said.

A. Peter and John Arrested

4:1 ¶ Now as they spoke to the people, the priests, the captain of the temple, and the Sadducees came upon them,

And as they spake unto the people, the priests, and the captain of the temple, and the Sadducees, (suddenly) came upon them,

Verses 1 through 4 describe the results of Peter's sermon in chapter 3. This captain is in charge of the thirty guards stationed throughout the temple.

Peter's sermon, like Jesus' sermons, will result in the salvation of some and adverse reactions by others. Opposition to Peter's message will come from organized religion, just as it had in Jesus' ministry.

4:2 being greatly disturbed that they taught the people and preached in Jesus the resurrection from the dead.

Being grieved (agitated, displeased) that they taught the people, and preached through Jesus the resurrection from the dead.

These religious men are upset and angered because the disciples preach without first asking their permission. The council is also frustrated because many people believe the message being preached, and the lame man stood before them as evidence of the truth of that message.

Peter is preaching and teaching. (He is teaching because many who had been born again on the day of Pentecost and afterward are present in the crowd [2:41, 47].) Peter once again brings out the essence of the gospel in this sermon just as he had in his first (2:23–31): the resurrection gives the gospel its power to deliver and save. Because Jesus was resurrected, believers will also be raised from the dead (1 Corinthians 15:12–20).

However, the Sadducees do not believe in angels or the resurrection (23:8). It is bad enough for them to hear doctrine they do not believe; it is worse to see the people accepting and following that doctrine.

4:3 And they laid hands on them, and put *them* in custody until the next day, for it was already evening.

And they laid hands (seized violently) on them, and put them in hold (jail cell) unto the next day: for it was now eventide (after 6:00 pm).

The immediate reaction of the religious leaders is an attempt to stop people from being saved. Their efforts will prove ineffective. Even after the arrest of Peter and John, thousands in the crowd will receive Jesus Christ as their Lord.

Because it was illegal to have a trial after sundown, they put them in prison for the night. Interestingly, it was these same Sadducees who had tried Jesus after sundown in a completely illegal manner, just before Passover.

4:4 However, many of those who heard the word believed; and the number of the men came to be about five thousand.

Howbeit many of them which heard the word (*logos*) believed; and the number of the men (males) was about five thousand.

"Howbeit" shows that despite the attempts of the Sadducees, a great number of the crowd believe in Jesus and are born again. It is difficult for the religious leaders to stop people from believing when a miracle standing directly in front of them, and they have just heard the gospel preached under the anointing of the Holy Spirit.

> **4:5 ⸿ And it came to pass, on the next day, that their rulers, elders, and scribes,**

And it came to pass on the morrow, that their rulers (of the Sanhedrin), and elders (of the temple), and the scribes (those who knew Old Testament law),

B. The Council

> **4:6 as well as Annas the high priest, Caiaphas, John, and Alexander, and as many as were of the family of the high priest, were gathered together at Jerusalem.**

Annas was a ringleader in extortion. He headed up a political group that took money from the bandits in the Negev, along the shores of Galilee. This is one area Herod cleaned up. He caught and confiscated the money of many of the bandits who hid in the caves along the shore.

Annas also accumulated money by selling sacrificial animals at inflated prices in the temple. Jesus displayed His disdain for this practice in Matthew 21:12–13 when He overturned the tables of the moneychangers.

Caiaphas was the son-in-law of Annas. They worked together (Luke 3:2; John 18:13, 24). John and Alexander were probably two of Annas's sons. Much of the remaining ruling body of the Sanhedrin was comprised of relatives of Annas and Caiaphas. This ruling body could be labeled a "kangaroo court." It was considered the supreme Jewish court of the land.

There were three parts of the Sanhedrin:

1. The rulers (24): chief priests

2. The elders (24): political leaders

3. The scribes (22): theologians

4:7 And when they had set them in the midst, they asked, "By what power or by what name have you done this?"

And when they had set (stood) them in the (their) midst, they asked, By (in) what power (*dunamis*), or by (in) what name, have ye done this?

Their question is concerning the group with which Peter and John are affiliated. The Sanhedrin is looking for a political or religious group Peter and John represent, much like people today would question the denomination backing a particular minister.

C. Peter Addresses the Council

4:8 ¶ Then Peter, filled with the Holy Spirit, said to them, "Rulers of the people and elders of Israel:

Apparently Peter has been praying in tongues during his night in prison, so he has a ready answer. Here Peter demonstrates the importance of staying filled with the Spirit (Ephesians 5:18). It is the fulfillment of Matthew 10:18–20.

1. The Issue of the Healed Man

4:9 If we this day are judged for a good deed *done* to a helpless man, by what means he has been made well,

Peter is now being sarcastic and embarrassing the court officials. They have asked Peter to name the authority who sent him, but Peter reminds them the whole incident began with the healing of an incurable, well-known cripple, a man who is standing with Peter (14).

Peter recognizes the diversion tactic used by the court. Their strategy is to draw him away from the real issue (the man being healed), but Peter keeps the issue clear and focused.

2. The Stone Which the Builders Rejected

4:10–11 let it be known to you all, and to all the people of Israel, that by the name of Jesus Christ of Nazareth, whom you crucified, whom God raised from the dead, by Him this man stands here before you whole. 11 This is the 'stone which was rejected by you builders, which has become the chief cornerstone.'

Verse 11 is a quote from Psalm 118:22 and 23. It was also quoted by Jesus to the same group of religious leaders in Matthew 21:42 through 44. These verses refer to Jesus and His resurrection. He had been rejected by His own and crucified, but God the Father raised Him from the dead and placed Him as the chief foundation stone of the church. All others are built upon Him (Ephesians 2:20–22).

"Stone" is a common title for Jesus in the Word of God, whether prophetically or symbolically:

> a) The Rock of Salvation (Exodus 17:1–7)
>
> b) The Rock of Judgment (Isaiah 8:14, 1 Peter 2:8)
>
> c) The Rock of Provision (Isaiah 26:3–4)
>
> d) The Foundation Rock (Psalm 118:22–23, Isaiah 28:16, 1 Corinthians 3:11)
>
> e) The Foundation of the Church (Matthew 16:18, Ephesians 2:20–22)
>
> f) The Rock of Judgment for the Unbeliever (Daniel 2:35, Matthew 21:44)

3. Salvation in None Other

4:12 Nor is there salvation in any other, for there is no other name under heaven given among men by which we must be saved."

Peter informs them that Jehovah, the redeemer of the Old Testament, is the same Jesus they crucified. This is the same Jesus in whom Abraham, Isaac, Jacob, Moses, and others put their trust and received salvation.

D. The Council's Response

1. Boldness Observed by Council

4:13 ¶ Now when they saw the boldness of Peter and John, and perceived that they were uneducated and untrained men, they marveled. And they realized that they had been with Jesus.

Now when they saw the boldness of Peter and John, and perceived that they were unlearned and ignorant men, they marveled (wondered); and they took knowledge of (remembered) them, that they had been with Jesus.

Boldness is a manifestation of the infilling of the Holy Spirit. Peter and John are not intimidated or fearful of being before these leaders. The council discerned Peter and John had no formal education, yet were speaking things which could only come by revelation. By remembering Peter and John had been with Jesus in His earthly ministry, they begin to comprehend that the same miracle working power and anointing that had been on Jesus was now on His followers. The counsel were the very ones who put Jesus on the cross, and now they were being confronted by a multitude of "little Jesuses" — Christians.

4:14 And seeing the man who had been healed standing with them, they could say nothing against it.

It is difficult to argue with a miracle, especially when the miracle is widely known and standing before the accusers. Peter, who was speechless at the crucifixion, even denying the Lord, now render these men speechless.

2. The Council Confers

4:15 But when they had commanded them to go aside out of the council, they conferred among themselves,

The council weighed the evidence in secret.

4:16 saying, "What shall we do to these men? For, indeed, that a notable miracle has been done through them is evident to all who dwell in Jerusalem, and we cannot deny it.

Religion is contradictory. It does not care about people, yet it fears them. The real desire of the council is to get rid of Peter and John, but they fear the reaction of the multitudes. The religious leaders recognize it is the people who provide money and power to them, but they care nothing about the people. They do not want to offend the people, yet they realize their religious empire is at stake.

3. The Council's Command

4:17 But so that it spreads no further among the people, let us severely threaten them, that from now on they speak to no man in this name."

The council releases Peter and John with a strong threat that their message go no further, yet the message will soon go worldwide. (Religion fears the name of Jesus because of its power.) Peter and John have broken no laws. In fact, they have healed a person, which should bring praise from the city leaders. Law is supposed to protect people from the evil ones not threaten the innocent.

4:18 ¶ So they called them and commanded them not to speak at all nor teach in the name of Jesus.

Again, it is the name which has so much power that threatens the Sadducees.

4. Peter and John Respond

4: 19 But Peter and John answered and said to them, "Whether it is right in the sight of God to listen to you more than to God, you judge.

Peter tells the council to make the decision for themselves. They are judges over natural men. Now they can be judges over God's will.

4:20 For we cannot but speak the things which we have seen and heard."

Peter and John in essence say, "We are nothing more than errand boys." They tell the Sanhedrin they can only say and do what they saw Jesus say and do.

E. Peter and John Released

4:21 So when they had further threatened them, they let them go, finding no way of punishing them, because of the people, since they all glorified God for what had been done.

The council tell Peter and John they will not beat them, but threaten to do so if they refused to stop preaching in the name of Jesus. The religious leaders do not beat Peter and John immediately because they are heroes in the eyes of the people because of the healing of the crippled man.

4:22 For the man was over forty years old on whom this miracle of healing had been performed.

For the man was above forty years old, on whom this miracle (*semeion*: sign) of healing was shown.

This man who is healed had been laid at the gate since he was young. He had been laid at that same gate for over thirty years and so was recognized and well-known by everyone in the city.

Peter & John

4:23 ¶ And being let go, they went to their own *companions* and reported all that the chief priests and elders had said to them.

"Their own companions" is the church which began in chapter 2. It is the "household of God" (Ephesians 2:19), the local church or expression of His universal church. Persecution did not drive the people away from the church; it drove them to it. The religious leaders did not keep their threats a secret, but made them known to all who were present. Church met each day, and immediately after leaving the Sanhedrin, Peter and John go directly to church.

II. Believers in One Accord (24–33)

In response to the report of persecution, the believers lift their voice to God in unity and release the outcome of the threats against them to the Lord. They acknowledge the guarantee of their deliverance is the resurrection of Jesus Christ. They then pray for boldness to speak the Word of God and for signs and wonders to follow the preaching of the Word.

A. Response to Religious Opposition

4:24 So when they heard that, they raised their voice to God with one accord and said: "Lord, You *are* God, who made heaven and earth and the sea, and all that is in them,

And when they (the congregation) heard that, they lifted up their voice to God with one accord, and said, Lord, thou art God, which hast made (designed) heaven, and earth, and the sea, and all that in them is:

The report of persecution causes the entire congregation to turn their voice to God. They do not become despondent, but instead worship God and put Him in remembrance of His Word.

They remind God the entire universe and earth are made after His own design. God designed the universe, Jesus created it (Colossians 1:16–17). If God had a plan for the earth, He must have a design and plan for His church.

If the earth can cope with opposition in nature, surely God has designed a plan for the church to cope with opposition from religion. If the earth can overcome the curse, so can the church. Even the wicked judges who have just threatened Peter and John are created by God. If God created them, He can also handle them.

4:25 who by the mouth of Your servant David have said:

> 'Why did the nations rage,
> And the people plot vain things?

Ps 2:1-2

Who (Christ) by the mouth of thy servant David hast said, Why did the heathen (national leaders) rage, and the people imagine (meditate on) vain (empty, futile) things?

Old Testament prophets spoke God's Word, not their own (2 Peter 1:21). The minister of the church now quotes Psalm 2, verses 1 and 2, where David prophesied of God's attitude toward national governments who try to stop the impact of gospel on society.

B. To Attack Believers Is To Attack the Lord

Hab 2:1-2

> 4:26 The kings of the earth took their stand,
> And the rulers were gathered together against the
> Lord and against His Christ.'

Psalm 2:2 calls Christ "his anointed." The word "Christ" means "anointed one." Jesus was anointed when he arose from the dead and was seated at the right hand of the Father (Hebrews 1:3–9). Throughout history, the leaders of nations and religions have stood against the Father and against the Lord. They have all fallen, and the congregation knows this situation will be no different. To attack miracles and the message is to attack the Lord; to attack the people of the Lord is to attack the Lord Himself (Matthew 25:40, Acts 9:4).

Blessing (Power) of Lord

4:27 ¶ "For truly against Your holy Servant Jesus, whom You anointed, both Herod and Pontius Pilate, with the Gentiles and the people of Israel, were gathered together

Isa. 43:25-26

Put God in remembrance of what He has done for you.

For of a truth against thy holy child (sinless humanity) Jesus, whom thou hast anointed, both Herod, and Pontius Pilate, with the Gentiles, and the people of Israel, were gathered together,

"Gathered together" fulfills Psalm 2:1. The congregation first applies Psalm 2 to the crucifixion of Jesus. Next, they apply the verse to their own situation. If God could deliver Jesus from the mob of people and evil rulers, bring Him out of hell, and raise Him from the dead to be seated in heaven, He could deliver them from any crisis that comes their way. The same is true for us!

C. The Resurrection: Guaranteed Deliverance

4:28 to do whatever Your hand and Your purpose determined before to be done.

The congregation releases the outcome of the threats of these judges into the hand of God and out of their own hands. They are taking God at His Word that vengeance belongs to Him (Romans 12:19). They are also acknowledging they have more important things to do than try to get even with men who have wrongly accused them. They must spread the gospel and have churches to build. They will do their part and expect God to do His.

Our guarantee of deliverance is the resurrection of Jesus. The crucifixion, attitudes, and actions of the people do not take God by surprise. In His foreknowledge, God knew the action of the people would be against His plan of the cross (2:23). God did not ordain the opposition, but He did know it would happen and planned the resurrection around it. God knows of our problems and has a plan for each opposition (1 Corinthians 10:13). God uses the devices and plans of men to bring glory to Himself and deliverance to us (Romans 8:28).

D. A Prayer for Boldness

4:29 Now, Lord, look on their threats, and grant to Your servants that with all boldness they may speak Your word,

This group of believers is in essence saying, "Lord, the heathen are at it again — they are threatening us." God promised deliverance by the mouth of David, and it is repeated throughout the Old Testament. In their own lifetime, they have seen the crucifixion, burial, and resurrection of Jesus out of the hands of evil men. Now, God will do it again. This occasion took God no more by surprise than any other, including the crucifixion of Jesus. Our attitude in prayer should simply be to bring the accusations of men before the Lord.

The believers in Jerusalem are doing what Hezekiah did when he faced an invasion by the army of Sennacherib. Hezekiah spread the evil report written by the heathen king before the Lord (Isaiah 37:14). The heathen were not bringing an evil report against the people; they were bringing an evil report against the Lord. Both Hezekiah and the congregation of Jerusalem were informing God of what was being spoken about Him. The congregation now asks God for boldness to speak His Word and the name of Jesus even more.

> **4:30 by stretching out Your hand to heal, and that signs and wonders may be done through the name of Your holy Servant Jesus."**

By stretching forth thine hand to heal; and that signs and wonders may be done by the name of thy holy child (spotless humanity of) Jesus.

In addition to asking for boldness, they are asking God for signs and wonders to accompany the preaching of the Word (Mark 16:20). The "hand" of the Lord is the power of the Holy Spirit. This power will work through their hands because they are the body of Jesus in the earth. Their hands and mouths are really His. His words and power are displayed through them.

We have been given dominion over the works of Jesus' hands (Psalm 8:6). Although healing comes through our hands, the power comes from God. We are only agents of God's healing power.

> **4:31 ¶ And when they had prayed, the place where they were assembled together was shaken; and they were all filled with the Holy Spirit, and they spoke the word of God with boldness.**

There are results when true worship and adoration are given to God and His Son, Jesus (16:26). Here God answers their prayer with a wonder: He shakes the meeting place. God also answers their prayer for boldness: They are filled with the Holy Spirit. This group of believers must have gone from praying in a known tongue to praying and praising God in unknown tongues of the Holy Spirit.

E. One Heart

4:32 ¶ Now the multitude of those who believed were of one heart and one soul; neither did anyone say that any of the things he possessed was his own, but they had all things in common.

And the multitude of them that believed were of one heart (love) and of one soul (purpose): neither said any of them that aught of the things which he possessed was his own; but they had all things common.

Not only is this a review of Acts 2:45, but also an introduction to Acts 5. Although all are said to be of one love and purpose toward each other and God, an exception will soon be found in Ananias and Sapphira.

4:33 And with great power the apostles gave witness to the resurrection of the Lord Jesus. And great grace was upon them all.

And with great power (*dunamis*: inherent power) gave the apostles witness of the resurrection of the Lord Jesus: and great grace (favor) was upon them all.

The power referred to is miracle power (1 Corinthians 12:10). The miracle received is semeion, which was found in verse 16. A miracle performed is *dunamis*, found in this verse. This verse also notes that miracles and signs are for witnessing (1:8). Each miracle proclaims that the primary reason Jesus was raised from the dead was to be our personal Savior. One of the benefits following a life of power and holiness is great grace or favor (2:47), which the disciples walked in.

III. Possessions Pooled (34–37)

Many of these first believers sold their land or homes so distribution could be made toward those in need, especially the widows. This giving was strictly voluntary on the part of the people. No one coerced them into doing so.

4:34 Nor was there anyone among them who lacked; for all who were possessors of lands or houses sold them, and brought the proceeds of the things that were sold,

The same thing will happen twice in the next chapter. Barnabas is one individual who will sell his land to give to the gospel and be blessed. He will be truthful with the people and the Holy Spirit. Ananias and Sapphira, however, will lie and receive judgment.

4:35 and laid *them* at the apostles' feet; and they distributed to each as anyone had need.

The giving of possessions is voluntary, and the people are free to participate or not participate. Many choose to pool their possessions, property, and finances because if they don't "own" anything, the government can't take it away. Part of the group who receives benefit from the common collection is the widows (6:1). The pooling of resources does not produce power, but is an outward sign of the unity which the disciples already possess.

4:36 ¶ And Joses, who was also named Barnabas by the apostles (which is translated Son of Encouragement), a Levite of the country of Cyprus,

And Joses (Joseph), who by the apostles was surnamed Barnabas, (which is, being interpreted, The son of consolation), a Levite, and of the country of Cyprus,

This is the beginning of the ministry of Barnabas:
1. He later became a prophet and teacher (13:1, 14:14).
2. He introduces Paul to the other apostles (9:25–27).
3. He began the church at Antioch (11:22–23).
4. He sent for Paul to teach the congregation (11:25–26).
5. He eventually became a pastor at Antioch and missed God through legalism (Galatians 2:13).
6. He finally became reconciled to Paul (1 Corinthians 9:6).

4:37 having land, sold *it*, and brought the money and laid *it* at the apostles' feet.

The church at Jerusalem is the only church that operated in this manner. This does not give the church immunity to persecution or destruction. After Saul's conversion, the church at Jerusalem begins to decline. Paul mentions later in the epistles (to Corinth and Philippi) the great needs at Jerusalem. Offerings will be given and distributed to them as a result. Thessalonica and Philippi will be great contributors to the saints in Jerusalem.

5:1–42 Preaching and Prison

The Challenge of Chapter Five

The following story of Ananias and Sapphira should cause us to examine our own heart motives in giving to the Lord. It should also cause us to realize the seriousness of lying to the Holy Spirit and the results.

We are told in Timothy that "all who desire to live godly in Christ Jesus will suffer persecution" (2 Timothy 3:12), something that we see clearly in chapter 5. Religion hates the gospel and will do everything to stop its influence in the world. But Jesus told us, "In the world ye shall have tribulation: but be of good cheer; I have overcome the world."

Living a godly life according to the Word of God will cause persecution in our lives. Similar to the first apostles, we will suffer tribulation in this life, but we can be of good cheer knowing the gospel cannot be stopped because Jesus has already won!

I. Ananias and Sapphira (1–11)

This chapter highlights the sin unto death as Ananias and Sapphira demonstrate the result of committing that sin. Individual accountability before God is also highlighted.

A. The Sin unto Death

Until this time, the attacks against the church have been external, through the Sanhedrin, the scribes, and the Pharisees. But beginning in chapter 5, the main attacks of Satan turn toward internal dissension.

This sin unto death, unlike the unpardonable sin, is not one particular sin committed exclusively by believers. This sin is the final in a series of sins.

    1. The principle is taught in the Old and New Testaments:

        a) Psalm 118:17–18

        b) Ezekiel 18:23–24

        c) 1 John 5:16–17

    2. There are seven biblical case histories of the sin unto death:

        a) Achan (Joshua 7)

        b) Saul's consultation with the witch of Endor (1 Samuel 28:15–19)

        c) Hezekiah's disobedience (Isaiah 38)

        d) Ananias and Sapphira's lies to the Holy Spirit (Acts 5:1–11)

e) The Corinthian man's incestuous relationship (1 Corinthians 5:1–5)

f) A believer's carnality at the Lord's table (1 Corinthians 11:30–31)

g) Hymenaeus and Alexander's Apostasy (1 Timothy 1:19–20)

B. Ananias Lies to the Holy Spirit

1. Ananias and Sapphira Conspire

5:1 ¶ But a certain man named Ananias, with Sapphira his wife, sold a possession.

Ananias and Sapphira are wealthy land owners in Jerusalem. They probably decide to duplicate Barnabas' gift, but give out of a wrong heart motive.

They are not living to please the Lord but to receive the praise and applause of men. They are carnal. They have been outdone by a spiritual man, Barnabas, and they want to have the attention turned away from Barnabas and toward them.

Many things may inspire us to give. We may be inspired by the example of another who has given, but our giving must always be motivated out of a love for God.

5:2 And he kept back *part* of the proceeds, his wife also being aware *of it*, and brought a certain part and laid it at the apostles' feet.

This sin is parallel to that of Achan in Joshua 7. Ananias and Sapphira do not have to bring the full amount of their possession. There is no pressure by Peter or any other church leader. We give as we purpose in our own heart, not grudgingly or of necessity (2 Corinthians 9:7). The purpose of this story is not to cause people to feel guilty for not giving. The purpose is to prevent people from lying about their giving. Do not give a portion and say you gave all.

Ananias comes to the meeting alone, and Sapphira comes later. They wanted to split the glory and make it last longer. She will arrive approximately three hours later (v. 7).

2. Peter Confronts Ananias

5:3 But Peter said, "Ananias, why has Satan filled your heart to lie to the Holy Spirit and keep back *part* of the price of the land for yourself?

Peter receives a word of knowledge by the Holy Spirit. Satan cannot possess a believer, but can persuade minds when we are carnal. Although Ananias and Sapphira are believers, they are under the control of Satan.

5:4 While it remained, was it not your own? And after it was sold, was it not in your own control? Why have you conceived this thing in your heart? You have not lied to men but to God."

Whiles it remained, was it not thine own? and after it was sold, was it not in thine own power (authority)? why hast thou conceived this thing in thine heart? thou hast not lied unto men, but unto God.

While he owned it and sold it, he was free to do with it as he pleased. The Word is strong on individual ownership of property — free enterprise.

3. Ananias Gives Up the Ghost

5:5 ¶ Then Ananias, hearing these words, fell down and breathed his last. So great fear came upon all those who heard these things.

And Ananias hearing (having heard) these words fell down, and gave up the ghost (his spirit): and great fear came on all them that heard these things.

Even after hearing these words, Ananias has an opportunity to repent. "Having heard" indicates he understands the situation and does not want to admit his sin or repent. This sin is premeditated. Ultimately, he lies to God and dies under the judgment of God, the sin unto death. This judgment brings great reverence to the people of the church.

5:6 And the young men arose and wrapped him up, carried *him* out, and buried *him*.

Ananias is bound up in grave clothes and buried quickly. (Burials were performed immediately in the ancient world.)

The "young men" of the congregation are those studying for the ministry. They could have been students or new converts, but they are doing the tasks of the ministry. In the Word of God, the younger men are usually responsible for the work of the ministry in preparation for preaching in the pulpit.

C. Sapphira Lies to the Holy Spirit

1. Peter Questions Sapphira

5:7 ¶ Now it was about three hours later when his wife came in, not knowing what had happened.

Not one man or woman has gone to Sapphira and told her what had happened to her husband. They all stay in the service and worship the Lord. All present have a renewed reverence for the Lord.

5:8 And Peter answered her, "Tell me whether you sold the land for so much?" ¶ She said, "Yes, for so much."

Peter gives Sapphira an opportunity to tell the truth before the congregation, but she also lies. She is not held accountable for her husband's sin unless she is in agreement with it. Her answer reveals her heart.

2. Peter Confronts Sapphira

5:9 ¶ Then Peter said to her, "How is it that you have agreed together to test the Spirit of the Lord? Look, the feet of those who have buried your husband *are* at the door, and they will carry you out."

Now a word of wisdom comes to Peter and he explains what is about to happen to her. The same men who had buried her husband will bury her.

3. Sapphira Gives Up the Ghost

5:10 Then immediately she fell down at his feet and breathed her last. And the young men came in and found her dead, and carrying *her* out, buried *her* by her husband.

The same sin brought the same judgment. Ananias and Sapphira are not judged because they did not bring all the money they received. They are judged because they lied.

5:11 So great fear came upon all the church and upon all who heard these things.

The honeymoon period of Acts 2 is over, and a new commitment has settled into the hearts of the people.

This story teaches of the importance of commitment to the Word of God and the local church. Acts 2:42 showed these believers began with a commitment, "they continued steadfastly in the apostle's doctrine."

II. Signs and Wonders by the Apostles' Hands (12–16)

The deaths of Ananias and Sapphira bring great reverence for God. Many other signs and wonders are performed through the hands of the apostles, and although some sinners do not join themselves to the apostles, the church has a good report among them.

As a result of the signs and wonders, new believers are added as the unsaved are drawn to the healings performed.

> **5:12 ¶ And through the hands of the apostles many signs and wonders were done among the people. And they were all with one accord in Solomon's Porch.**

Great reverence for God allows the Holy Spirit to do more signs and wonders through the church leadership.

> **5:13 Yet none of the rest dared join them, but the people esteemed them highly.**

Sinners do not join themselves to the apostles, but speak very highly of the believers and church leaders. The church has a good rapport with people who do not agree with their beliefs and doctrines.

> **5:14–15 And believers were increasingly added to the Lord, multitudes of both men and women, 15 so that they brought the sick out into the streets and laid *them* on beds and couches, that at least the shadow of Peter passing by might fall on some of them.**

More unity brings more signs and wonders. More signs and wonders bring more souls into the kingdom of God. There are so many people receiving the Lord, numbers are no longer mentioned. In chapter 2, three thousand were added. In chapter 4, five thousand were added. Now "multitudes" are added.

The healing ministry brings great popularity to the disciples with the unsaved multitudes who need healing.

Healing comes in many different ways in the Bible. The woman with the issue of blood was healed through the anointing in Jesus' clothes. Paul later sees people healed through handkerchiefs and aprons. The anointing for healing radiates from the minister. Here, Peter's shadow does not heal, but the power of God which radiates through Peter brings the healing. The faith of the people is not in Peter but in God's power.

> **5:16 Also a multitude gathered from the surrounding cities to Jerusalem, bringing sick people and those who were tormented by unclean spirits, and they were all healed.**

Whether through hands, shadows, clothes, or any other means, God's purpose is to heal all just as it is to save all (2 Peter 3:9). These are the same results that accompanied the healing ministry of Jesus. Jesus also healed all (Matthew 4:23, 24, 8:16, Acts 10:38). Now, the disciples continue with Jesus' ministry.

III. The Second Arrest of the Apostles (17–24)

The high priest and Jewish religious leaders are enraged by the popularity Christianity is gaining. They arrest the apostles and put them in prison. As a sign to the Sanhedrin, an angel releases the apostles from prison. The next day, it is reported to the religious leaders that the apostles were found teaching in the temple.

A. The Apostles Thrown in Jail

> **5:17 ¶ Then the high priest rose up, and all those who *were* with him (which is the sect of the Sadducees), and they were filled with indignation,** *Religion people are indignant of christian*

Then the high priest rose up, and all they that were with him (which is the sect of the Sadducees), and were filled with indignation,

Those with the high priest are Annas, Caiaphas, and members of the Sanhedrin. We have already seen them in 4:6. The Sadducees are mentioned because of their stand against angels. Interestingly, it is an angel that God will use to deliver the disciples here and on many other occasions.

> **5:18 and laid their hands on the apostles and put them in the common prison.**

over is man anything

This is the public prison which houses all who have been arrested during the day. They are put in holding cells before they are brought to trial.

B. Angels Deliver the Apostles

5:19-20 But at night an angel of the Lord opened the prison doors and brought them out, and said, 20 "Go, stand in the temple and speak to the people all the words of this life."

The angel is not seen by the prisoners or guards who are close by. For the disciples, the angel's presence confirms that God is pleased with their stand for the gospel and their boldness to minister to the sick in the name of Jesus. The angel also instructs them to teach the whole Word of God.

People being born again because of the preaching of the Word is only the beginning. They must also be instructed in the whole Word of God, so they will not become disciples, not just converts.

5:21 ¶ And when they heard *that*, they entered the temple early in the morning and taught. But the high priest and those with him came and called the council together, with all the elders of the children of Israel, and sent to the prison to have them brought.

While the officers of the Sanhedrin are looking for the prisoners in the jail cells, the disciples are already in the temple teaching. Their deliverance is a clear indication of God's attitude toward governments who try to stop the teaching and ministering of the Word of God. It is also a clear teaching on what our attitude should be toward government leaders who try to restrain the ministry of the Word.

C. Officers Report to Religious Leaders

5:22-23 ¶ But when the officers came and did not find them in the prison, they returned and reported, 23 saying, "Indeed we found the prison shut securely, and the guards standing outside before the doors; but when we opened them, we found no one inside!"

The officers explain to the leaders that they had done their job the night before. The prison doors were not only closed, safety locks were in place and guards were stationed outside the prison doors. Even though no one was inside the prison, the guards had properly performed their duty. In other words, the only explanation for the prisoners being freed is a miracle.

> **5:24 Now when the high priest, the captain of the temple, and the chief priests heard these things, they wondered what the outcome would be.**

The leaders of the Sanhedrin are at a loss for words. Their desire is to keep this movement from growing, and they do not know what to do to stop it.

IV. The Third Arrest of the Apostles (25–27)

When the religious leaders discover the apostles teaching the Word of God in the temple, they arrest them again. Because they fear the crowd's reaction, the captain arrests them quietly.

> **5:25 So one came and told them, saying, "Look, the men whom you put in prison are standing in the temple and teaching the people!"**

The leaders of the government are so out of touch with what has taken place, the disciples are already in the temple teaching the Word of God, and they know nothing about it. While these same leaders are preparing to interrogate the disciples, the disciples are in the temple doing the will of God.

> **5:26 ¶ Then the captain went with the officers and brought them without violence, for they feared the people, lest they should be stoned.**

The first reaction of the captain and officers is to grab the apostles and make a public display of them. However, they recognize the popularity of the disciples, and the people are gathering by the thousands to hear them speak and see the miracles they are performing.

The captain and officers then decide to arrest them without making a scene. They fear the reaction of the crowd.

The disciples willingly go with the temple guards when they are asked, demonstrating their submissive hearts.

V. The Apostles Brought Before the Council (27–42)

The council confronts the disciples about continuing to preach the gospel. But the disciples make it clear they must obey God. Peter then accuses the religious leaders of crucifying Jesus. The council is so enraged they want the disciples to be put to death immediately. Gamaliel reasons with the council, and the council listens. Again they only threaten the disciples and release them. The disciples rejoice at suffering and continue to teach and preach.

A. Interrogation by the High Priest

5:27 And when they had brought them, they set *them* before the council. And the high priest asked them,

Notice the question is not "How did you escape from prison?" The council was afraid of the response they would receive if they asked that question. Instead, they interrogate the disciples over preaching in the name of Jesus.

5:28 saying, "Did we not strictly command you not to teach in this name? And look, you have filled Jerusalem with your doctrine, and intend to bring this Man's blood on us!"

Satan hates the name of Jesus, and religion is backed by Satan and demons. But the name of Jesus has been exalted above them all.

By this time, the teaching of the disciples has saturated Jerusalem and everyone is talking about the words, signs, and wonders of the disciples. Yet these religious leaders believe the disciples are preaching to blame them for the death of Jesus. However, these same leaders had already accepted this blame when Jesus was taken to be crucified (Matthew 27:24–25).

This verse reveals the corruption of the religious leaders. They are more concerned about themselves than the people.

B. Peter's Response

5:29 ¶ But Peter and the *other* apostles answered and said: "We ought to obey God rather than men.

The Bible commands us to obey the laws of the land (Romans 13) because government is of the Lord. But when government oversteps its limits and dictates when and where to preach the gospel, believers must go with the Word. When men in authority contradict God's Word, then and only then do Christians have a right to disobey the law.

5:30 The God of our fathers raised up Jesus whom you murdered by hanging on a tree.

"Our fathers" includes the religious leaders Peter is addressing. These men defied the will of the God they claim to serve.

5:31 Him God has exalted to His right hand *to be* Prince and Savior, to give repentance to Israel and forgiveness of sins.

Peter explains that God overrode their decision to crucify Jesus by raising Him up and giving Him the highest position in heaven. Peter is, in essence, saying, "You are not the leaders over Israel, and your religion does not offer salvation." Jesus is both leader and savior. He is the only one who can remove sin. He is also savior of the nation of Israel.

5:32 And we are His witnesses to these things, and *so* also *is* the Holy Spirit whom God has given to those who obey Him."

Peter and the disciples are natural witnesses. The Holy Spirit is the supernatural witness.

5:33 ❡ When they heard *this*, they were furious and plotted to kill them.

The Greek says, "their heart was divided with rage and anger." While the disciples stood before them, the religious leaders made the decision to put them to death.

C. Gamaliel Speaks

5:34 Then one in the council stood up, a Pharisee named Gamaliel, a teacher of the law held in respect by all the people, and commanded them to put the apostles outside for a little while.

Gamaliel is a respected Pharisee of his day and is the grandson of Hillel who founded a theological school. Gamaliel has oversight of the school and was one of Paul's teachers (Acts 22:3). He requests the disciples be removed from the room for a time so he can discuss the issue with others on the Sanhedrin.

5:35–36 And he said to them: "Men of Israel, take heed to yourselves what you intend to do regarding these men. 36 For some time ago Theudas rose up, claiming to be somebody. A number

of men, about four hundred, joined him. He was slain, and all who obeyed him were scattered and came to nothing.

History (Josephus) tells us that Theudas rose up, caused a small revolution and declared himself to be Messiah. He had approximately four hundred followers. The Romans captured and beheaded him. They left his head in the streets to show the people that Caesar was still lord. Theudas's followers quickly scattered.

5:37 After this man, Judas of Galilee rose up in the days of the census, and drew away many people after him. He also perished, and all who obeyed him were dispersed.

Judas of Galilee rebelled during the taxation recorded in Luke 2:1.

5:38 And now I say to you, keep away from these men and let them alone; for if this plan or this work is of men, it will come to nothing;

Gamaliel is advising the council to remove the pressure and opposition they have against the disciples.

5:39 but if it is of God, you cannot overthrow it—lest you even be found to fight against God."

Gamaliel's argument and advice:
1. If the movement be of man, it will fall apart by itself. Either God or the men involved will destroy it (i.e. Theudas and Judas).
2. If the movement be of God, the Sanhedrin has placed itself in a position of fighting against God.
3. If it is of God, man cannot stop it.
4. Leave it alone.

5:40 ¶ And they agreed with him, and when they had called for the apostles and beaten *them*, they commanded that they should not speak in the name of Jesus, and let them go.

The Sanhedrin agrees with Gamaliel while he is standing before them, but still do their best to hinder the disciples. Their new threats will accomplish no more than their previous threats had. The disciples are resolute in their decision to obey God and preach and teach in the name of Jesus even more than they already had been.

D. The Disciples Depart from the Council

5:41 So they departed from the presence of the council, rejoicing that they were counted worthy to suffer shame for His name.

The disciples are fulfilling Philippians 4:4, 1 Thessalonians 5:18, and James 1:2. They have learned to "count it all joy" when they fall into trials and tests. They consider it an honor to be persecuted for the name of Jesus. They believe it is a mark of blessing to know they have caused enough damage in Satan's kingdom to be persecuted.

5:42 And daily in the temple, and in every house, they did not cease teaching and preaching Jesus *as* the Christ.

The entire congregation meets in the temple, but in every house they meet for meals and fellowship. The persecution does not stop the Word, but increases the teaching and preaching of it.

6:1–15 The First Local Church

The Challenge of Chapter Six

Belonging to and participating in a local church is of utmost importance for every born-again believer. The main function of the members of the local church is to relieve the pastor of the daily responsibilities so he may dedicate himself to prayer and the study of God's Word. Ushers, greeters, counselors, hospital workers, children, and youth workers are all vital to the successful and effectual functioning of the local church.

Just as in the first local church, there are no perfect churches because there are no perfect people. But we can strive to walk free of strife and in the unity of faith with a heart to serve one another in the body of Christ. God offers His divine wisdom to all who will ask. We can walk in the same wisdom in which Stephen operated if we will only ask.

I. The Local Church

Much is written in the New Testament about the daily operation of the local church, especially in the book of Acts. Foundational principles are established because the first local church at Jerusalem is far from perfect. Very little of what is written is being followed today.

A. The Pastor

The pastor is the final authority in the local church, and it's his responsibility is to teach the Word of God. This is his only responsibility. Anything else is subject to his own personal desires, strengths and weaknesses, and ability to delegate. He is given a number of titles:

1. Elder (*presbuteros*): Describes his person and maturity. "The elders which are among you I exhort, who am also an elder, and also a partaker of the glory that shall be revealed" (1 Peter 5:1).

2. Bishop (*episkopos*: overseer): Describes the pastor's responsibility and work. "Take heed therefore unto yourselves, and to all the flock, over the which the Holy Ghost hath made you overseers, to feed the church of God, which he hath purchased with his own blood" (Acts 20:28). Also 1 Peter 5:2: "Feed the flock of God which is among you, taking the oversight thereof, not by constraint, but willingly; not for filthy lucre, but of a ready mind; . . ."

3. Pastor (*poimen*: shepherd): Describes the pastor's spiritual gift, responsibility to his congregation, and his qualifications (Acts 20:28,

Ephesians 4:11, Colossians 1:25–29, 1 Timothy 3:7, 4:15–16, 2 Timothy 4:1–3, Titus 1:5–9, 1 Peter 5:1–4).

4. Deacon (*diakonos*): Describes the pastor's attitude toward the ministry: "But we will give ourselves continually to prayer, and to the ministry of the word" (Acts 6:4).

B. Areas of Responsibility in the Local Church

Other people in areas of responsibility are needed in the local church to enhance the pastor's role.

1. Elders rule and teach, e.g. Sunday school teachers, staff, etc. (Philippians 1:1, 1 Timothy 3:1–7, Titus 1:5–9).

2. Bishops are overseers, e.g. Sunday school superintendents (Philippians 1:1, 1 Timothy 3:1–7).

3. Deacons are helps ministers, e.g. ushers, communion servers, and greeters (Acts 6:3, 1 Timothy 3:8–13).

C. Principles Established in the Local Church

No church is perfect. The government laid down in the word is not rules, but principles. Often, believers want to look back at the early church and emulate its ways. But the early church had strife, schisms, and divisions. We have everything the early church had and more. We have the same problems and the same Holy Spirit, but the word is now complete.

II. Early Development of the Local Church (1–7)

Every growing church goes through pains and difficulties even when disciples are multiplying. Growth in numbers is usually met with murmuring. Most complaints are usually "Things are not like they used to be."

The first major church problem is the treatment of Greek and Hebrew widows. Because the primary responsibility of the apostles is prayer and study, the people choose seven men to alleviate the problem. Again, the Word of God increases and the number of disciples multiply.

A. Murmuring of Grecians Against the Hebrews

6:1 ¶ Now in those days, when *the number of* the disciples was multiplying, there arose a complaint against the Hebrews by the Hellenists, because their widows were neglected in the daily distribution.

And in those days, when the number of the disciples was multiplied, there arose a murmuring of the Grecians against the Hebrews, because their widows were neglected in the daily ministration (*diakonos*).

The first major internal problem of the Jerusalem church is racial. Grecian widows feel they are not being cared for as well as the Hebrew widows. A faction arises as the Greeks rally around their widows.

Inequality probably did exist since the church leaders are Hebrew, but the problem was probably not intentional. The word "ministration" comes from the Greek word *diakonos*, which means service or work. The service being administered is the distribution of food and goods. Those distributing the goods are favoring the Hebrew widows over the Greek.

B. Solution to Inequality

6:2 Then the twelve summoned the multitude of the disciples and said, "It is not desirable that we should leave the word of God and serve tables.

Then the twelve called the multitude of the disciples unto them, and said, It is not reason (pleasing to God) that we should leave the Word of God, and serve (*diakonos*) tables.

The solution proposed by the people is for the church leaders to distribute the provisions. However, the apostles quickly see that their true calling and responsibility is in jeopardy.

The typical solution given by people for solving problems in a church is for the church leaders to personally handle the situations. They desire the pastor to pray for the sick, visit those in prison, and witness to those who need salvation. However, the pastor is not responsible for taking care of everyone, only to ensure that everyone is taken care of.

The true meaning of *diakonos* is brought out in this verse. It is the serving of tables. The deacon's ministry is to serve others. This is the practical side of the ministry. Without the practical side, the Word could not be effectively taught to the people. When numbers increase, organization must change. Change is an important part of any growing organization.

C. The Selection of Deacons

6:3 Therefore, brethren, seek out from among you seven men of *good* reputation, full of the Holy Spirit and wisdom, whom we may appoint over this business;

The first qualification for the newly chosen helpers is an "honest report" (1 Timothy 3:7). They must be well-thought-of throughout the church and the community. Second, they must be filled with the Holy Spirit (Ephesians 5:18) and speak with tongues daily. Finally, they must be filled with the Word (Colossians 3:16), so they can operate in divine wisdom.

The "business" spoken of here is not the financial business of the church. It is "this business" of taking care of the widows. Many churches believe this verse means deacons watch over the business area of the church. But deacons watch over "this business," the serving of the needs of the people.

> **6:4 but we will give ourselves continually to prayer and to the ministry of the word."**

But we will give ourselves continually (primarily) to prayer, and to the ministry (*diakonos*) of the word.

Prayer and preparation of the Word of God takes much time and concentration. Any ministry by a deacon or elder also takes extended times of preparation and concentration. One person, the pastor, cannot do both and effectively feed the sheep (Acts 20:28).

Moses faced the same problem with the children of Israel. His father-in-law, Jethro, proposed the same solution. Moses was to choose men to help him watch over the people so he could minister in prayer and the teaching of the Word (Exodus 18:19–22). In both Exodus and Acts, prayer is mentioned before the ministry of the Word. Prayer hears from God to know His mind concerning what to give to the people. The Holy Spirit is the agent and power of prayer. He leads us into the Word. The pastor is also seen in this passage as a deacon. Just as every believer has work and service to perform, the pastor's duty is to serve the Word of God to the people.

D. Seven Men Chosen

> **6:5 ¶ And the saying pleased the whole multitude. And they chose Stephen, a man full of faith and the Holy Spirit, and Philip, Prochorus, Nicanor, Timon, Parmenas, and Nicolas, a proselyte from Antioch,**

Notice each man chosen has a Greek name. Whether these men are fully or partially Greek is not known. All are probably Greek speaking and understand the needs of the Greek widows.

These are the seven men chosen and presented to the church leadership:

1. **Stephen** means "victor's crown." He is a teacher of the Word of God and will teach with deep conviction before the religious crowd. He is an excellent example and great tribute to the potential of promotion in the office of a deacon (1 Timothy 3:13). Stephen will also become the subject of Acts 7, as well as the first martyr of the church.

2. **Philip** means "lover of horses." Philip will become the subject of Acts 8. He will become the first evangelist of the New Testament (Acts 21:8).

3. **Prochorus** means "leader of a chorus."

4. **Nicanor** means "victorious."

5. **Timon** means "honorable."

6. **Parmenas** means "abiding."

7. **Nicolas** means "victor of the people." Nicolas is a born-again Greek who was also circumcised. He later became apostate and founded one of the early cult movements that opposed Christianity, a group known as the Nicolaitans (Revelation 2:6, 15). He mingled Christianity with the worship of Aphrodite and formed a brotherhood which added other beliefs. Many Christians were drawn away. John associates their teachings with the doctrine of Balaam.

The choosing of Nicolas reveals that regardless of how well leaders are chosen, some will turn away. We sometimes blame ourselves or wonder where we went wrong when individuals turn against us. But this group of believers is doing their best to be led by the Holy Spirit. The seven men selected are even brought before church leadership. Even with all these safety checks in place, Nicolas easily became a deacon in the church.

God does not punish us today for what we will do in the future. He rewards us today for our present faithfulness.

6:6 whom they set before the apostles; and when they had prayed, they laid hands on them.

Although the people chose these seven men, they were ultimately approved by the church leadership. The people may have chosen people who looked good outwardly, but often, leadership is in a position to know things others do not know.

E. Increase of the Word

6:7 ¶ Then the word of God spread, and the number of the disciples multiplied greatly in Jerusalem, and a great many of the priests were obedient to the faith.

Before this time, the number of the disciples was multiplying (v. 1). Now the disciples multiplied greatly because the Word of God increased. When the church leadership is given the freedom to give more of their time to prayer and the ministry of the Word of God, the Word is able to increase. It is a simple progression. When dedicated members of the church (disciples) give themselves to helping the work of the ministry, the pastor is free to give himself in a greater way to prayer and preparation of the Word. The result is an even greater number of disciples arising and multiplying. Those disciples then go out and preach the Word, and the most difficult cases, the religious people, are won to the Lord. Those who witness to the religious crowd are not the pastor and church staff; they are the people of the congregation. One of those deacons who witnessed to the religious crowd was Stephen. He would soon give his life for the gospel.

III. The Arrest of Stephen (8–15)

Stephen, one of the seven men selected to be a deacon, eventually teaches the Word with signs and wonders following. Stephen operates in the wisdom of God, and the religious leaders of the time cannot dispute his wisdom, so they bring false witnesses against him and have him arrested.

A. Dispute Against Stephen

6:8 ¶ And Stephen, full of faith and power, did great wonders and signs among the people.

And Stephen, full of faith and power (*dunamis:* inherent power), did great wonders and miracles (*semeion:* signs) among the people.

Stephen is one who listened to the Word taught in the church. Because of this, faith came, and the power of the Holy Spirit is a result. Stephen witnesses in the city of Jerusalem and signs and wonders follow his teaching ministry, which causes an uproar among the religious leaders.

6:9 Then there arose some from what is called the Synagogue of the Freedmen (Cyrenians, Alexandrians, and those from Cilicia and Asia), disputing with Stephen.

Then there arose certain of the synagogue, which is called the synagogue of the Libertines (liberated slaves), and Cyrenians (a Greek trade center of North Africa) and Alexandrians (Jews from Alexandria), and of them of Cilicia (a city of Asia Minor), and of Asia, disputing with Stephen.

Descendants of Jewish slaves make up the "synagogue of the Libertines." Their ancestors had been slaves under Rome who had been released. They are one of the groups who join together to dispute Stephen. Cilicia is one of the groups mentioned, and from this group comes Saul of Tarsus (7:58). He might have even been one of the men arguing with Stephen.

6:10 And they were not able to resist the wisdom and the Spirit by which he spoke.

And they were not able (*ischus*: endowed with enough) to resist the wisdom (word) and the spirit (anointing) by which he spake.

Stephen's wisdom is from studying the word, and his anointing comes from prayer. If Saul is one of the men arguing with Stephen, we can see his humiliation. New Christians should have been too ignorant to know any of the word, and certainly too ignorant to humiliate a Pharisee in a public debate.

B. False Witnesses

6:11 Then they secretly induced men to say, "We have heard him speak blasphemous words against Moses and God."

Then they suborned (bribed) men, which said, We have heard him speak blasphemous words against Moses, and against God.

Because the Pharisees cannot not out-debate Stephen, they resort to illegal proceedings. Even the accusation is illegal because it is hearsay and not acceptable in court. But this does not matter to the Pharisees. They will falsely accuse Stephen just as they had Jesus.

6:12–13 And they stirred up the people, the elders, and the scribes; and they came upon *him*, seized him, and brought *him* to the council. 13 They also set up false witnesses who said, "This man does not cease to speak blasphemous words against this holy place and the law;

They mention the temple first, and the Word second.

6:14 for we have heard him say that this Jesus of Nazareth will destroy this place and change the customs which Moses delivered to us."

The temple will be destroyed, but it won't be by Jesus. Jesus never said He would destroy the temple, and neither did the early church. The temple would be destroyed later by the Romans (Luke 21:20–24). And by this time, the customs and ceremonies were already changing because Jesus fulfilled them all.

C. Stephen's Face Shines

6:15 And all who sat in the council, looking steadfastly at him, saw his face as the face of an angel.

The men in the courtroom cannot take their eyes off Stephen. God's sense of humor is now displayed. The council has used Moses as evidence against Stephen, but God uses the same confirmation of His presence with Stephen as He had with Moses: Stephen is covered with the glory of God, and his face begins to shine just as Moses' face had (Exodus 34:30). The disciples have also observed this same manifestation of the glory of God, when Moses appeared before Jesus on the mountain (Matthew 17:2).

7:1–60 Stephen's Sermon and Defense

The Challenge of Chapter Seven

Regardless of the circumstances we may face, we must always keep our eyes fixed on God's Word. The Word will give us boldness in the face of religion, false accusations, and even death.

The last enemy to be destroyed will be death (1 Corinthians 15:26). But as believers, we should not fear death. First Corinthians 15:55 says, "O death, where is thy sting? O grave, where is thy victory?" Just as Stephen's eyes are opened to the spirit realm, heaven, and Jesus awaiting him when facing death, the same is true for every child of God. We must not fear death, but live our lives fearlessly proclaiming God's Word, even when confronted with severe opposition.

I. Stephen Testifies (1–50)

In response to false accusations, Stephen preaches a sermon reminding them of those who preceded them. Through recounting the history of Israel and the patriarchs, the Holy Spirit (through Stephen) is revealing to the council that God cannot be confined to a temple made with the hands of men.

A. Abraham

7:1 ¶ Then the high priest said, "Are these things so?"

"These things" is a reference to 6:13–14. In other words, the high priest is asking Stephen, "Are you guilty?" But beginning in verse 2, Stephen will refer to Jesus. Stephen will begin with the call of Abraham and recount the history of Israel up until the time of Moses. He will also show how the ritual and ceremony of the temple is changed by Jesus' fulfillment of the law.

1. A Supernatural Race

7:2 ¶ And he said, "Brethren and fathers, listen: The God of glory appeared to our father Abraham when he was in Mesopotamia, before he dwelt in Haran,

"The God of glory" is the Lord Jesus Christ. Glory is the visible image of God, the manifested presence of deity. Mesopotamia is Ur of the Chaldees (Genesis 12:1–9). Jesus appeared to Abraham when he was a sinner, a Gentile.

He became a Jew when he believed and thus the father of the Jewish nation (Genesis 15:6).

The Jews were the last race to be formed on the earth. All other races were formed from the sons of Noah and were natural races (Genesis 10). Then God dispersed these races (Genesis 11) around the world and confused their languages.

One race that came from Noah was the Chaldeans, who were sons of Shem. They settled in Mesopotamia. God called out one man from this race — Abram — and when he believed in the Lord, God also changed his race. The Jews are a supernatural race. Their origin is not based upon natural seed, but upon faith.

This Jewish race is a type of Jesus, who was virgin born. It is also a type of the church, which is based on spiritual birth, regeneration. The story of Abraham leaving Ur of the Chaldees and traveling to Haran is told in Genesis 11:31.

2. Abraham Instructed to Leave Ur

7:3 and said to him, 'Get out of your country and from your relatives, and come to a land that I will show you.'

The country Abraham was to leave was Ur and the kindred were his father and nephew, Lot. Abraham obeyed the first command, but not the second. He ran into continual trouble until he separated from his father (unbelievers) and Lot (carnal believers).

7:4 Then he came out of the land of the Chaldeans and dwelt in Haran. And from there, when his father was dead, He moved him to this land in which you now dwell.

Abraham was stopped in Haran because he would not fully obey God and separate from relatives. He was in Haran thirteen years until his father died (Genesis 11:31–12:5). Abraham became wealthy in Haran, yet he was miserable.

3. God's Promise to Abraham

7:5 And God gave him no inheritance in it, not even enough to set his foot on. But even when Abraham had no child, He promised to give it to him for a possession, and to his descendants after him.

Abraham was given God's promises while he was in Ur of the Chaldees, and he left for the land promised him in faith. But because of his unbelief, he failed to claim any promise in the land except his son Isaac. When Abraham arrived in Canaan, there was a famine. Rather than standing in faith, he traveled to Egypt.

Eventually, Abraham returned to Canaan, but he brought Egypt with him when he returned with Hagar. For nearly twenty-five years Abraham tried everything in the natural to fulfill the promise God had given him. Haran, Lot, Eliazar, Egypt, Hagar, and Ishmael all had to be dealt with before Abraham would see the fulfillment of any of God's promises to him. After all of these leaning props fell out from under him, Abraham finally leaned on the Word (Romans 4:20–21). God promised it, God would perform it.

7:6 But God spoke in this way: that his descendants would dwell in a foreign land, and that they would bring them into bondage and oppress *them* four hundred years.

Abraham finally became strong and trusted God even to the point of offering Isaac. He knew God would raise him from the dead (Genesis 22). Under Isaac, the Israelites continued downhill until they went into captivity under Joseph. Seventy-five people went into captivity and, four hundred years later, two million came out.

7:7 'And the nation to whom they will be in bondage I will judge,' said God, 'and after that they shall come out and serve Me in this place.'

4. The Covenant of Circumcision

7:8 Then He gave him the covenant of circumcision; and so *Abraham* begot Isaac and circumcised him on the eighth day; and Isaac *begot* Jacob, and Jacob *begot* the twelve patriarchs.

Circumcision was instituted to show the coming new covenant — the new birth. It was a continual reminder of Israel's spiritual foundation, a nation which began supernaturally after all other races and nations. Circumcision meant new beginnings. Children were circumcised on the eighth day. The number eight meant nothing to the Jews. They would have related more to the number seven (Sabbath, Jubilee, etc). Circumcision was also a continual reminder of the Abrahamic covenant, which was established on faith.

Having the father or doctor perform the circumcision was a reminder of the grace of God. As the child grew, his circumcision was a sign of something that occurred while he was completely dependent. Finally, circumcision was a reminder of the coming Messiah.

Today, we do not worship on the seventh day or even the first day. We worship on the eighth day. We are living in the new covenant, the day of new beginnings (2 Corinthians 5:17).

B. Joseph

1. Sold Into Slavery

7:9 ¶ "And the patriarchs, becoming envious, sold Joseph into Egypt. But God was with him

The brothers who sold Joseph into slavery were a type of the Jews who crucified Jesus. The patriarchs sold Joseph to the Gentiles to get rid of him and unknowingly sold themselves into slavery for the next four hundred years. God was with Joseph and he became the governor over the Egyptians, the Gentiles. The Jews (especially Judas) "sold" Jesus to the Romans, yet he went on to become the head of the church. Meanwhile, the Jews have gone into dispersion and will remain in that condition until Jesus returns.

2. Governor of Egypt

7:10 and delivered him out of all his troubles, and gave him favor and wisdom in the presence of Pharaoh, king of Egypt; and he made him governor over Egypt and all his house.

Just as Joseph was raised from prison, Jesus was raised from the dead and hell. Just as God favored Joseph, God favored Jesus, made Him the head of the church, and gave Him dominion in heaven and earth.

3. Famine in the Land

7:11 Now a famine and great trouble came over all the land of Egypt and Canaan, and our fathers found no sustenance.

Now there came a dearth (famine and drought) over all the land of Egypt and Canaan, and great affliction (hunger and death): and our fathers (Israel) found no sustenance.

Because of their sins, these brothers were the cause of the trials and tribulations that confronted their own family and nation. God spared Egypt because of Joseph's presence and gave that nation supernatural guidance to prepare and overcome the famine.

7:12–13 But when Jacob heard that there was grain in Egypt, he sent out our fathers first.[13] **And the second *time* Joseph was made known to his brothers, and Joseph's family became known to the Pharaoh.**

There is coming a time in which Jesus, who was sold and now became the ruler of heaven and earth, will receive the Jewish nation to Himself, and they will again be in God's favor.

7:14 Then Joseph sent and called his father Jacob and all his relatives to *him*, seventy-five people.

Included in this number are Jacob's sons, their wives, children, and grandchildren. They are the ones who will settle in Egypt and go into slavery. They will also come out of captivity four hundred years later, numbering over two million.

4. Death of Jacob

7:15–16 So Jacob went down to Egypt; and he died, he and our fathers. [16] **And they were carried back to Shechem and laid in the tomb that Abraham bought for a sum of money from the sons of Hamor, *the father* of Shechem.**

Jacob and his sons were buried in Shechem when they first died, but Joseph was not. Joseph's bones remained unburied for four hundred years. They were eventually carried by the children of Israel to Shechem and buried there (Genesis 50:22–26, Joshua 24:32, Hebrews 11:22).

5. Evil Against Israel

7:17–18 ¶ "But when the time of the promise drew near which God had sworn to Abraham, the people grew and multiplied in Egypt [18] till another king arose who did not know Joseph.

But when the time of the promise drew nigh (400 years later), which God had sworn to Abraham, the people grew and multiplied in Egypt, til another king arose, which knew not Joseph. This is found in Exodus 1:8–22.

7:19 This man dealt treacherously with our people, and oppressed our forefathers, making them expose their babies, so that they might not live.

The same dealt subtly with (schemed against) our kindred, and evil entreated our fathers, so that they cast out their young children, to the end they might not live.

The Pharaoh was so enraged that these people multiplied even under hardship and slavery, he made a decree to kill all the young male children to hold down the population.

C. Moses
1. Birth

7:20 At this time Moses was born, and was well pleasing to God; and he was brought up in his father's house for three months.

Moses was given an Egyptian name. He was found by the daughter of the Pharaoh Tutmos. She named him after her father, calling him Moses, which means "out of the water" (Exodus 2:5–10). His true mother nursed him for three months, weaned him and gave him to Pharaoh's house (Hebrews 11:23).

7:21–22 But when he was set out, Pharaoh's daughter took him away and brought him up as her own son. 22 And Moses was learned in all the wisdom of the Egyptians, and was mighty in words and deeds.

Moses became a great speaker and worker. When Moses told God he could not speak, it was not true (Exodus 4:10). God made Aaron his mouthpiece and during the fifth plague, Moses pushed Aaron aside and spoke for himself from that time forward.

2. Moses Attempts to Deliver

7:23 ¶ "Now when he was forty years old, it came into his heart to visit his brethren, the children of Israel.

God spoke to Moses at the same time he was offered the Egyptian empire and Moses chose to go with his own people, Israel (Hebrews 11:24–27).

7:24 And seeing one of *them* suffer wrong, he defended and avenged him who was oppressed, and struck down the Egyptian.

Moses was naturally a very strong man. With one blow, he killed the Egyptian man. Moses was also brilliant and a great speaker. He had many reasons in the natural to trust in his own ability. Pride was one of the areas God had to rid Moses of during his forty years on the backside of the wilderness.

7:25 For he supposed that his brethren would have understood that God would deliver them by his hand, but they did not understand.

God spoke to his heart, and Moses knew he was the deliverer of Israel. Moses assumed because he knew he was the deliverer, the whole nation of Israel would also recognize he was their deliverer. But they did not. They believed Moses sided with the Egyptians.

7:26 And the next day he appeared to *two of* them as they were fighting, and *tried to* reconcile them, saying, 'Men, you are brethren; why do you wrong one another?'

After the Egyptian taskmaster had gone, the Jews began to fight among themselves.

7:27 But he who did his neighbor wrong pushed him away, saying, 'Who made you a ruler and a judge over us?

The children of Israel did not understand that Moses was their deliverer. This was eye-opening for Moses. Moses needed preparation. He was called, but not separated (Romans 1:1). He needed to understand his calling could not be revealed by force. Fists and human strength only confuse the issue (Titus 1:7). Let God reveal you in His time: "Not by might, nor power, but by my spirit . . ." (Zechariah 4:6).

7: 28 *Do you want to kill me as you did the Egyptian yesterday?'*

The people had witnessed the outward act of Moses but did not know his heart or the call of God on his life.

3. Moses Flees Egypt

7:29 Then, at this saying, Moses fled and became a dweller in the land of Midian, where he had two sons.

Moses saw his mistake and fleed to the desert. He was in fear for his life. Moses needed to go to a place where he would learn to depend on God's Spirit alone. In the desert, Moses could not depend on his own strength. Fists do not solve problems with sheep. God was preparing Moses for two wilderness experiences. The first would be with sheep, the next with people (human sheep).

4. The Burning Bush

7:30 ¶ "And when forty years had passed, an Angel of the Lord appeared to him in a flame of fire in a bush, in the wilderness of Mount Sinai.

The time for Moses has arrived, but now he will not stand in his own strength; he will stand in the power of God.

7:31 When Moses saw *it*, he marveled at the sight; and as he drew near to observe, the voice of the Lord came to him,

Moses saw a bush burning, but it was not being consumed. This is a type of the anointing God would saturate Moses with, but Moses would not be consumed. God places His anointing on people, but their personality and personal strengths and weaknesses remain the same.

7:32 *saying, 'I am the God of your fathers—the God of Abraham, the God of Isaac, and the God of Jacob.' And Moses trembled and dared not look.*

Saying, I am the God of thy fathers, the God of Abraham, the God of Isaac, and the God of Jacob. Then Moses trembled and durst not behold (did not want to look).

7:33 *'Then the Lord said to him, "Take your sandals off your feet, for the place where you stand is holy ground.*

The ground was holy. This is very important to the message Stephen is giving. The religious Jews hearing this sermon preach that the temple is holy. The place where Moses stood was holy, but it was in Arabia, the land of cursing. Moses was not in Zion. Stephen is revealing that a holy place exists anywhere God is.

5. Moses Sent to Deliver

7:34 *I have surely seen the oppression of My people who are in Egypt; I have heard their groaning and have come down to deliver them. And now come, I will send you to Egypt."*

Now is the time of Moses' separation. God, not Moses and his fists, is going to deliver the people.

7:35 ¶ "This Moses whom they rejected, saying, 'Who made you a ruler and a judge?' is the one God sent to be a ruler and a deliverer by the hand of the Angel who appeared to him in the bush.

Forty years earlier, the Jews had asked Moses, "Who made you ruler?" Now he was returning in God's power to answer that question.

7:36 He brought them out, after he had shown wonders and signs in the land of Egypt, and in the Red Sea, and in the wilderness forty years.

The "He" who brought them out was the Lord Jesus Christ.

7:37 ¶ "This is that Moses who said to the children of Israel, 'The Lord your God will raise up for you a Prophet like me from your brethren. Him you shall hear.'

This is that Moses, which said unto the children of Israel, A prophet shall the Lord your God raise up unto you of your brethren, like unto me; him shall ye hear (Deuteronomy 18:15, 18).

7: 38 ¶ "This is he who was in the congregation in the wilderness with the Angel who spoke to him on Mount Sinai, and *with* our fathers, the one who received the living oracles to give to us,

This is he (Moses), that was in the church (tabernacle) in the wilderness with the angel which spake to him in the Mount Sinai, and with our fathers: who received the lively (living) oracles (law) to give unto us:

6. Israel Murmurs

7:39–40 whom our fathers would not obey, but rejected. And in their hearts they turned back to Egypt, 40 saying to Aaron, 'Make us gods to go before us; as for this Moses who brought us out of the land of Egypt, we do not know what has become of him.'

When Moses went to the mountain to receive the law, the people rejected him and turned to idols. Aaron was weak, and the people knew this. They were afraid of Moses, but knew they could sway Aaron. They waited until Moses was gone and began to work on Aaron.

These religious men interrogating Stephen have accused him of rejecting Moses, yet they are just as Israel was in the wilderness. They are accepting the law but rejecting Moses's prophecy of a great prophet who would come. This prophet (Jesus) has always been with Israel and Moses.

7. The Golden Calf

7:41 And they made a calf in those days, offered sacrifices to the idol, and rejoiced in the works of their own hands.

The golden calf made in "those days" was no more of an idol than the law was on the day Stephen stands before the religious leaders. They too, have turned the laws and sacrifices of God into idols and rejoice in their own works.

7:42 Then God turned and gave them up to worship the host of heaven, as it is written in the book of the Prophets:

> *'Did you offer Me slaughtered animals and sacrifices*
> *during forty years in the wilderness,*
> *O house of Israel?*

The "host of heaven" were the Egyptian gods of the stars. The quote here is from Amos 5:25. The Israelites had disobeyed the commands of God by worshiping idols and sacrificing to heathen gods instead of the true God.

7:43 *You also took up the tabernacle of Moloch,*
And the star of your god Remphan,
Images which you made to worship;
And I will carry you away beyond Babylon.'

The god of the Canaanites (Amorites) was an ox-headed statue that had two hoofs extended in front of his body. Children were placed on these hoofs , a fire was lit underneath, and the children were burned to death. Because the dying children would scream, the worshipers would loudly beat drums to drown out their screams.

The Hebrew word for drums is *toph*. One word for hell is *tophet*, which emphasizes the screams accompanying the flames.

The star of Remphan was Saturn. The Israelites followed the idolatry of the Canaanites and, as a result, eventually went into captivity in Babylon for seventy years.

7:44 ¶ "Our fathers had the tabernacle of witness in the wilderness, as He appointed, instructing Moses to make it according to the pattern that he had seen,

The purpose of the tabernacle, its worship, sacrifices, furniture, and law was to witness and teach about Jesus.

D. Joshua, David, Solomon

7:45–46 which our fathers, having received it in turn, also brought with Joshua into the land possessed by the Gentiles, whom God drove out before the face of our fathers until the days of David, 46 who found favor before God and asked to find a dwelling for the God of Jacob.

Moses brought the law to Israel, but David discovered grace. David knew more about God's grace than any Old Testament writer. David's reign will be compared to the grace of God in our own dispensation (Acts 15:16). David also experienced more of God's grace and forgiveness than anyone else in the Old Testament. He was called the man after God's own heart and wrote about it much in the Psalms.

7:47 But Solomon built Him a house.

In Acts 15:16, David's reign will be compared to the church but his tabernacle was a tent in Zion. It was Solomon who was chosen by God to build the temple. Solomon's reign is a type of the millennial reign of the Lord Jesus, which is to come. During David's reign, there was much war, and David was called a man of war. During Solomon's reign there was little war and a great span of peace. This is a type of the millennium.

Stephen presents three names: Moses, David, and Solomon. Each of these men span the three time periods of Israel's history following their deliverance from Egypt: the law, the church age, and the millennium.

7:48 ❡ "However, the Most High does not dwell in temples made with hands, as the prophet says:

This word comes from 2 Chronicles 2:6. Stephen now turns the table on his accusers and becomes their judge. They believe God lives in their temple, but they are as apostate as their ancestors.

7:49 'Heaven is My throne,
And earth is My footstool.
What house will you build for Me? says the Lord,
Or what is the place of My rest?

This is a quote from Isaiah 66, verses 1 and 2. God is deity, therefore He is omnipresent. He can be in heaven and, at the same time, make the earth His footstool.

7:50 Has My hand not made all these things?'

Only apostate people try to put God in a temple built by man. God created everything in heaven and earth. He cannot be contained.

II. Stephen Accuses the Council (51–53)

Upon the conclusion of his sermon, Stephen accuses the council of being hardened against God and His Word even as their fathers had been. He boldly charges them guilty of killing the Messiah and not keeping the law because of their rejection of Him.

7:51 ❡ "You stiff-necked and uncircumcised in heart and ears! You always resist the Holy Spirit; as your fathers did, so do you.

Stephen now concludes his sermon. He accuses them of being hardened against God and His Word. They are uncircumcised in heart because they have not received Jesus, the Messiah, as their savior. They have purposely shut off their hearts by purposely shutting their ears to the gospel. He is now accusing them of being sinful and rejecting God as their fathers had before them. These religious leaders take pride in not being as bad as the Old Testament fathers had been, yet they actually show themselves to be worse.

7:52 Which of the prophets did your fathers not persecute? And they killed those who foretold the coming of the Just One, of whom you now have become the betrayers and murderers,

Stephen is telling them the same thing they heard from Jesus Himself (Matthew 21:28–46, 22:1–13, 23:29–32). Just as the fathers persecuted the prophets who foretold of the coming of Jesus, they have now killed the Holy One prophesied of. These Jewish leaders rid themselves of problems by killing them. They killed the prophets and they killed Jesus. Now they will repeat the pattern by killing Stephen.

7:53 who have received the law by the direction of angels and have not kept *it*."

In addition to the law, many of the books of the major and minor prophets were given by angels (Galatians 3:19). The purpose of the law was to teach of Jesus Christ. By rejecting, persecuting, and killing Jesus, they have not kept the law.

III. The Sanhedrin's Reaction (54–60)

The council is so convicted, they determine to stone Stephen. Stephen is dragged outside the city and stoned. While being stoned, he intercedes for all those responsible for his death.

A. Cut to the Heart

Verses 54 through 56 give the reaction of the Sanhedrin to Stephens message.

7:54 ¶ When they heard these things they were cut to the heart, and they gnashed at him with *their* teeth.

The council now understands the meaning behind Stephen's message, and become convicted in their hearts.

B. Dying Grace

7:55 But he, being full of the Holy Spirit, gazed into heaven and saw the glory of God, and Jesus standing at the right hand of God,

Stephen was under a strong anointing to preach; now he has a strong anointing to face death. Stephen has been given dying grace and is able to see both the natural and spiritual world simultaneously. The glory that took Jesus into heaven now surrounds Stephen.

7:56 and said, "Look! I see the heavens opened and the Son of Man standing at the right hand of God!"

Stephen refers to the anointing for death as the "opening of heaven." Jesus, who is usually seated in heaven, stands up to greet one of His saints who is about to arrive in heaven. Throughout the Word, saints are met with departed relatives, angels, and the Lord Jesus Himself. We will also be greeted by the same regal welcome at the rapture of the church (1 Thessalonians 4:16–17).

C. Religion's Reaction to the Truth

7:57 ¶ Then they cried out with a loud voice, stopped their ears, and ran at him with one accord;

The religious leaders fight the conviction they feel by killing Stephen in an attempt to stop his message. Since they are in a courtroom (6:15) and not in the streets surrounded by multitudes of people, they feel safe in attacking Stephen and dragging him outside to be stoned.

These religious leaders are now out of control. They are acting like wild animals. They scream in an attempt to drown out Stephen's voice. They also cover their ears to block themselves from hearing Stephen's sermon any longer. These men represent the highest court in the land, yet they are acting like maniacs. This is the reaction of religion when it is cornered.

D. Stephen's Stoning

7:58 and they cast *him* out of the city and stoned *him*. And the witnesses laid down their clothes at the feet of a young man named Saul.

Since the members of the religious council are sticklers about obeying the law, they stone Stephen outside the city. The witnesses of the stoning are the false witnesses who had been bribed by the court into giving a false testimony against Stephen (6:11–14).

7:59 And they stoned Stephen as he was calling on *God* and saying, "Lord Jesus, receive my spirit."

The counsel does not stone Stephen; they stand by and watch the false witnesses stone him. While Stephen is being stoned, he calls out for the Lord to receive his spirit.

7:60 Then he knelt down and cried out with a loud voice, "Lord, do not charge them with this sin." And when he had said this, he fell asleep.

Stephen, like Jesus on the cross, is interceding for the people who are stoning him. Those watching are just as guilty as those who stoned Stephen. Stephen's prayer, like that of Jesus on the cross, will be answered after his death. Jesus asked for those who crucified Him to be forgiven. Later, the Roman guard received salvation. Stephen's prayer results in the salvation of Saul of Tarsus who stands by, holding the coats of those who do the stoning. This prayer will be answered in chapter 9.

8:1–40 Influence for Revival

The Challenge of Chapter Eight

We may suffer persecution for believing in Jesus Christ, but like the persecuted and scattered church at Jerusalem, we must never stop boldly proclaiming the gospel of Jesus Christ. The power and associated gifts of the
Holy Spirit are never meant to draw attention to ourselves nor are they to
be used for the purpose of financial gain, rather, they should always glorify
God and lead others into salvation or a deeper walk with Him. God may
perform miracles and signs through our hands, not only to set people free,
but ultimately to cause sinners to come to the saving knowledge of Jesus
Christ. We must continue to grow in our knowledge of God's Word, continue to pray, and be quick to obey the Spirit. In doing so, we may be led across
the paths of those sincerely seeking the truth and cause sinners to be saved
from an eternity spent in hell.

Four men will appear in Acts 8 whose lives greatly affect the early church.
They will influence individual lives as well as entire nations. The first man
appears in the first half of chapter 8, Saul of Tarsus who later becomes Paul
the apostle. The second is Philip who becomes the first evangelist of the
church age and sees revival change an entire city at one time. The third is
Simon the Sorcerer whose stand against the gospel causes many to respond
and receive the Holy Spirit. The fourth is the Ethiopian eunuch whose conversion will change an entire nation.

I. Saul: Persecutor of the Church (1–4)

Saul, a witness to the stoning of Stephen is bringing great persecution to
the church at Jerusalem as he drags Christian men and women from their
homes and has them thrown into prison. Many believers flee the city, but
still boldly preach the gospel wherever they go.

A. Saul Persecutes the Church

Saul is a member of the Sanhedrin, a devoutly religious Jew deeply steeped
in Judaism (Philippians 3:4–9). As an unbeliever, Saul's mind is blinded (2
Corinthians 4:4) through religion, self-righteousness, and hypocrisy. Because of his religious background and persecution of the church, Paul con-
siders himself to be the worst man who ever lived (1 Timothy 1:12–16).

**8:1 ¶ Now Saul was consenting to his death. ¶ At that time a great
persecution arose against the church which was at Jerusalem;**

and they were all scattered throughout the regions of Judea and Samaria, except the apostles.

Stephen's death is the first in an extended period of persecution. Jerusalem, the headquarters of Judaism, wants Christianity out. The church is scattered and sent out of Jerusalem (Acts 11:19, James 1:1). This is a fulfillment of Jesus' prophecy found in chapter 1, verse 8.

The apostles, however, remain in Jerusalem to form the government and counsel of the church at Jerusalem. They remain as many of their congregation leave the city for safer, more peaceful places to preach the gospel.

8:2 And devout men carried Stephen *to his burial*, and made great lamentation over him.

Just as the young, devout men had buried Ananias and Sapphira in chapter 5, they now bury one of their own who had become a renowned teacher in the city of Jerusalem. The process is repeated. The young men who had buried the bodies of Ananias and Sapphira became the deacons in chapter 6 as the church began to grow. As those first deacons (which included Stephen) enter the ministry, new young and devout men are being raised up under them.

8:3 ¶ As for Saul, he made havoc of the church, entering every house, and dragging off men and women, committing *them* to prison.

Saul is a very committed and zealous man for the religion of the Jews. He believes what he is doing against the church is for God. At this point, Saul is Christianity's greatest adversary. Later he will refer to himself as the worst sinner who ever lived (1 Timothy 1:15).

Religion is the greatest enemy of the gospel. The religious person is the most difficult to win and the least receptive to the gospel of grace. Religious people are too consumed in their own human good and arrogance to believe they need a savior (Isaiah 64:6, Titus 3:5).

B. The Church Is Scattered

8:4 ¶ Therefore those who were scattered went everywhere preaching the word.

Therefore they that were scattered abroad (*diaspeiro*) went every where preaching the word.

The Greek word for "scattered" means "to throw out as seed" (see James 1:1). These believers are not thrown away nor do they run away in fear. They disperse to escape the persecution, but they are not silent about the Lord Jesus. For the Jews to believe they have gained a great victory over the Christians is as futile as believing they could get rid of seed by throwing it away on good soil.

Any rejoicing on the part of the Jews will be short-lived; Christians begin to crop up in the many places outside Jerusalem where believers have been dispersed.

II. Philip: The Evangelist (5–8)

Philip goes to Samaria and preaches Christ to them. He also performs miracles, casts out unclean spirits from those possessed, and heals many paralyzed and lame people by the power of God. There is great joy in the city.

A. A Revival in the City

8:5 Then Philip went down to the city of Samaria and preached Christ to them.

One of those who fled Jerusalem was the second deacon mentioned in Acts 6, Philip, who was called to be an evangelist (Acts 21:8, Ephesians 4:11). Unlike the office of a teacher (which Stephen walked in), the evangelist does not expound Scripture, but simply brings out Jesus and the new birth from any section of Scripture. Philip's message is the same whether he is addressing an entire city or an individual — salvation by faith in Jesus Christ. He does not preach sin, but Christ.

Philip is not the first to preach Christ in Samaria. This is the same city where Jesus met the woman at the well (John 4:5–42). Jesus informed His disciples that many had previously preached the gospel in Samaria. Some had planted, others had watered, and now God would receive the increase (John 4:37–38, 1 Corinthians 3:6–8).

Philip is entering a city which has entered revival. The gospel has been preached, and the city is prepared for even greater numbers of souls to be won.

8:6 And the multitudes with one accord heeded the things spoken by Philip, hearing and seeing the miracles which he did.

The ministry of the evangelist is accompanied by the power gifts, gifts of healing and working of miracles (1 Corinthians 12:28). The purpose of these gifts is to direct the focus of attention on salvation through the Lord Jesus Christ.

B. Demons Flee and Bodies Healed

8:7 For unclean spirits, crying with a loud voice, came out of many who were possessed; and many who were paralyzed and lame were healed.

At this time, Samaria is under the influence of the Greek culture and worships the demons of the Pantheon (1 Corinthians 10:21–22). Half of Samaria is comprised of a Jewish population and half is Gentile. The same is true of their worship. Citizens of Samaria acknowledge the God of Israel while at the same time acknowlede demonic gods.

Philip casts out devils *and* heals the sick. Not all sickness is a result of demons. A distinction is made between healing and casting out demons (Matthew 10:8, Acts 19:11–12). The same anointing delivers people from both, but we must depend on the gifts of the Holy Spirit to discern the difference.

8:8 And there was great joy in that city.

Joy is a fruit of the new birth, a result of salvation.

III. Simon: The Sorcerer (9–25)

Simon is a sorcerer who had once practiced sorcery in the city of Jerusalem and is now in Samaria proclaiming he is someone great. The people believe him because he astonishes them with magic. However, when Philip preaches Christ, many of the same people believed Philip's message, including Simon. Simon is amazed by the miracles and signs God performs through Philip and follows him as he preaches.

A. Simon Held in High Esteem

8:9 ¶ But there was a certain man called Simon, who previously practiced sorcery in the city and astonished the people of Samaria, claiming that he was someone great,

But there was a certain man, called Simon, which beforetime in the same city used sorcery (*mageuo*), and bewitched (*existemi*) the people of Samaria, giving out that himself was some great one:

Up until now, Simon has been highly renowned in the city. He uses witch-craft and the powers of demons to display satanic signs and wonders to the people. Now Philip becomes more esteemed among the people than Simon as the true power of God manifests through the ministry of Philip. A similar situation will later occur in Paul's ministry in Ephesus when com-pared to the seven sons of Sceva (19:13–14).

According to Justin Martyr, Simon was born in Gitton, a small village in Samaria. He was educated under Dositheus in Alexandria and became a gnostic. Simon's mixture of religion, philosophy, and magic had gained him a reputation in Samaria.

8:10 to whom they all gave heed, from the least to the greatest, saying, "This man is the great power of God."

Simon has much attention as a sorcerer. When Peter and John arrive, he will feel neglected and attempt to buy back his reputation among the people.

8:11 And they heeded him because he had astonished them with his sorceries for a long time.

Satan's ministry is to imitate the works of God.

B. Conversions in Samaria

8:12 But when they believed Philip as he preached the things concerning the kingdom of God and the name of Jesus Christ, both men and women were baptized.

Philip preaches three things: Christ (v. 5), the kingdom of God (v. 12), and the name of Jesus (v. 12).

8:13 Then Simon himself also believed; and when he was bap-tized he continued with Philip, and was amazed, seeing the miracles and signs which were done.

Coming from a background of sorcery, Simon has seen spiritual signs through demons. Now he is observing the true signs from God and is able to recognize the difference between the two. Simon is converted and strongly desires to operate in the gifts of the Holy Spirit. He follows Philip closely to learn how he is able to perform these miracles.

8:14 ¶ Now when the apostles who were at Jerusalem heard that Samaria had received the word of God, they sent Peter and John to them,

Hearing about the conversion of the Samaritans (the first Gentiles to be converted), Peter and John were sent to the converts and prayed for them to receive the baptism in the Holy Spirit.

Peter and John are gifted by the Holy Spirit in leading others into the infilling. Philip is gifted in leading others into the new birth and getting them healed. Philip's weakness is getting people filled with the Holy Spirit. These disciples serve as a reminder that we all need each other as team members in the body of Christ. One person is not gifted to operate in all areas.

C. Infillings in Samaria

8:15 who, when they had come down, prayed for them that they might receive the Holy Spirit.

The Holy Spirit, just like salvation and every gift of God, has already been given. The prayer is not for the Holy Spirit to fall or come on them; He has already come in chapter 2, on the day of Pentecost. The Holy Spirit is already present and desires to fill these new believers.

The hindrance is not the Holy Spirit, but the will of the people. They need to be taught and prayed for to receive the Holy Spirit. This is the key to everything in the Christian life. Everything has been given in grace (2 Peter 1:3). Faith responds and receives the grace, the gifts which have already been given.

Peter and John are not prejudice against these people and neither are the leaders at Jerusalem (at this time). They are happy and rejoice with the Samaritans when they hear of their new births and the revival which hits the city. Peter and John are joyous when these new converts received the same Holy Spirit and the same experience they had received at Pentecost.

8:16 For as yet He had fallen upon none of them. They had only been baptized in the name of the Lord Jesus.

Philip had ministered to them the new birth, healings, miracles, and baptism.

8:17 Then they laid hands on them, and they received the Holy Spirit.

Peter and John lay hands on the Samaritan believers and they received the Holy Spirit. The assumption can be made that the infilling of the Samaritan believers was accompanied by speaking in tongues. Simon would have sought what the apostles had because there had been some manifestation.

D. Simon Tries to Buy Power

8:18 ⸹ And when Simon saw that through the laying on of the apostles' hands the Holy Spirit was given, he offered them money,

Simon now wants the popularity and position of prominence he once held in Samaria returned to him and offers money to have this power.

8:19 saying, "Give me this power also, that anyone on whom I lay hands may receive the Holy Spirit."

God does give this authority, but never to exalt a man, and never for money.

8:20 ⸹ But Peter said to him, "Your money perish with you, because you thought that the gift of God could be purchased with money!

Simon is headed toward the sin unto death, as was the case with Ananias and Sapphira. He is not headed toward hell, because he has received Jesus Christ as his Lord and Savior. Instead, Simon has opened himself up to the destruction of his physical body because of his thoughts and words against the gospel and the will of God.

8:21 You have neither part nor portion in this matter, for your heart is not right in the sight of God.

Thou has neither part nor lot in this matter (*logos*: utterance) for thy heart is not right in the sight of God.

The utterance given by the people is speaking in tongues. Simon wants the authority associated with the Holy Spirit, but his motives are wrong. Peter tells Simon he has no part in operating in the power of God because of his wrong heart.

To fully enter into the plan of God, our motives and desires should be to help others, not to enhance who we are. The focus should be on God, not on us!

E. Peter Calls Simon to Repentance

8:22 Repent therefore of this your wickedness, and pray God if perhaps the thought of your heart may be forgiven you.

Sin always begins with the thought of the heart. Not only should we ask forgiveness for the act of sin, we should also ask forgiveness for the thought of the sin (1 John 1:9).

8:23 For I see that you are poisoned by bitterness and bound by iniquity."

Peter perceives in his spirit that Simon's heart was not right before God (Mark 2:8, Luke 9:47).

8:24 ¶ Then Simon answered and said, "Pray to the Lord for me, that none of the things which you have spoken may come upon me."

As far as we know, Simon never becomes a notable believer.

8:25 ¶ So when they had testified and preached the word of the Lord, they returned to Jerusalem, preaching the gospel in many villages of the Samaritans.

Testimonies have a place when the Word is also taught. Peter and John continue preaching in many of the small cities of Samaria and then return to Jerusalem. Philip is still in Samaria and will receive supernatural instruction to go to Gaza.

IV. The Ethiopian Eunuch (26–40)

Next, an angel instructs Philip to take a road from Jerusalem to Gaza. Philip obeys and comes upon an Ethiopian eunuch of great authority, reading the book of Isaiah. In explaining the scripture, Philip preaches Jesus to the eunuch who receives Jesus and then asks Philip to baptize him in water. The moment Philip and the eunuch come up out of the water, Philip is caught away by the Holy Spirit, and the eunuch goes his way rejoicing. Philip is carried away by the Spirit to Azotus, where he continues to preach from there all the way to Caesarea.

A. The Ethiopian Comes to Worship

8:26–27 ¶ Now an angel of the Lord spoke to Philip, saying, "Arise and go toward the south along the road which goes down from Jerusalem to Gaza." This is desert. 27 So he arose and went. And behold, a man of Ethiopia, a eunuch of great authority under Candace the queen of the Ethiopians, who had charge of all her treasury, and had come to Jerusalem to worship,

The Ethiopian is third in power in his kingdom and is treasurer to the queen. He is very dedicated to his office, his call as a eunuch, and to the Lord. When Philip finds him, the Ethiopian is searching for the Lord more than in a religious way. The eunuch is searching the scriptures when Philip finds him. He has become a Jewish proselyte and is traveling back from Jerusalem where he traveled for the express purpose of worship. He had probably been there for six weeks, from Passover to Pentecost.

His sincere desire to know the Lord causes the angel to give supernatural guidance to Philip. Because of one man's desire to find God, God sends Philip miles out of his way to minister to him (compare Luke 7:1–10).

8:28 was returning. And sitting in his chariot, he was reading Isaiah the prophet.

The chariot is either moving slowly or standing still. The Ethiopian's chariot is similar to a stagecoach with a driver. The eunuch is sitting in the back of the chariot reading the scriptures when Philip arrive. Later, he will command the driver to stop the chariot (v. 38).

B. Philip Obeys the Spirit

8:29 Then the Spirit said to Philip, "Go near and overtake this chariot."

Philip now understands why the Lord has sent him into the desert. He does not know who the Ethiopian is, but it does not matter. Philip is one man who has been responsible for the salvation of many in his home country.

8:30 ¶ So Philip ran to him, and heard him reading the prophet Isaiah, and said, "Do you understand what you are reading?"

The Holy Spirit speaks to Philip and tells him to go to the chariot. Again, Philip is quick to obey. He actually runs! When he arrives, he hears the eunuch reading aloud at the very place of Isaiah's prophecy.

8:31 ¶ And he said, "How can I, unless someone guides me?" And he asked Philip to come up and sit with him.

This is the purpose of ministry, to guide, not to dominate or run the lives of others. Guidance is still the cry of people today. When we act under the guidance of the Holy Spirit, His job becomes ours. He is sent to guide us into all truth.

8:32–33 The place in the Scripture which he read was this:

> *"He was led as a sheep to the slaughter;*
> *And as a lamb before its shearer is silent,*
> *So He opened not His mouth.*

> *33 In His humiliation His justice was taken away,*
> *And who will declare His generation?*
> *For His life is taken from the earth."*

Phillip is quoting Isaiah 53:7–8 here.

8:34 ¶ So the eunuch answered Philip and said, "I ask you, of whom does the prophet say this, of himself or of some other man?"

The eunuch has been blinded by religion and Satan and is unable to understand the simplest of scriptures (2 Corinthians 4:4). God will use Philip to help lift the veil.

8:35 Then Philip opened his mouth, and beginning at this Scripture, preached Jesus to him.

Philip preaches the crucifixion, death, burial, and resurrection of Jesus.

C. The Eunuch Is Baptized

8:36 Now as they went down the road, they came to some water. And the eunuch said, "See, *here is* water. What hinders me from being baptized?"

Philip also preaches water baptism to the eunuch, as he had to the Samaritans (v. 12).

8:37 ¶ Then Philip said, "If you believe with all your heart, you may." ¶ And he answered and said, "I believe that Jesus Christ is the Son of God."

Water baptism should come only after a person has believed on the Lord Jesus. It is not part of salvation but an action that accompanies salvation. Water baptism is an outward act showing the inward faith a person has toward the Lord; it is an outward expression of salvation, not part of the new birth.

8:38 ¶ So he commanded the chariot to stand still. And both Philip and the eunuch went down into the water, and he baptized him.

Water baptism is a complete immersion. Philip and the eunuch both go into the water and after the eunuch is immersed, they both arise from the water, signifying the eunuch's passage from spiritual death to life.

D. Philip Caught Away

8:39 Now when they came up out of the water, the Spirit of the Lord caught Philip away, so that the eunuch saw him no more; and he went on his way rejoicing.

Although the Bible doesn't tell the story, this man's life influences all of Ethiopia. For the next 600 years, Ethiopia resists the Muslims. Through the life of one man, the gospel infiltrated the government of his land.

8:40 But Philip was found at Azotus. And passing through, he preached in all the cities till he came to Caesarea.

Azotus is the ancient city of Ashdod in Philistia. The Greeks will be the next group of people Philip will evangelize. Philip will then travel from Azotus up the northern coast.

9:1-43 Saul's Conversion

The Challenge of Chapter Nine

God's mercy, forgiveness, and salvation are extended to all who will receive them, even to the worst of sinners. No place in the Bible can we see this as clearly as we do with Saul, one of the biggest enemies of the early church.

Saul's dramatic conversion caused many to believe in Jesus Christ, and the letters written by the Holy Spirit through his hand still instruct and encourage saints today.

Ananias's willingness to obey God in ministering to Saul, even through the fear and doubt he experienced, is a lesson to us that our obedience canbe the difference between heaven and hell for someone's soul. In leading a person to the Lord, we may never know in this lifetime how God might use that life to impact the kingdom of God.

Even when faced with the most severe persecution, we must never stop boldly proclaiming Jesus Christ.

Part of the salvation Jesus provided includes healing, and just as the healings of Aeneas and Dorcas in this chapter result in salvations, the same is true today of healings and miracles. We believers need to be bold to do as the Bible instructs and lay hands on the sick and expect to see them recover.

I. The Road to Damascus (1–19)

Saul is still threatening and murdering the disciples of Jesus. He has gone to the high priest of the temple in Jerusalem and asked for letters to give to the leaders of the synagogues in Damascus. These letters would give him the right to bind up any follower of Jesus and bring them back to Jerusalem.

But as he approaches Damascus, a light shines from heaven, he falls to the ground, and he has a direct encounter with the Lord Jesus Christ.

A. Introduction

This chapter contrasts the emerging ministry of Saul (1–31) with the disappearing ministry of Peter (32–43). Because of the deteriorating conditions in Jerusalem, Peter, who is called to the Jews, finds his calling moving toward the Gentiles, beginning at Caesarea. In contrast, Saul's main call will be to the emerging Gentile nations. His call will also include the Jews, but Saul's main priority is the Gentiles (verse 15). His ministry begins with the Gentiles and eventually leads to a few opportunities to minister to the Jews.

In this chapter, Saul becomes the twelfth apostle.

B. Saul's Persecution of Christians

9:1 ¶ Then Saul, still breathing threats and murder against the disciples of the Lord, went to the high priest

In 1 Timothy 1:12–15, Saul refers to himself as the worst of all sinners because of his early persecution of the church. Prior to his conversion, his name is the same as that of King Saul of the Old Testament. Just as King Saul was possessed with hatred for David, this Saul is possessed with hatred for the church and is breathing out his anger against it.

9:2 and asked letters from him to the synagogues of Damascus, so that if he found any who were of the Way, whether men or women, he might bring them bound to Jerusalem.

And desired of (from) him letters to Damascus to the synagogues, that if he found any of this way (5:20: ". . . this life"), whether they were men or women, he might bring them bound unto Jerusalem.

Damascus is 150 miles north of Jerusalem. This shows Saul's dedication to arrest Christians and put them in jail.

C. A Light from Heaven

9:3 ¶ As he journeyed he came near Damascus, and suddenly a light shone around him from heaven.

The light mentioned in this verse is the glory of God manifesting, and it causes Saul to fall to the ground.

9:4 Then he fell to the ground, and heard a voice saying to him, "Saul, Saul, why are you persecuting Me?"

Saul was so stubborn Jesus had to lay him on his back to get his attention. When Saul persecutes the church, he is persecuting the Lord Jesus Himself. Jesus did not say, "Why are you persecuting Christians?" (See Matthew 25:40).

D. Jesus Speaks

9:5 ¶ And he said, "Who are You, Lord?" ¶ Then the Lord said, "I am Jesus, whom you are persecuting. It is hard for you to kick against the goads."

And he said, Who art thou, Lord? And the Lord said, I am Jesus whom thou persecutest: [it is] hard for thee to kick against the pricks.

The phrase ". . . it is hard for thee to kick against the pricks" is not found in many of the oldest manuscripts. The Greek word for "pricks" means an ox goad. The Lord had been goading Saul like a farmer goads a plowing ox headed in the wrong direction. A rebellious ox will turn and kick against the goad. The idea behind goading an ox is that the farmer knows best.

The Lord knows what is best, and Saul has reached a crossroads in his life. He will either continue to kick against the goad and be put to death like a rebellious ox, or he will submit his will to God's. Saul has reached the end of God's patience towards him. If Saul is not stopped or is unwilling to change, many more Christians will die at his command, and the work of the Lord will suffer great harm.

Saul asks who is speaking to him. He is confused because he realizes it is the Lord but does not know who the Lord is. He has fought the concept that Jesus Christ is the Lord Jehovah. Now that he has experienced a taste of God's power, he is willing to ask and accept any answer he receives. Saul, who has worshiped the Lord for many years, misunderstood who the Lord was. He had been worshiping the lord of religion. He is now confronted by what he had feared, the Lord is Jesus Christ.

E. Saul Obeys

> **9:6–7 ¶ So he, trembling and astonished, said, "Lord, what do You want me to do?" ¶ Then the Lord *said* to him, "Arise and go into the city, and you will be told what you must do." 7 ¶ And the men who journeyed with him stood speechless, hearing a voice but seeing no one.**

The men with Saul do not see the vision he has. They do hear the sound of a voice, but cannot distinguish the words that are spoken. This also happened in Jesus' ministry when God spoke to Him from heaven; some in the crowd heard the voice as thunder and others as the voice of an angel (John 12:28–29).

> **9:8 Then Saul arose from the ground, and when his eyes were opened he saw no one. But they led him by the hand and brought *him* into Damascus.**

Saul is immediately obedient to the command of the Lord. He now becomes submissive to the one he has fought for many years. Saul opens his natural eyes and is blind. This is part of the divine plan of the Lord. God wants Saul to experience three days of natural blindness as a demonstration of the spiritual blindness Saul walked in his entire life (1 John 4:4).

Even though Saul believes himself to be a spiritual leader, he is really in the position of a blind person leading the blind (Matthew 15:14). Religion and its leaders are blind. Those who follow religion are blind and head toward hell and ultimately to the Lake of Fire. Saul is physically experiencing the blindness he has walked in for so many years.

During these three days, Saul does not eat or drink, but prays until Ananias comes and lays hands on him for the recovery of his sight.

F. Ananias Instructed to Go to Saul

> **9:9–10 And he was three days without sight, and neither ate nor drank. 10 ¶ Now there was a certain disciple at Damascus named Ananias; and to him the Lord said in a vision, "Ananias." ¶ And he said, "Here I am, Lord."**

The name "Ananias" means protected by the Lord. He is not in the fivefold ministry. He is a layman, a church worker the Lord uses to point Saul in the right direction.

Because of his arrogance, Saul might expect a minister from the local church like Peter, John, or one of the original disciples to come and lay hands on him. But God wants Saul to learn early the power of any man or woman dedicated to the Lord. A man's position and power before he is born again is of no value to the Lord. God will invest much time to work the religious background and pride out of Saul of Tarsus. Just as Moses had to learn humility in the backside of the wilderness, Saul also learns humility and becomes the apostle Paul.

Ananias is referred to as a "certain" disciple because God uses him to direct one of God's most influential ministers (22:12–13). Ananias receives a vision from God (2:17) and is obedient to it. He also understands grace and will lay hands on Saul, yet will keep this fact hidden from others. Most men, if given this task would brag about being used by God to lay hands on a figure as prominent as Saul of Tarsus. But Ananias is humble, and God knows he can be trusted.

9:11 ¶ So the Lord *said* to him, "Arise and go to the street called Straight, and inquire at the house of Judas for *one* called Saul of Tarsus, for behold, he is praying.

All but one street in Damascus wound and curved through the city. This street was called "Straight Street" and still exists in Damascus today, one of the oldest cities in the world.

Saul is still blind and still praying, waiting to hear from the Lord. He refuses to move until he knows with a certainty he is responding to the will of God. Saul continues to be obedient to what he knows, which is very little.

9:12 And in a vision he has seen a man named Ananias coming in and putting *his* hand on him, so that he might receive his sight."

God prepares both Saul, who will be prayed for, and Ananias, who does the praying. God in His goodness verifies His will with both parties involved. God will do the same thing with Peter and Cornelius when the new birth and infilling come to the city of Caesarea in chapter 10.

Distance does not bother the Lord. In matters of great importance, He will work over many miles to verify His will.

9:13 ¶ Then Ananias answered, "Lord, I have heard from many about this man, how much harm he has done to Your saints in Jerusalem.

Saul has saturated the city of Jerusalem with his evil toward believers, and his reputation has spread to many cities. Ananias has also heard in advance of the coming persecution Saul is bringing to the saints at Damascus.

9:14 And here he has authority from the chief priests to bind all who call on Your name."

The answer Ananias gives is typical of many that God speaks to. He immediately begins to expound on the circumstances from his human viewpoint. He informs God of the details as if God is completely ignorant of the circumstances. In verses 15 and 16, God gives Ananias the divine viewpoint.

G. Ananias Obeys the Lord's Command

9:15 ¶ But the Lord said to him, "Go, for he is a chosen vessel of Mine to bear My name before Gentiles, kings, and the children of Israel.

God doesn't give Ananias any more information. Even though Ananias is reluctant, God simply instructs him to go.

Saul will "bear" the Lord's name. The Greek word for "bear" is *bastazo,* which means to lift with the hands a flag or standard. God reveals to Ananias something that will not be seen for another fifteen years: First, Saul (Paul) will carry the gospel to the Gentiles, Romans and Greeks. Second, he will carry the gospel to kings, Nero and Agrippa. Finally, he will carry redemption to the children of Israel, the religious leaders of Gentile capitals, and Jerusalem.

God lists these according to their priority. God's main call on Paul's life is to carry the gospel to the Gentiles. Paul will eventually become confused through pride and put ministering to the Jewish people above ministering to the Gentiles. Because of it Paul will end up being shipwrecked and thrown into prison for five years.

9:16 For I will show him how many things he must suffer for My name's sake."

Before Paul ever ministers, God shows him that he will suffer greatly.

9:17 ¶ And Ananias went his way and entered the house; and laying his hands on him he said, "Brother Saul, the Lord Jesus, who appeared to you on the road as you came, has sent me that you may receive your sight and be filled with the Holy Spirit."

This is one of the first recorded cases of laying on of hands by someone outside of the fivefold ministry. Peter and John have laid hands on the Samaritans to receive the Holy Spirit (8:17), but until now, no layman has used this ministry. However, the ministry of laying on of hands is available to all believers (Mark 16:18) and Ananias uses it to lift the scales from Saul's eyes and get him filled with the Holy Spirit. (Jesus must have instructed him to lay his hands on Saul).

Ananias also calls Saul "brother." Ananias took the Lord at His word. Saul is now a believer and called into the ministry. Ananias has to forget everything he had heard about Saul and refuse to be moved by what he sees. He chooses to accept the word of the Holy Spirit.

H. Saul's Eyes Opened

9:18 Immediately there fell from his eyes *something like* scales, and he received his sight at once; and he arose and was baptized.

Saul's eyes are immediately opened as if someone has lifted blinders from them.

9:19 ⸿ So when he had received food, he was strengthened. Then Saul spent some days with the disciples at Damascus.

Saul's first teacher is Ananias. Next, he is taught by disciples in Damascus. None of the disciples who instruct Saul are well-known in the churches. At this time, there is not even an organized church in Damascus, even though there is a great concentration of believers.

In Galatians 1:17, Paul writes that he does not counsel with anyone who was an apostle. The disciples in Damascus lay a foundation in him of the simple truths of the Word of God and the new birth. Although Saul is very knowledgeable about the Old Testament, he is a baby in the kingdom of God.

Many of the gaps in Saul's timeline from this period can be filled in by also looking at Galatians 1. After Saul is instructed by Ananias and many of the disciples, he leaves Damascus and travels to Arabia in the desert (Galatians 1:17). He then returns to Damascus (Galatians 1:17, Acts 9:23–25) where he receives death threats from the Jews who live there. Saul then travels to Jerusalem after escaping from Damascus by rope over the wall (Galatians 1:18, Acts 9:26–29). Then, from Jerusalem, he travels to Tarsus (9:30–31) and there spends six to nine years.

II. Saul Preaches (20–22)

Saul immediately begins preaching Jesus is the Son of God in the synagogues of Damascus. Saul continues to increase in strength, confounding the Jews in Damascus and proving Jesus is the Christ.

9:20 ⸿ Immediately he preached the Christ in the synagogues, that He is the Son of God.

And straightway (immediately) he preached Christ (Greek: Jesus) in the synagogues, that he is the Son of God.

As a new convert, Saul is eager to preach. He proclaims Jesus in the only place he knows to preach, the synagogue. Since his audience knows him well, they are shocked and begin to spread the news that Saul is now a Christian and preaching the gospel he once refuted.

9:21 ❡ Then all who heard were amazed, and said, "Is this not he who destroyed those who called on this name in Jerusalem, and has come here for that purpose, so that he might bring them bound to the chief priests?"

These Jewish religious leaders in Damascus are shocked to hear of Paul's change from Judaism to Christianity on his short journey from Jerusalem to Damascus. They had expected him to speak of arrests and prison terms for Christians, but instead they hear his testimony.

9:22 ❡ But Saul increased all the more in strength, and confounded the Jews who dwelt in Damascus, proving that this *Jesus* is the Christ.

But Saul increased the more in strength, and confounded the Jews which dwelt at Damascus, proving (demonstrating) that this is very (indeed) Christ.

Saul increased in spiritual strength, the ability to preach the gospel with greater clarity, and in the teaching of the Word of God. The very scriptures Saul once used to teach against Jesus he now used as a defense for Jesus. His demonstration of the gospel to the Jews had to be signs and wonders. Just as Stephen had performed miracles in the sight of the Jewish leaders (6:8), Saul is now teaching and preaching the same Old Testament as a defense of Jesus and performing the same miracles, signs, and wonders.

III. Saul Escapes to Jerusalem (23–31)

Between verses 22 and 23, Saul travels to Arabia for a time (Galatians 1:17). When he gets back, the Jews at Damascus plot to kill Saul, but he is helped to escape and he flees to Jerusalem.

Once there, Saul tries to join the disciples, but they do not believe he has truly converted. Barnabas comes to Saul's defense, confirming that he has truly had an encounter with the Lord and has been boldly preaching in Damascus in the name of Jesus.

The Hellenists in Jerusalem try to kill Saul, and when the believers learn of it, they take him to Caesarea and then send him to Tarsus. Following this, the churches throughout Judea, Galilee, and Samaria have peace and are multiplied.

A. The Disciples Help Saul Escape

9:23 ❡ Now after many days were past, the Jews plotted to kill him.

Saul was in Arabia for the "many days" referred to in this verse. He now returns to Damascus and the Jews decide the only way to eliminate this situation is to kill Saul.

> **9:24 But their plot became known to Saul. And they watched the gates day and night, to kill him.**

Either one of the disciples learn of the Jews' plot or it is revealed to Saul through a word of knowledge, and the Jews are watching the gates (main entrance and exit of the city) day and night. They are so infuriated with Saul they are ready to kill him even in broad daylight.

> **9:25 Then the disciples took him by night and let *him* down through the wall in a large basket.**

The disciples let Saul down by a rope usually used to transfer people from one ship to another at sea. Saul is let down over the wall in a remote area where it is difficult for anyone to observe his escape. This location is far from the gates, and the Jews watch for many days, not realizing Saul has already escaped.

B. Barnabas Confirms Saul's Conversion

> **9:26 ¶ And when Saul had come to Jerusalem, he tried to join the disciples; but they were all afraid of him, and did not believe that he was a disciple.**

These are the same disciples Saul had tried to kill just a few years earlier. They still fear him.

> **9:27 But Barnabas took him and brought *him* to the apostles. And he declared to them how he had seen the Lord on the road, and that He had spoken to him, and how he had preached boldly at Damascus in the name of Jesus.**

Barnabas is a forgiving man. He operates in the grace of God (4:30) and will be the one who quickly forgives John Mark when he fails on the first missionary journey (15:38–39). He now defends this new convert before his accusers. Barnabas most likely reminded them of the grace of God, which extends forgiveness and salvation to them.

Every child of God begins as a sinner and we cannot blame or condemn others for their evil past. Once a sinner has confessed Jesus, it doesn't take long before the fruits of his righteousness become apparent. Saul has demonstrated these fruits of righteousness in his life. Barnabas testifies to the reality of this as evidenced in Paul's preaching,teaching, and the signs and wonders performed through him in the city of Damascus.

9:28 So he was with them at Jerusalem, coming in and going out.

Saul wins the confidence of the people by association before he ever speaks in the church at Jerusalem.

9:29 And he spoke boldly in the name of the Lord Jesus and disputed against the Hellenists, but they attempted to kill him.

And he spake boldly in the name of the Lord Jesus, and disputed against the Grecians (Hellenists: Greek-speaking Jews): but they went about to slay him.

Apparently, the church has experienced trouble with the Hellenistic leaders. They can handle the religious Jews, but the converted Jews could debate them and win! Saul however argues so convincingly against them, they resort to violence in an attempt to stop him.

Saul's gift is to the Gentiles (Galatians 2:7) as revealed in this verse.

C. Saul Sent to Tarsus

9:30 When the brethren found out, they brought him down to Caesarea and sent him out to Tarsus.

Just as the believers had at Damascus, the believers at Jerusalem now help Saul escape with his life.

9:31 ¶ Then the churches throughout all Judea, Galilee, and Samaria had peace and were edified. And walking in the fear of the Lord and in the comfort of the Holy Spirit, they were multiplied.

This was the immediate purpose for Saul's conversion. The chief leader of the persecution is now a believer and the Jews have to go home, lick their wounds, and regroup. During this time there is great peace in the body of Christ and souls are won and discipled with little or no persecution.

IV. Aeneas and Tabitha (32–43)

In verses 32 through 43, Peter once again becomes the subject. His calling to the Jews is diminishing, and his leading to the Gentiles is increasing. He travels to a small village west of Jerusalem where he heals Aeneas, a man who has been paralyzed for eight years.

After this, Dorcas, a highly regarded godly woman in Joppa, becomes sick and dies. Peter prays and Dorcas immediately opens her eyes. Both this miracle and Aeneas's healing, cause many to receive Jesus Christ.

A. Peter Heals Aeneas

9:32 ¶Now it came to pass, as Peter went through all *parts of the country*, that he also came down to the saints who dwelt in Lydda.

Lydda is the same place as Lud in 1 Chronicles 1:17.

9:33 There he found a certain man named Aeneas, who had been bedridden eight years and was paralyzed.

Aeneas has been paralyzed for eight years and is bedfast. Since verse 32 says Peter passed through and came to the "saints" at Lydda, it seems Aeneas is already a believer.

9:34 And Peter said to him, "Aeneas, Jesus the Christ heals you. Arise and make your bed." Then he arose immediately.

And Peter said unto him, Aeneas, Jesus Christ maketh (Greek: has made) thee whole: arise, and make thy bed. And he arose immediately.

Peter introduces Jesus as the healer of Aeneas' body. The same redemption that forgave sin also heals the man's body (Psalm 103:3). Aeneas now needs to accept his healing just as he received his righteousness.

9:35 So all who dwelt at Lydda and Sharon saw him and turned to the Lord.

This is the Valley of Sharon, which produces grapes and other crops. In this place of great commerce, Aeneas is well known. When people witness he is now walking, many accept the Lord as their Savior. Again, signs and wonders serve as a tool to bring people to salvation.

The healing and consequent salvations here parallel the results Philip participates in at Samaria in chapter 8. Many times the book of Acts records an act of healing which results in a revival and great multitudes being saved.

B. Tabitha Raised from the Dead

9:36 ¶ At Joppa there was a certain disciple named Tabitha, which is translated Dorcas. This woman was full of good works and charitable deeds which she did.

Tabitha's name means "gazelle." She is apparently very pretty and gracious. She is known throughout the area for her care of other Christians and her giving to the poor.

9:37 But it happened in those days that she became sick and died. When they had washed her, they laid *her* in an upper room.

And it came to pass in those days, that she was sick (*astheneo*), and died (suddenly died): whom when they had washed, they laid her in an upper chamber (upstairs bedroom).

Her sickness had been progressive. The Greek word for sickness, *astheneo*, means to be weak or sickly (James 5:14). Apparently, Dorcas had become sick and, over several days, became weak. No one had been overly concerned about her because they do not realize the seriousness of her condition until she dies suddenly. She is laid in an upstairs bedroom until she can be buried.

Her situation is similar to what had transpired with Lazarus. When Peter arrives, she has not been dead for as long as Lazarus had been, but she has been dead long enough for people to know. There is no way her death could be mistaken for a coma. She will be raised from the dead, and everyone will know it.

9:38 And since Lydda was near Joppa, and the disciples had heard that Peter was there, they sent two men to him, imploring *him* not to delay in coming to them.

Peter will go and raise Dorcas from the dead because messengers have been sent to him about her death. Peter responds because of a need. In the next story, Peter will be prepared by the Lord through a vision to meet a need in Caesarea. Whether we have a vision or not, God wants us to use the authority He has given us to bring deliverance to people.

> **9:39 Then Peter arose and went with them. When he had come, they brought _him_ to the upper room. And all the widows stood by him weeping, showing the tunics and garments which Dorcas had made while she was with them.**

Many who come for healing try to prove their worth but are no more worthy to receive healing than they are salvation. Even when the Jews were sent to represent the Roman centurion, they besought Jesus by saying the centurion was worthy (Luke 7:3–5). However, worthiness is never a requirement for healing or salvation. Peter does not raise Dorcas from the dead because of her good deeds but because of the finished work of Jesus. Peter had just healed a man who was lame and paralyzed. Because of his condition, this man had been unable to do any good works or give to the poor. In fact, he had probably even begged for years, yet Jesus healed him. The same will occur with Dorcas.

> **9:40 But Peter put them all out, and knelt down and prayed. And turning to the body he said, "Tabitha, arise." And she opened her eyes, and when she saw Peter she sat up.**

In the story of Jarius's daughter, Jesus had removed the mourners because of their unbelief and ridicule (Matthew 9:25). However, Peter removes the mourners here because they confuse the issue.

> **9:41 Then he gave her _his_ hand and lifted her up; and when he had called the saints and widows, he presented her alive.**

Peter touches her hand, then takes it to lift Dorcas up.

C. Many Believed

> **9:42 And it became known throughout all Joppa, and many believed on the Lord.**

Again, the purpose of miracles, signs, and wonders is to bring about the greatest miracle of all: salvation. Signs and wonders are not an end in themselves, but a means to an end — the new birth.

9:43 So it was that he stayed many days in Joppa with Simon, a tanner.

A tanner is one who deals with the hides of animals. According to Jewish law, a tanner is unclean because to tan animal hides requires dead (unclean) animals to be touched. Peter is staying in the home of a man whose shop would be forbidden to enter by many Peter knows in Jerusalem. Because Peter has raised Dorcas from the dead, the people have opened their city and this particular home to him, Peter is staying with the tanner as an act of courtesy toward the people of Joppa. Not only is the home considered unclean, the smells in the home are probably offensive. This is a good place for God to give Peter a housetop vision and open his eyes to the needs of the "unclean" people, the Gentiles.

10:1-48 Peter's Housetop Vision

The Challenge of Chapter Ten

Just like Cornelius, there are people who have hearts toward God that have not yet heard the message of salvation. We must always remember God is searching for hearts that hunger after Him, regardless of how they look or talk. We must always guard against prejudice, exclusivity, and disrespect of people because of their nationality, race, gender, or social status. Obeying God and the leading of the Holy Spirit ministering to all people should be a vital and integral part of our daily Christian life.

I. Snapshot

In fulfillment of Jesus' promise in the Acts 1:8, witnesses have taken the gospel to "Jerusalem [the Jews]" (Chapter 2), and "Judea [the Samaritans]" (Chapter 8). Now, in Acts 10, They will now take the gospel to "the uttermost part of the earth."

In this chapter, Peter will receive a clearer understanding of God's will for the entire world. But while Peter's vision is becoming clearer, the vision of the church at Jerusalem is becoming more clouded. In Acts 11, Peter will be challenged about ministering to the Gentiles, because church leaders have forgotten the admonition of Jesus. They do eventually recover, but only temporarily. Seeds of discrimination and bigotry have already arisen in the church against other nations receiving the goodness and blessing of the Lord.

II. An Angel Appears to Cornelius (1–8)

Cornelius is a devout man who prays and is generous in giving money to those in need. An angel appears to him instructing him to send a delegation to find Peter. Cornelius obeys and sends men to Joppa.

A. The City of Caesarea

Herod the Great built Caesarea as a seaport for the Jews. It took Herod ten years to dredge the cliffs along the Mediterranean before he could build this great city. He then named the city after his close friend, Julius Caesar.

When the Romans took over Palestine, they made Caesarea their headquarters. It then became despised by the Jews because it represented heathenism to them. Greek culture took over, and the city later became the nerve center of the Gentile world.

B. The Vision

10:1 ¶ There was a certain man in Caesarea called Cornelius, a centurion of what was called the Italian Regiment,

Cornelius was a leader among the Roman armies. Since he was from Caesarea, he was probably part of the general's staff. He is called a "certain man" and will become a major key to the revival and the outpouring of the Holy Spirit on the Gentiles.

10:2 a devout *man* and one who feared God with all his household, who gave alms generously to the people, and prayed to God always.

Although Cornelius is sincere (vv. 22, 35, 37), he is an unbeliever (11:14, 15:7, 8). However, he has a genuine desire to know the Lord, and out of his heart he cries to God to know Him. Cornelius wants someone to bring him the message of righteousness and is an example of someone consciously wanting to know the Lord.

Because of his heart's cry, God is under obligation to send someone to Cornelius. God will give the assignment to Peter. The motivation behind Cornelius' prayers and giving to the Lord was a heart of love.

10:3 About the ninth hour of the day he saw clearly in a vision an angel of God coming in and saying to him, "Cornelius!"

Three o'clock in the afternoon is the Jewish time of prayer. It is amazing that a Gentile, a Roman, would observe this tradition. It shows that Cornelius had probably researched salvation as much as possible by looking into Jewish traditions.

10:4 ¶ And when he observed him, he was afraid, and said, "What is it, lord?" ¶ So he said to him, "Your prayers and your alms have come up for a memorial before God.

Memorial represents intent. This word "memorial" is also used in Mark 14:9 and Matthew 26:13 when Mary of Bethany broke the ointment over Jesus' head. Jesus had called it a memorial of His burial and resurrection. In this passage, Cornelius's memorial is prayer and giving with an attitude of devotion and worship.

10:5 Now send men to Joppa, and send for Simon whose surname is Peter.

Joppa is another seaport where Jews preferred to stay. It is a smaller, natural seaport, thirty miles south of Caesarea. Cornelius, a soldier high in the Roman aristocracy sends for Peter, a low-class, Jewish fisherman.

10:6 He is lodging with Simon, a tanner, whose house is by the sea. He will tell you what you must do."

Since these men are not from Joppa and Peter is lodging temporarily in the city, the angel is exact in describing Peter's location. He does not want Cornelius' men to be wasting time searching for him. Because Joppa is not Peter's hometown and very few people knew where he was staying, it would have been difficult for the men to find him if they had not been directed by the angel.

C. Cornelius Obeys

10:7 And when the angel who spoke to him had departed, Cornelius called two of his household servants and a devout soldier from among those who waited on him continually.

Cornelius obeys immediately. He sends three men (v. 19) to find Peter and bring him to Caesarea.

10:8 So when he had explained all *these* things to them, he sent them to Joppa.

Apparently, these men start their journey late in the day and have to stop and spend the night on their way to Joppa (v.9).

III. Peter's Vision (9–23)

The next day, as Peter is on the housetop praying, he has a vision of a sheet lowered to the earth filled with animals that, according to Jewish tradition, are unclean. This happens three times accompanied by a voice from heaven. As Peter is pondering the meaning of this vision, the men Cornelius has sent arrive. Peter goes with them to Caesarea.

Cornelius was first Gentile

A. The Housetop *to hear the gossip.*

10:9 ¶ The next day, as they went on their journey and drew near the city, Peter went up on the housetop to pray, about the sixth hour. *(lunch time)*

In that day, it was common to have gardens on rooftops. In 2 Samuel 11:2, David was walking on the rooftop when he saw Bathsheba. In Matthew 24:17, Jesus warned those alive during the tribulation to come down from the rooftops.

Peter has gone to the rooftop at noontime It is a tranquil place for Peter to relax and pray.

While the men sent by Cornelius resume their journey and approach Joppa, Peter is praying.

10:10 Then he became very hungry and wanted to eat; but while they made ready, he fell into a trance

Peter is trying to pray but smells the lunch being prepared in the home below. While waiting for the cooks to call him, he slips into a trance. This is an open vision where the functions of his body are suspended.

10:11 and saw heaven opened and an object like a great sheet bound at the four corners, descending to him and let down to the earth.

The "open" heaven is the opening of the curtain that separates the spiritual realm from the natural. This is the meaning of the name revelation (*apokalupsis*). This sheet is immense, and all four corners are tied at the top. Like being held by a giant hand from the knot at the top, the sheet is let down to the earth and opens when it touches the ground.

10:12 In it were all kinds of four-footed animals of the earth, wild beasts, creeping things, and birds of the air.

These "beasts" are all unclean animals that are forbidden to be eaten according to Old Testament law.

10:13 And a voice came to him, "Rise, Peter; kill and eat."

In Greek, these are three commands given in the imperative mood: rise, kill, eat.

10:14 ¶ But Peter said, "Not so, Lord! For I have never eaten anything common or unclean."

Peter knows the voice of the Lord, but also knows the commandments of the Old Testament. He is resisting the voice of the Lord, and must be greatly confused by the vision and the command.

10:15 ¶ And a voice *spoke* to him again the second time, "What God has cleansed you must not call common."

God is preparing Peter to help the Gentiles come to know the Lord. When God cleanses a person through the new birth, their nationality becomes insignificant. At the very moment God is preparing Peter for the arrival of Cornelius's men at the house, the house of Cornelius is preparing for the arrival of Peter. God is working on both ends of this visitation.

10:16 This was done three times. And the object was taken up into heaven again.

Peter is acquainted with the grace of God, but he still harbors many prejudices against the Gentile people. This vision will be answered in a few minutes as the group from Caesarea is arriving at this very moment.

B. Peter Sought Out

10:17 ¶ Now while Peter wondered within himself what this vision which he had seen meant, behold, the men who had been sent from Cornelius had made inquiry for Simon's house, and stood before the gate.

Peter is perplexed because God asked him to do something contrary to the law, which was part of God's Word. He does not fully understand the change in dispensations.

10:18 And they called and asked whether Simon, whose surname was Peter, was lodging there.

And called (shouted), and asked whether Simon, which was surnamed (nicknamed) Peter, were lodged there.

10:19 ¶ While Peter thought about the vision, the Spirit said to him, "Behold, three men are seeking you.

Peter cannot not hear the men shouting because the gate is a great distance from the house. Also, Peter is concentrating on the vision and is not aware of the men.

10:20 Arise therefore, go down and go with them, doubting nothing; for I have sent them."

The Holy Spirit tells Peter of Cornelius' men and their arrival. Not only has the Holy Spirit prepared both sides for their meeting, he alerts Peter the time has arrived to meet. The Holy Spirit instructs Peter not to doubt. He is to go meet the men in faith.

10:21 ¶ Then Peter went down to the men who had been sent to him from Cornelius, and said, "Yes, I am he whom you seek. For what reason have you come?"

Although the Holy Spirit tells Peter of the men and their arrival, He does not inform Peter about their mission. Peter has to ask them a question.

10:22 ¶ And they said, "Cornelius *the* centurion, a just man, one who fears God and has a good reputation among all the nation of the Jews, was divinely instructed by a holy angel to summon you to his house, and to hear words from you."

And they said, Cornelius the centurion, a just (*dikaios*) man, and one that feareth (*phobeo*: reverences) God, and of good report (*martureo*: witness) among all the nation of the Jews, was warned from God by an holy (*hagios*) angel to send for thee into his house, and to hear words of (from) thee.

These men give Peter all of Cornelius's qualifications. They attempt to convince Peter to go based on the man's merits. Although Peter does want to know something about Cornelius, he travels with them only because God has instructed him to do so.

10:23 Then he invited them in and lodged *them.* ¶ On the next day Peter went away with them, and some brethren from Joppa accompanied him.

The Lord is honoring Simon the tanner. Although he is considered ceremonially unclean because he is a tanner, God allows him to witness an important moment in the spiritual history of the Gentile church. Not only does he have Peter, the greatest spiritual leader of the Jewish church, in his home, Roman representatives from the house of Cornelius, a top ranking official in the Italian band, have come. The very people who will witness the Holy Spirit's transition into the Gentile nations are in Simon's home.

IV. The Meeting of Peter and Cornelius (24–33)

Upon meeting Cornelius, a Gentile, Peter explains his vision and God's instruction. Peter then asks Cornelius to explain why he had been summoned. Cornelius recounts the angel's visitation four days earlier.

A. Cornelius Waits

10:24 ¶ And the following day they entered Caesarea. Now Cornelius was waiting for them, and had called together his relatives and close friends.

And the morrow (morning) after (leaving Joppa) they entered into Caesarea. And Cornelius waited for them, and had called together his kinsmen (relatives) and near (close) friends.

During the absence of his men, Cornelius had rounded up his relatives and close friends to hear the message Peter would bring. He has never seen or heard of Peter but is relying completely on the report of the angel. *Heb. 11*

B. Peter Arrives at the Home of Cornelius

10:25 As Peter was coming in, Cornelius met him and fell down at his feet and worshiped *him.*

Cornelius knows better than to fall down and worship Peter, but he has been waiting three days, and it is customary to bow before an emperor. He confuses the messenger with the God who sent him.

10:26 But Peter lifted him up, saying, "Stand up; I myself am also a man."

Peter immediately informs Cornelius that he is not a god nor is he the angel who spoke to him.

10:27 And as he talked with him, he went in and found many who had come together.

Peter is probably surprised to find a crowd waiting for him.

C. Jews and Gentiles

10:28 Then he said to them, "You know how unlawful it is for a Jewish man to keep company with or go to one of another nation. But God has shown me that I should not call any man common or unclean.

Peter's tradition begins to arise as he sees the company awaiting him in the next room. This was not the law but customs and traditions instituted by the legalistic religious leaders of Israel. The Mosaic law does not forbid fellowship or marriage to Gentiles, only to unbelievers.

10:29 Therefore I came without objection as soon as I was sent for. I ask, then, for what reason have you sent for me?"

Peter lets Cornelius know that despite his Jewish prejudice, he is quick to obey the Lord when He speaks.

D. Cornelius Recounts His Vision

10:30–33 ¶ So Cornelius said, "Four days ago I was fasting until this hour; and at the ninth hour I prayed in my house, and behold, a man stood before me in bright clothing, 31 and said, 'Cornelius, your prayer has been heard, and your alms are remembered in the sight of God. 32 Send therefore to Joppa and call Simon here, whose surname is Peter. He is lodging in the house of Simon, a tanner, by the sea. When he comes, he will speak to you.' 33 So I sent to you immediately, and you have done well to come. Now therefore, we are all present before God, to hear all the things commanded you by God."

Cornelius explains to Peter that four days earlier, an angel appeared to him and instructed him to have Peter brought to Caesarea to share whatever God instructed him to share. He then describes how the angel had given Peter's name and where to find him.

V. The Outpouring of the Holy Spirit on the Gentiles (34–48)

Peter preaches to the household of Cornelius, and the Holy Spirit is poured out on all the Gentiles. The Jews with Peter are astonished because they hear the Gentile believers speaking in tongues and magnifying God, just as they had. The new converts are then baptized in water.

A. Peter Preaches

10:34 ¶ Then Peter opened his mouth and said: "In truth I perceive that God shows no partiality.

Peter knows this is true from the scripture, but now he sees it firsthand. God does not judge anyone according to nationality, color, social status, or sex.

10:35 But in every nation whoever fears Him and works righteousness is accepted by Him.

But in every nation he that feareth him, and worketh (*ergozomai*: works out) righteousness, is accepted with (by) him.

This passage lines up with the verse of scripture Peter used in his sermon on the day of Pentecost from Joel 2:28.

10:36 The word which *God* sent to the children of Israel, preaching peace through Jesus Christ—He is Lord of all—

Jesus Christ is the Lord of all things, people, and nations (Colossians 1:16–21). The purpose of the Old Testament is for the Jew to preach God's message to the Gentiles, the message of reconciliation through Jesus Christ. Old Testament and New, Jesus has always been the means of salvation, and reconciliation has always been the message in the Old Testament (Isaiah 52:7) and New Testament (Ephesians 2:17, Colossians 1:20). This is the removal of the barrier of sin. Old Testament speaks of the reconciliation to come, and the New Testament says it has already been accomplished.

10:37 that word you know, which was proclaimed throughout all Judea, and began from Galilee after the baptism which John preached:

Peter reminds these Roman Gentiles the message of Jesus is nothing new; they know of Jesus. They have heard of His miracles and teachings. He not only came to the Jewish people, He lived in the Roman Empire. Both nations had dealings with Jesus.

John's baptism was mainly for Jews to repent of their sins and apostasy. It is from this point that the message of Jesus spread throughout the empire and into Caesarea, which has brought Cornelius to the present point of hearing the gospel.

10:38 how God anointed Jesus of Nazareth with the Holy Spirit and with power, who went about doing good and healing all who were oppressed by the devil, for God was with Him.

How God anointed Jesus of Nazareth with the Holy Ghost and with power (*dunamis,* Mark 5:30) who went about doing (*energeia*: producing) good, and healing all that were oppressed of the devil; for God was with him.

The Holy Spirit anointed the humanity of Jesus and was given for His teaching ministry as well as His miracles (Luke 4:16–21). Another name for the power which anointed Jesus is virtue (Mark 5:30, Luke 6:19).

10:39 And we are witnesses of all things which He did both in the land of the Jews and in Jerusalem, whom they killed by hanging on a tree.

Peter is addressing Romans. Romans tried Him, beat Him, and crucified Him; yet Peter blames the Jews. Religion put Jesus on the cross, not the Roman government.

10:40 Him God raised up on the third day, and showed Him openly,

Him God raised up the third day, and shewed him openly (publicly).

10:41 not to all the people, but to witnesses chosen before by God, *even* to us who ate and drank with Him after He arose from the dead.

Jesus was able to eat and drink with His resurrection body.

10:42 And He commanded us to preach to the people, and to testify that it is He who was ordained by God *to be* Judge of the living and the dead.

Jesus, who was judged, will be the judge of the spiritually living and dead.

10:43 To Him all the prophets witness that, through His name, whoever believes in Him will receive remission of sins."

The Holy Spirit will break in at the perfect time. While Peter gives the simplicity of salvation, Cornelius and his household believe (John 8:30). Jews and Gentiles are told in the Old Testament that faith in Jesus (the Messiah) brings remission or cleansing of sins.

B. The Holy Spirit Falls

10:44 ¶ While Peter was still speaking these words, the Holy Spirit fell upon all those who heard the word.

Now that these men are born again, just as on the day of Pentecost in Jerusalem, the Holy Spirit falls, and they are filled with the Spirit.

10:45 And those of the circumcision who believed were astonished, as many as came with Peter, because the gift of the Holy Spirit had been poured out on the Gentiles also.

And the circumcision (Jews) which believed were astonished (astounded), as many as came with Peter, because that on the Gentiles also was poured out the gift of the Holy Ghost.

This verse tells us the Holy Spirit falls on the Gentiles (non-Jews).

10:46 For they heard them speak with tongues and magnify God. ¶ Then Peter answered,

The Jews know the Gentiles are filled with the Holy Spirit because they are speaking with tongues. Apparently, they also prophesy because they are filled with the Spirit. We see later in Ephesus, Gentiles who have been filled with the Spirit will also prophesy (19:6).

10:47 "Can anyone forbid water, that these should not be baptized who have received the Holy Spirit just as we *have*?"

Peter now changes his sermon to include water baptism as an outward sign of their new birth.

10:48 And he commanded them to be baptized in the name of the Lord. Then they asked him to stay a few days.

Peter and his friends stay for a few days to teach and disciple the new converts.

11:1-30 Expansion of the Gospel

The Challenge of Chapter Eleven

There is always a tendency for legalism to creep into the church, but we are saved by grace through faith, not through any effort on our part. It is a gift from God (Ephesians 2:8). We cannot add anything to the gift of our salvation and must guard against becoming legalistic in our relationship with the Lord and others. Our righteousnesses, achieved through human works is as filthy rags (Isaiah 64:6) when compared to the righteousness of God we receive at salvation. Salvation is available to anyone who will receive it. We must ever strive to live in the grace of God in our daily lives.

I. Opposition to the Spreading of the Gospel (1–18)

With the rapid spread of the gospel, Gentiles are being born again and filled with the Holy Spirit. The elders of the church at Jerusalem dispute with Peter because he has gone into the home of uncircumcised men and eaten foods forbidden by Jewish law. Peter describes the vision he received when regarding the Gentiles. This temporarily assuages their legalism.

The church is now expanding both geographically and racially. What began in Jerusalem on the day of Pentecost has now spread, and the elders of the Jerusalem church are becoming legalistic. They do not want other races or cities to receive the gospel. They are trying to combine law and grace, and the "little leaven" is destroying the "lump."

A. Peter Challenged

11:1-2 ¶ Now the apostles and brethren who were in Judea heard that the Gentiles had also received the word of God. 2 And when Peter came up to Jerusalem, those of the circumcision contended with him,

The Jews begin an argument with Peter for taking the gospel to the Gentiles. They seem to have forgotten about Jesus declaring the message of the gospel would extend from Jerusalem to "the uttermost parts of the earth." They have turned their focus toward and begun emphasizing the law of circumcision.

The reaction of these men is typical of many denominations today. They are "religious," judging spirituality by actions that any sinner could perform.

11:3 saying, "You went in to uncircumcised men and ate with them!"

After Peter and his men stayed with Cornelius for a few days, they were free to eat with him and the other Gentile believers. This means Peter has eaten food forbidden under Jewish law. He probably ate some of the meat he saw in the vision on the housetop.

B. Peter Recounts His Housetop Vision

11:4 ¶ But Peter explained *it* to them in order from the beginning, saying:

Peter will share the story told in chapter 10 without omitting a single detail. He will describe the events in chronological order so those listening understand the involvement of the Holy Spirit from both sides of the situation.

Verses 5 through 17 recount the salvation and infilling of the Holy Spirit in the house of Cornelius (which would begin the great revival among the Gentiles).

11:5–10 "I was in the city of Joppa praying; and in a trance I saw a vision, an object descending like a great sheet, let down from heaven by four corners; and it came to me. 6 When I observed it intently and considered, I saw four-footed animals of the earth, wild beasts, creeping things, and birds of the air. 7 And I heard a voice saying to me, 'Rise, Peter; kill and eat.' 8 But I said, 'Not so, Lord! For nothing common or unclean has at any time entered my mouth.' 9 But the voice answered me again from heaven, 'What God has cleansed you must not call common.' 10 Now this was done three times, and all were drawn up again into heaven.

Peter might not have visited the home of a Gentile apart from the vision and the Lord speaking directly to him concerning the vision.

C. Peter Recounts the Events of His Journey to Caesarea

11:11–17 At that very moment, three men stood before the house where I was, having been sent to me from Caesarea. 12 Then the Spirit told me to go with them, doubting nothing. Moreover these six brethren accompanied me, and we entered the man's house. 13 And he told us how he had seen an angel standing in his house, who said to him, 'Send men to Joppa, and call for Simon whose surname is Peter, 14 who will tell you words by which you and all your household will be saved.' 15 And as I began to speak, the Holy Spirit fell upon them, as upon us at the beginning. 16 Then I remembered the word of the Lord, how He said, 'John indeed baptized with water, but you shall be baptized with the Holy Spirit.' 17 If therefore God gave them the same gift as He *gave* us when we believed on the Lord Jesus Christ, who was I that I could withstand God?'"

All of Peter's prejudice and religious thinking are gone at this display of the grace and sovereignty of God concerning the Gentiles.

D. Legalism Temporarily Defeated

11:18 ¶ When they heard these things they became silent; and they glorified God, saying, "Then God has also granted to the Gentiles repentance to life."

Legalism is temporarily defeated in Jerusalem. Peter's recounting of the event helps for a time, but legalism eventually creeps back in, destroying the church and ultimately Jerusalem itself in 70 AD. As goes the church, so goes the nation. The men at this conference are silenced by the words of Peter. The love of God that has confronted Peter is now causing a change in the thinking of the legalistic Jews.

II. The Church at Antioch (19–30)

A number of the Jews who scattered in chapter 8 have gone to Antioch to start a church. A revival begins with such an impact that even the believers in Jerusalem three hundred miles away hear about it. Barnabas understands the grace of God and sees that grace in operation in the church at Antioch. He is instrumental in bringing Paul to Antioch to instruct the new converts in the Word of God.

Prophets from Jerusalem arrive in Antioch, and Agabus prophesies about a famine coming to Jerusalem. The saints in Antioch take up an offering for the church at Jerusalem in response to this prophecy.

11:19 ¶ Now those who were scattered after the persecution that arose over Stephen traveled as far as Phoenicia, Cyprus, and Antioch, preaching the word to no one but the Jews only.

In verses 19 through 30, the discussion returns to the Jews scattered at the beginning of chapter 8. Part of those scattered travel to Antioch and begin a church.

11:20 But some of them were men from Cyprus and Cyrene, who, when they had come to Antioch, spoke to the Hellenists, preaching the Lord Jesus.

Some Jews witnessed to other Jews alone (v. 19) while others also witnessed to Gentiles (v. 20).

A. Signs and Wonders

something is about to happen.

11:21 And the hand of the Lord was with them, and a great number believed and turned to the Lord.

When "the hand of the Lord" is mentioned, it is a reference to signs and wonders. The miracles draw attention to the gospel, and many Gentiles are born again.

B. Striving to Maintain Grace

Man of encouragement

11:22 ¶ Then news of these things came to the ears of the church in Jerusalem, and they sent out Barnabas to go as far as Antioch.

From his humble beginnings, when he first gave to the church in Jerusalem (4:36), Barnabas has become a great minister. He understands grace and will later become the leader of the Antioch church and travel with Paul on his first missionary journey.

11:23 When he came and had seen the grace of God, he was glad, and encouraged them all that with purpose of heart they should continue with the Lord.

Barnabas remains in Jerusalem with the disciples after the stoning of Stephen (8:1). He continues in Jerusalem through the decline of the church and has been disturbed by what he has observed. He knows something is wrong, but has not identified the problem and is praying to discover what it is. God then sends Barnabas to Antioch, and he is so impressed with the attitude of grace he observes in these believers that he exhorts them to maintain it (Galatians 5:1).

Barnabas remains a man of grace, and what is so visible in Antioch is the grace of God. This is a stark contrast to Jerusalem. Peter later discovers this same grace (Galatians 2:11–21).

Barnabas is not legalistic. If he had been, he would have been angry at the freedom he saw in Antioch. Grace always irritates legalistic people. Legalistic people will try to pull others down into their traditions and works. Christians must strive to maintain grace (Hebrews 4:11).

> **11:24 For he was a good man, full of the Holy Spirit and of faith. And a great many people were added to the Lord.**

For he was a good man (in God's sight), and full of the Holy Ghost (prayed in tongues) and of faith (studied the word): and much people was added unto the Lord.

When a church emphasizes the grace of God, many people are born again. The church in Antioch became the spiritual center for many years. Paul's first three missionary journeys began at Antioch.

Barnabas recognizes the need for good leadership in the church at Antioch. He does not return to Jerusalem to ask Peter, James, or any other elder in Jerusalem to come to Antioch. Instead, Barnabas travels to Tarsus and finds Paul, the man who had the greatest revelation of the grace of God.

C. Barnabas Seeks for Saul

> **11:25 ¶ Then Barnabas departed for Tarsus to seek Saul.**

Barnabas was not jealous of Paul's superior knowledge and gifts. He was only interested in the growth of the saints in Antioch.

> **11:26 And when he had found him, he brought him to Antioch. So it was that for a whole year they assembled with the church and taught a great many people. And the disciples were first called Christians in Antioch.**

In his search for Paul, Barnabas is not supernaturally guided as in the case of Peter and Cornelius. Barnabas seeks out Paul for himself. When Paul arrives in Antioch, he teaches the people for one year.

New converts need teaching. The first teachings converts receive should establish them in the grace of God. Teaching and training transforms converts into disciples.

The name "Christian" means Christlike. You do not become Christlike until you become a disciple. The disciples were called Christians, but it was a derogatory term when first used by Gentiles against believers.

D. The Office of the Prophet

11:27 ⸏ And in these days prophets came from Jerusalem to Antioch.

The office of the prophet found in the New Testament is very similar to the prophet (or seer) of the Old Testament. In the New Testament, God uses prophets to warn of the attacks of Satan and to judge prophecy (1 Corinthians 14:9).

11:28 Then one of them, named Agabus, stood up and showed by the Spirit that there was going to be a great famine throughout all the world, which also happened in the days of Claudius Caesar.

Agabus is an accurate prophet. He rises up from among the prophets and prophesies of a famine that would come to the area of Jerusalem, which was fulfilled. This prophecy is probably made before the leaders of the church rather than the congregation. The word is received and an offering started for the saints at Jerusalem.

The drought came to pass in the days of Claudius Caesar, two years later. Claudius Caesar was the cousin of Caligula, the third emperor of the Roman Empire and was assassinated after just four years as emperor.

Agabus is the same man who later prophesies to Paul of his impending danger and imprisonment (21:10). He warned Paul not to return to Jerusalem. Paul did not heed his warning.

E. The Church at Antioch Gives

11:29 Then the disciples, each according to his ability, determined to send relief to the brethren dwelling in Judea.

The members of Antioch are not forced or coerced into giving. Each gives according to their ability, which is mature giving, in response to Agabus's prophecy. They also give because the believers in Jerusalem are their spiritual brothers and sisters. Distance is never an issue in the body of Christ. We are all members of the family of God (Ephesians 3:15), and we never leave the family.

11:30 This they also did, and sent it to the elders by the hands of Barnabas and Saul.

The people of the church give the money to their church leaders who, in turn, give it to the leaders of the Jerusalem church. This demonstrates their maturity. If they had sent the money directly to congregational members of the Jerusalem church, it might have been viewed by the church leaders as trying to "buy" the "sheep" without their knowledge. They trust the elders of the church at Jerusalem to distribute the money fairly. Unfortunately, the Jerusalem church does not appreciate their offering and later tries to destroy the church at Antioch.

12:1–25 Peter's Escape from Prison

The Challenge of Chapter Twelve

We should never fear the world's attitude toward the spreading of the gospel. If persecution comes, imprisonment, or even the possibility of death, we can experience God's divine peace while trusting His ability to deliver us supernaturally. The gospel cannot and will not be stopped, and Jesus will return to establish His kingdom in the earth.

I. Herod Persecutes the Church (1–4)

With the spreading and growing influence of the gospel, Herod begins to persecute the Church. He kills James the brother of John and because James' death so pleases the Jews, he captures and imprisons Peter. He plans to also put Peter to death after the days of unleavened bread have passed.

> **12:1 ¶ Now about that time Herod the king stretched out *his* hand to harass some from the church.**

Now about that time Herod the king stretched forth his hands to vex (persecute and kill) certain (key members) of the church.

The phrase "about that time" refers to the time of the drought in Jerusalem. Herod Agrippa is the king mentioned in this verse. He is the grandson of Herod the Great. Herod, like his grandfather, embraces Judaism and wants to please the Jews. He learns of their hatred for Christians and is determined to persecute the church. This is primarily a political move on his part. Being a military man, he knows the best way to instill fear and discouragement into a group is to kill one of their leaders (5:36–37). Typically, when a leader of a movement is killed, the followers disperse rapidly. However, in this particular instance, that plan backfires on Herod. Peter will remain alive, and Christianity will survive and flourish.

A. James Is Killed

> **12:2 Then he killed James the brother of John with the sword.**

James, the brother of John is decapitated. Jesus had nicknamed James and John the "Sons of Thunder" (Mark 3:17). Their mother had asked for each of her sons to be seated beside Jesus in His kingdom (Matthew 20:20–23).

Following the death of Stephen, James is the next apostle to be killed. John will be the last.

This extreme persecution arises as a result of the legalism in Jerusalem. James' death could have been prevented through the prayers of the saints. However, because of James's death, when Peter is thrown in prison, the church immediately begins to intercede for him.

B. Peter Is Seized

12:3 And because he saw that it pleased the Jews, he proceeded further to seize Peter also. Now it was *during* the Days of Unleavened Bread.

Peter is held in prison temporarily with the plan to later execute him only because the Jews had a law that no one could be executed during a feast day.

12:4 So when he had arrested him, he put *him* in prison, and delivered *him* to four squads of soldiers to keep him, intending to bring him before the people after Passover.

And when he had apprehended him, he put him in prison, and delivered him to four quaternions of soldiers to keep him; intending after Easter (Passover) to bring him forth to the people.

A "quaternion" is the smallest division in the Roman army consisting of four soldiers. There is one quaternion for each watch of the day (six hours). Two soldiers are chained to Peter, one on each arm. The other two soldiers watch the door. Herod's intention is to leave Peter in prison until the Passover week is completed and then to publicly execute him.

II. Peter Miraculously Freed (5–17)

As the church in Antioch prays without ceasing for Peter, an angel appears and the chains that bind Peter fall from his wrists. The angel instructs Peter to follow him, which he does. Peter eventually finds himself in the street outside the gates of the prison. He immediately goes to the house of Mary where the believers are praying.

A. Church Prays Without Ceasing

12:5 ¶ Peter was therefore kept in prison, but constant prayer was offered to God for him by the church.

The prayer made "without ceasing" is intercessory prayer. This prayer could have lasted as long as one week during the Feast of Unleavened Bread. This verse also tells us the church is not a building but a people. Buildings do not pray. People pray.

> **12:6 And when Herod was about to bring him out, that night Peter was sleeping, bound with two chains between two soldiers; and the guards before the door were keeping the prison.**

Peter has been in jail for many days and was sleeping the night before his execution. This is the gift of faith in operation (1 Corinthians 12:9). The same gift was in operation when Daniel was in the lion's den and when Paul was on board a ship destined to be shipwrecked (Acts 27).

The gift of faith can operate in one of two ways. A person can become bold under this gift as Samson did or as David did before Goliath. Other times, this gift causes a person to become peaceful during a time of tribulation, like Jesus sleeping through the storm.

B. An Angel Appears

> **12:7 Now behold, an angel of the Lord stood by *him*, and a light shone in the prison; and he struck Peter on the side and raised him up, saying, "Arise quickly!" And his chains fell off *his* hands.**

The angel of the Lord described in this verse is not a visitation from the angel of the Lord (Jesus) in the Old Testament. This particular angel comes to rescue Peter. The light that shines in the prison is the glory surrounding the angel. Peter is consistent. He slept while Jesus prayed in Gethsemane (Matthew 26:39–41), and now he is sleeping while the church is praying for him.

Peter has improved the cause for his sleep. Unlike the time in the Garden of Gethsemane when he was supposed to be watching and praying for Jesus, he now is sleeping because he has God's peace and the gift of faith operating in his life. In fact, Peter is in such a deep sleep, the angel has to hit him on the side to wake him up.

> **12:8 Then the angel said to him, "Gird yourself and tie on your sandals"; and so he did. And he said to him, "Put on your garment and follow me."**

What Peter could do, the angel commands him to do. But what Peter could not do, the angel does for him. The angel does not dress Peter or put his shoes on him. The angel did not carry Peter out of the prison. Peter could do that himself. However, Peter could not free himself. The chains fell off his wrists by supernatural power.

C. Peter Follows the Angel

12:9 So he went out and followed him, and did not know that what was done by the angel was real, but thought he was seeing a vision.

Peter is still not quite awake and thinks he is having another housetop vision.

12:10 When they were past the first and the second guard posts, they came to the iron gate that leads to the city, which opened to them of its own accord; and they went out and went down one street, and immediately the angel departed from him.

Peter comes to himself once he is outside the prison. The air in his face probably fully awakens Peter, and as he stands in the streets of Jerusalem, he realizes a true miracle has just taken place. This is Peter's second miraculous deliverance from prison (5:19).

D. Peter Comes to Himself

12:11 ¶ And when Peter had come to himself, he said, "Now I know for certain that the Lord has sent His angel, and has delivered me from the hand of Herod and *from* all the expectation of the Jewish people."

Peter is delivered from the Jews and the Romans simultaneously.

12:12 ¶ So, when he had considered *this*, he came to the house of Mary, the mother of John whose surname was Mark, where many were gathered together praying.

Peter has some time to think about what has just happened before he arrives at the prayer meeting. Peter does not consider fleeing. Instead, as he had done previously, he goes to his "own company" (4:23).

Those who are praying for Peter have gathered together in the home of Mark's mother, Mary. Mark wrote the book of Mark based on accounts he

Jesus spoke to demons once (handwritten)

received from Peter. This is our first introduction to Mark. He is the same man who will accompany Paul and Barnabas on their first missionary journey from Antioch (v. 25, 13:5)

E. Rhoda at the Gate of Mary's House

12:13–14 And as Peter knocked at the door of the gate, a girl named Rhoda came to answer. 14 When she recognized Peter's voice, because of *her* gladness she did not open the gate, but ran in and announced that Peter stood before the gate.

Rhoda is probably a servant girl working in Mary's home. She is a believer, and although she is not praying with the others, she is concerned for Peter's deliverance from prison. When she sees Peter outside the gate, she is so excited, she runs to tell everyone and leaves Peter standing at the gate.

12:15 But they said to her, "You are beside yourself!" Yet she kept insisting that it was so. So they said, "It is his angel."

The intercessory, prevailing prayer of those gathered has been effective. Their prayers manifested so quickly, no one is ready to stop praying. They had planned to pray for a long period of time for Peter's deliverance and are surprised when the answer comes.

They initially think the girl has seen an angel. It should be easier to believe Peter is outside the gate than an angel. An angel would appear to them in their prayer room rather than knocking on the gate.

12:16 ¶ Now Peter continued knocking; and when they opened *the door* and saw him, they were astonished.

But Peter continued knocking: and when they had opened the door, and saw him, they were astonished (speechless).

The group finally goes to the gate to see if Peter is really there.

F. Peter's Testimony of Being Delivered from Prison

12:17 But motioning to them with his hand to keep silent, he declared to them how the Lord had brought him out of the prison. And he said, "Go, tell these things to James and to the brethren." And he departed and went to another place. *brother of Jesus* (handwritten)

Speak to demons at home (handwritten)

When they see it is Peter, they are initially speechless, but then begin talking so loudly Peter has to quiet them with his hand. He tells them the story of his deliverance and asks them to tell the church leaders what has happened.

After attending the prayer meeting in Mary's house, he departs for Antioch. Although he has been supernaturally delivered, he knows it is important to leave town quickly. The soldiers who have been left at the prison will be in danger for their lives and might come looking for Peter at Mary's house.

III. Response to Peter's Escape (18–20)

Herod is extremely angered by Peter's escape and searches for him unsuccessfully. Herod executes all of the guards who were on watch when Peter walked out of the prison.

> **12:18 ¶ Then, as soon as it was day, there was no small stir among the soldiers about what had become of Peter.**

In the natural realm, Peter's escape is impossible. The "stir" among the soldiers is comprised of confusion and disbelief which will then turn to anger.

> **12:19 But when Herod had searched for him and not found him, he examined the guards and commanded that *they* should be put to death. And he went down from Judea to Caesarea, and stayed *there*.**

At this point, Herod becomes angry and fearful for his kingdom and position as king. He has tried to please the Jews as much as possible, but now that things have become difficult, he returns to his true allegiance, the Romans. He flees to Caesarea, a Roman city.

> **12:20 ¶ Now Herod had been very angry with the people of Tyre and Sidon; but they came to him with one accord, and having made Blastus the king's personal aide their friend, they asked for peace, because their country was supplied with food by the king's *country*.**

A border dispute has broken out in this area of Phoenicia and has lasted for many years. Herod is angry at them during this time. While he is in Caesarea, the people of Tyre and Sidon come with a united front to meet with Herod and make peace because they fear he will cut off financial aid to their countries. They bribe Blastus to arrange a meeting for them with Herod.

IV. The Death of Herod (21–22)

Herod gives a speech, and the audience heralds him as a god. Because Herod does not give glory to God for his position, an angel of God strikes him dead.

A. Herod Deified

12:21 ¶ So on a set day Herod, arrayed in royal apparel, sat on his throne and gave an oration to them.

Herod decides to make a big show of extending peace to the people of Tyre and Sidon. He is full of arrogance, and expects the people to revere him.

12:22 And the people kept shouting, "The voice of a god and not of a man!"

Because of fear of losing their finances, the people play into Herod's arrogance.

B. Herod and the Angel

12:23 Then immediately an angel of the Lord struck him, because he did not give glory to God. And he was eaten by worms and died.

According to the historian Josephus, the entire process of Herod's sickness from worms to death took approximately five days. The angel referred to in this verse is probably the same angel who delivered Peter from prison. Now he is delivering Peter from Herod. The assumption can be made that someone is still interceding for Peter's safety and for the government of the land. When a government plays God, it will be judged. Herod becomes weak and dies, but the church cannot be destroyed (Matthew 16:18).

V. The Gospel Continues to Spread (24–25)

Neither the death of James nor the imprisonment of Peter hinders the spread of the gospel.

12:24 ¶ But the word of God grew and multiplied.

Out of persecution, the church, the Word, and the disciples increase. They also increase in power. Whenever the Word increases, so does the number of disciples. When the number of disciples increases, so does the number of converts (6:7).

12:25 ¶ And Barnabas and Saul returned from Jerusalem when they had fulfilled *their* ministry, and they also took with them John whose surname was Mark.

Barnabas and Saul are given the mission to deliver money collected by believers in Antioch to the saints in Jerusalem (11:27–30). When they return to Antioch, Barnabas and Saul take Mark with them on their first missionary journey.

13:1-52 Revival Spreads

The Challenge of Chapter Thirteen

Missions spread the gospel and teach the message of grace to those who have not heard it. Sending people God has called to specific missions should be an integral part of the local church. We should be bold to preach God's Word, even in the midst of persecution, but if an individual or group rejects the message of the gospel, we need to move on to others whose hearts are open.

I. The Birth of Missions

Missionary activity emanating from a local church begins in Antioch. Throughout many of the remaining chapters in the book of Acts, this church becomes the central launching place for spreading the gospel.

Previously, individual men had gone in response to a directive from God after a mission work had already been established (Acts 8). However, not only is it God's desire to send people out in alignment with His will, but it is his desire for them to be recognized and sanctioned by church leaders.

The Great Commission is a joint effort by God and man. God chooses Antioch as the place the mission team will be sent from. Antioch becomes the center of missionary activity for many chapters to come.

The church at Antioch is successful because:

1. It is not founded by the apostles; it has been founded by common men who were disciples of Cyprus and Cyrene (11:29).
2. It grows under Barnabas, a man of grace (11:22–23). Saul, whose life was dedicated to Gentiles and whose gift was teaching, grounds the church at Antioch (11:26). They are instructed in grace from the start.
3. Antioch is a giving church. They give to Jerusalem, a legalistic church (11:29–30). They give because it is their nature to give, not because of the nature of those in need. They operate in true love.

II. The Separation of Barnabas and Saul to Ministry (1–3)

A group of prophets and teachers are spending time together ministering to the Lord. As they fast and pray, the Lord speaks to them to separate Barnabas and Saul. In response, the men with Barnabas and Saul pray, lay hands on them, and send them away.

A. Leadership in the Church at Antioch

13:1 Now in the church that was at Antioch there were certain prophets and teachers: Barnabas, Simeon who was called Niger, Lucius of Cyrene, Manaen who had been brought up with Herod the tetrarch, and Saul.

Previously we studied about the prophets who left the fading church at Jerusalem to become part of the growing church at Antioch (11:27–28). During this time, others may have been rising up in the congregation and receiving the call of God while learning under the leadership of the prophets who were present. Prophets primarily give leadership from the Holy Spirit. Teachers give leadership from the Word of God.

The name of the church at Antioch is given to identify its location as home base from which ministers will travel. Although these particular ministers primarily travel from church to church and city to city, they are sent from and return to the local church.

Many fallacies have been based on Acts 13. Some teaching purports each church must have prophets and apostles who attend and officiate, that they must be part of the government of the local church. This is not correct. Although prophets and apostles are mentioned as being in leadership positions in the Antioch church, the office of the pastor had not yet been established and local churches were not being established in the many cities where mission activity will occur. The names of the prophets and teachers are mentioned and called "certain." These are key and unique leaders in the church at Antioch.

1. **Barnabas**: Previously discussed as one of the founders of the church.
2. **Simeon**: called Niger (the Nigerian), a black prophet from North Africa.
3. **Lucius**: of Cyrene, a fellow worker with Paul (Romans 16:21).
4. **Manaen**: Stepson of Herod by a Samaritan woman named Malfauke. He is a wealthy aristocrat who became born again and a gifted teacher at Antioch. His brothers Antipas and Archelaus, were both unbelievers. Antipas is the king who beheaded John the Baptist.
5. **Saul**: In this chapter, Saul is nicknamed Paul (v. 9), and is called Paul from this point on.

B. Ministering to the Lord

13:2 As they ministered to the Lord and fasted, the Holy Spirit said, "Now separate to Me Barnabas and Saul for the work to which I have called them."

As they ministered (*leitourgeo*: were ministering) to the Lord, and fasted (were fasting), the Holy Ghost said, Separate (*aphorizo*) me Barnabas and Saul for (because of) the work whereunto I have called them.

The Greek word for "ministered" means to minister sacrificially at your own expense (cf. Romans 13:6, 15:16, 27; Hebrews 1:7, 8:2, 10:11).

In this instance, Barnabas, Simeon, Lucius, Manaen, and Saul are ministering directly to the Lord. It is part of their priestly duty (1 Peter 2:9), and apparently, these five leaders meet together to minister to the Lord quite often.

C. The Holy Spirit Speaks

As they are ministering, the Holy Spirit speaks through one of the prophets and gives the call for separation to Barnabas and Saul. They will be separated to the Lord's calling, and from other ministers they have grown close to in the church. The Greek word for "separate" means to mark off by boundaries. God is calling Saul and Barnabas both from something and to something. The calling is past tense, and the separation is present. There is a time period between their calling and their separation. God had everything to do with the calling, and they have everything to do with the separation. The point of separation comes because of their faithfulness in the ministry. The Holy Spirit does the choosing and the separating, but the point of separation is dependent on the one called. This is why many are called, but few are chosen. Most Christians will not pay the price of faithfulness to reach the point of separation. Paul is separated into the ministry because of his faithfulness (1 Timothy 1:12). In verse 3, men see the faithfulness and calling on men and lay hands on them in recognition. God calls and separates, men agree.

D. Barnabas and Saul Sent

13:3 Then, having fasted and prayed, and laid hands on them, they sent *them* away.

Until this time, they had fasted and ministered. Now they need guidance and they pray. Simeon, Lucius, and Manaen lay their hands on Barnabas and Saul. The purpose is twofold:

1. Their hands represented their agreement with the leadership of the Holy Spirit.
2. Laying hands on Barnabas and Saul indicates the transference of the power of the Holy Spirit to the call upon their lives.

The hands of these men represent the hand of the Lord and the power of the Holy Spirit. Until this time, hands have only been used for the infilling of the Holy Spirit and healing. This is the first case of hands being laid on individuals for separation into ministry.

III. Preaching in Cyprus (4–12)

Barnabas and Paul travel from Antioch to the city of Seleucia, just south of Antioch and, from there, sail to the island of Cyprus. They arrive in the city of Salamis where they preach to the Jews in the synagogues. From there they travel to Paphos, and the proconsul calls for them because he wants to hear the Word of God. Present with the proconsul is a sorcerer who tries to turn him from the message of faith. Saul (Paul) filled with the Holy Spirit, confronts the man, who suddenly becomes blind and requests to be led out of the room by his hand. When the proconsul sees this "wonder," he believes.

A. Seleucia

> **13:4 ¶ So, being sent out by the Holy Spirit, they went down to Seleucia, and from there they sailed to Cyprus.**

Even though men sent them forth, Barnabas and Saul consider this the work of the Holy Spirit. Seleucia is the port where they caught a ship to Cyprus, an island in the Mediterranean. This island is valuable to the Romans for its mineral wealth, mainly copper. The Latin name for copper is *cyprium,* and so the island was named Cyprus for its copper.

B. Salamis

> **13:5 And when they arrived in Salamis, they preached the word of God in the synagogues of the Jews. They also had John as *their* assistant.**

And when they (Barnabas and Saul) were at Salamis, they preached the word of God in the synagogues of the Jews: and they had also John to their minister (*huperetes*).

Salamis, the eastern seaport of Cyprus, is known as the Greek harbor. When they land, they preach their first message in the synagogues (Romans 1:16).

Preaching the Word of God in denominational churches is nothing new. Paul and Barnabas do this on their first missionary journey at their first stop. John Mark ,who has been mentioned before, now joins them. Mark is probably the nephew of Barnabas.

C. The Underrower

Mark wrote the book of Mark from notes and stories Peter had shared with him. The Greek word for "minister" means underrower. For slaves, this was the lowest position on a Roman ship. There were three levels of rowers, and the newest slaves were placed on the bottom level. It was considered a promotion to be raised to the second level. A slave could rise to the highest position on the first level of the ship. Paul and Barnabas are probably first level rowers and Mark traveled with them to carry their suitcases, book their hotel and transportation, and prepare the churches for when they arrived to speak.

Although Paul and Barnabas are top level rowers, they are still rowers. The passengers who ride on the deck are the greatest. The congregations are the ones who make the ministry possible.

D. Bar-Jesus the Sorcerer

> 13:6 ¶ Now when they had gone through the island to Paphos, they found a certain sorcerer, a false prophet, a Jew whose name *was* Bar-Jesus,

Paphos is a seaport on the western end of Cyprus known as the Phoenician harbor. It was famous for the occult and the worship of Venus (v. 19). Bar-Jesus was in league with Satan. He was demon possessed and the advisor to the ruler of the island (Daniel 10:13, 20).

> 13:7 who was with the proconsul, Sergius Paulus, an intelligent man. This man called for Barnabas and Saul and sought to hear the word of God.

Which was with (an advisor to) the deputy (pro counsel) of the country, Sergius Paulus, a prudent (intelligent) man; who called for Barnabas and Saul, and desired to hear the word of God.

Saul's name is Jewish. His Roman name is Paul or Paulus (v. 9). He and Sergius come from the same Roman heritage. They both have the name Paulus. As proconsul of the island, he desires to hear the gospel, but his demon-possessed advisor will try to block it from happening.

E. Elymas the Sorcerer

13:8 But Elymas the sorcerer (for so his name is translated) withstood them, seeking to turn the proconsul away from the faith.

Elymas means wise one in Arabian. He apparently tries to discredit both Saul and Barnabas in the presence of Sergius.

13:9 Then Saul, who also *is called* Paul, filled with the Holy Spirit, <u>looked intently at him</u>   *(the Spirit)*

Saul, who is also called Paul (like Sergius), has been praying in the Spirit for some time and now stares at Elymas. It is difficult for this demon-possessed person to look back into the eyes of a believer.

13:10 and said, "O full of all deceit and all fraud, *you* son of the devil, *you* enemy of all righteousness, will you not cease perverting the straight ways of the Lord?

And said, O full of all subtlety (guile) and all mischief (craftiness), thou child of the devil, thou enemy of all righteousness, wilt thou not cease to pervert the right ways of the Lord?

Paul now has the upper hand by exposing this man before all who are present. Paul asks Elymas if he is determined to continue perverting God's ways. If so, God will put a stop to it.

13:11 And now, indeed, the hand of the Lord *is* upon you, and you shall be blind, not seeing the sun for a time." ¶ And immediately a dark mist fell on him, and he went around seeking someone to lead him by the hand.

God immediately judges Elymas. In humiliation, the man who once was in control is now blind and must be led out by those who can see. Not only is he blind, his satanic roots have been exposed. He has fooled many for a long time, including the leader of the island. Now Jesus' greater power has revealed his true nature.

eyes are windows to the soul.

F. God's Word in Demonstration

13:12 Then the proconsul believed, when he saw what had been done, being astonished at the teaching of the Lord.

This man not only hears the doctrines and teachings of Paul, he sees the wonders that accompany the Word. Again, this is the purpose of miracles and the gifts of the Holy Spirit. This deputy believes in Jesus and is born again.

IV. Paul Preaches in Antioch (13–42)

From Cyprus, Paul and Barnabas travel to Antioch and John (Mark) returns to Jerusalem. When they arrive in Pisidia, they enter the synagogue on the Sabbath. Because they are visitors, they are invited to speak and Paul accepts. He begins by giving a brief history of the Jews, and like Stephen, he will use Jewish history to reveal that Jesus Christ is the God of Israel.

A. The Journey

Verse 13 begins the second half of their missionary journey. The first half of their journey is to the island of Cyprus. This is probably the suggestion of Barnabas since he came from Cyprus (4:36).

The second half of their journey is a return to the mainland, to Pamphylia.

B. Perga

13:13 ¶Now when Paul and his party set sail from Paphos, they came to Perga in Pamphylia; and John, departing from them, returned to Jerusalem.

Now when Paul and his company loosed (set sail) from Paphos, they came to Perga in Pamphylia (modern day Turkey): and John (Mark) departing from them returned to Jerusalem.

Perga in Pamphylia is a very ancient city where pirates and bandits lived for over four hundred years. The rocky coastline made good hangouts for these men, and no one traveled into this region unless accompanied by armed guards. The terrain further inland was mountainous, which also made good natural protection against military forces attempting to flush out these criminals.

The area was cleaned up by Rome approximately one hundred years later when Hannibal was defeated by Rome. Alexander the Great said the greatest opposition and fiercest fighting he had ever encountered was in Pamphylia. Paul also refers to this place in his account of trials he suffered recorded in 2 Corinthians 11:26.

C. Mark Departs

The conditions at Perga are the reason Mark deserts Paul and Barnabas. Although Paul keeps silent, he is tremendously upset by Mark's desertion. Even when Mark repents and expresses a desire to go on the second missionary journey, Paul does not forget. This will eventually become a point of division between Paul and Barnabas (15:37–40).

Mark returns to Jerusalem because this is where his mother lives (12:12) and probably the reason Paul is so bothered by his departure. Paul does not like to be deserted, especially by someone simply returning to his mother. Mark did fine as a traveling companion as long as God led them someplace prosperous and civilized like Cyprus. However, when the Spirit led them to the other extreme, Mark is moved by his senses and fear dominates his decision. Mark leaves Paul and Barnabas at a critical point (15:38). Paul and Barnabas are more seasoned in traveling by faith and go expecting a great harvest. Paul later admits he needed Mark (2 Timothy 4:11).

D. Paul and Barnabas Arrive in Antioch

13:14 But when they departed from Perga, they came to Antioch in Pisidia, and went into the synagogue on the Sabbath day and sat down.

Perga is the point where John Mark caught a ship back to Jerusalem and Paul and Barnabas travel to Antioch. Paul and Barnabas do not evangelize here but move directly to the interior. They will preach in Perga on the way out (14:25).

E. Paul's Sermon

13:15 And after the reading of the Law and the Prophets, the rulers of the synagogue sent to them, saying, "Men *and* brethren, if you have any word of exhortation for the people, say on."

The sermon begins with the priests commenting on sections of the Old Testament. They see strangers in the congregation, Paul and Barnabas, and ask if they have any comments or words for the people. They probably expect Paul and Barnabas to share where they are from and what business brings them to Pisidia in Antioch. They are recognized as Jews and are invited to speak.

13:16 ¶ Then Paul stood up, and motioning with *his* hand said, "Men of Israel, and you who fear God, listen:

Paul addresses both Jewish and Gentile unbelievers who are present (as well as those who may have already been born again). He asks them to pay attention since it is time for visitors to speak.

F. Jewish History Reveals Jesus

1. Introduction

Verse 17 is the beginning of Paul's sermon. The introduction sounds very similar to Stephen's sermon (7:2). Since Paul is mainly speaking to Jews, he will use Jewish history to reveal that the God of Israel was indeed the Lord Jesus Christ, just as Stephen once had.

2. The Exodus

13:17 The God of this people Israel chose our fathers, and exalted the people when they dwelt as strangers in the land of Egypt, and with an uplifted arm He brought them out of it.

Stephen had previously revealed the Lord Jesus Christ as the God of the fathers of Israel (7:52). By His foreknowledge of their faith in Him, God had chosen Israel (Romans 8:29–30; Ephesians 1:4).

Election has always been the pattern with the patriarchs (Malachi 1:2), and faith has always been the means of pleasing the Lord (Hebrews 11:6). God exalted the chosen nation of Israel because they trusted in Him.

This exaltation occurred when Israel was in captivity in Egypt. Despite the hardships, Israel grew in numbers and became a threat to Egypt (Exodus 1:7–20). During this time of 400 years, they grew from seventy-five people to over two million. Throughout the years, Jews had exalted themselves, but now they will hear about the true one who chose, exalted, and delivered Israel, the Lord Jesus Christ.

The "uplifted arm" is a reference to the salvation and supernatural deliverance God brought to the nation through the exodus, Passover, and parting of the Red Sea.

3. The Wilderness

13:18 Now for a time of about forty years He put up with their ways in the wilderness.

And about the time of forty years suffered (put up with) he their manners (obnoxious habits of unbelief) in the wilderness.

Their manners and habits included fear, worry, unbelief, and doubt. God tolerated this in grace and love for forty years. He came to the end of His longsuffering, and the first generation died. This freed up the second generation to go into Canaan led by Joshua.

13:19 And when He had destroyed seven nations in the land of Canaan, He distributed their land to them by allotment.

This verse speaks of the two divisions of the book of Joshua. The first half (chapters 1–12) speaks of the destroying of the seven nations (Deuteronomy 7:1). The second half (chapters 13–24) describes the dividing up of the land among the tribes. The land was divided by "lots," the casting of the Urim and Thummim, stones of the priesthood (Exodus 28:30, Leviticus 8:8, Deuteronomy 33:8) used to receive guidance from the Lord.

4. The Judges

13:20 ¶ "After that He gave *them* judges for about four hundred and fifty years, until Samuel the prophet.

For 450 years, judges ruled in Israel. Samuel was the last judge and the first of a new type of leader, the prophet. He was known in the Old Testament as the seer because of his ability to discern spiritual things and receive direction from the Lord. He gave supernatural guidance and utterance to the people.

5. King Saul

13:21 And afterward they asked for a king; so God gave them Saul the son of Kish, a man of the tribe of Benjamin, for forty years.

Before this time, Israel was a theocracy, ruled by God through chosen leaders. However, the people desired a king because they wanted to be like other nations (1 Samuel 8:4–9). God made them unique as a people and a nation, but they continued to have bad attitudes even after the wilderness. They forsook faith for sight. They wanted a status symbol and got Saul, a tall and handsome man. He ruled for forty years. God allowed this because of his mercy. He also allowed it to show the people the error of their choice.

6. King David

13:22 And when He had removed him, He raised up for them David as king, to whom also He gave testimony and said, 'I have found David the son of Jesse, a man after My own heart, who will do all My will.'

And when he had removed him, he raised up unto them David to be their king; to whom also he gave testimony (memorial), and said (1 Samuel 13:14), I have found David the son of Jesse, a man after mine own heart, which shall fulfil (establish) all my will (covenant).

Saul was removed because of the sin unto death (1 Chronicles 10:13–14). David was a man who hungered after God and sought Him day and night (Psalm 1:2). David sinned much but was a man quick to repent. God's will was fulfilled through David by the establishment of the Davidic Covenant, the promise that the Messiah, Jesus Christ, would come from his own loins (2 Samuel 7:8–16, Psalm 89:20–37, 132:8–11).

13:23 From this man's seed, according to *the* promise, God raised up for Israel a Savior—Jesus—

David's seed is the same as Abraham's seed. The "seed" is the Lord Jesus Christ. Paul is speaking of the humanity of Jesus coming from the lineage of David. The title "Son of David" is the messianic title for Jesus.

7. John the Baptist

13:24 after John had first preached, before His coming, the baptism of repentance to all the people of Israel.

When John had first preached (announced) before (beforehand) his coming the baptism of repentance (*metanoia*) to all the people of Israel.

John the Baptist was the herald of the King. He baptized believers, those who had repented and accepted Jesus as their savior.

13:25 And as John was finishing his course, he said, 'Who do you think I am? I am not *He*. But behold, there comes One after me, the sandals of whose feet I am not worthy to loose.'

Here Paul is quoting what John said in Matthew 3:11. John's "course" was the end of his life. Our lives are compared to a race (2 Timothy 4:7). John was a very controversial man among the religious leaders, and he confronted them many times. John also continued to confirm to his followers that he was not the Messiah though his ministry had become very powerful.

8. Jesus the Messiah

13:26 ¶ "Men *and* brethren, sons of the family of Abraham, and those among you who fear God, to you the word of this salvation has been sent.

Men (Gentiles) and brethren (Jews), children of the stock of Abraham, and whosoever among you feareth God, to you is the word (*logos*) of this salvation sent.

Paul is addressing both Jews and Gentiles, and those among them who are already believers in the Lord Jesus. The Old Testament was not written exclusively to Jews, but to all nationalities to inform them that Jesus is the only way to salvation in any time period.

9. Paul's Warning

13:27 For those who dwell in Jerusalem, and their rulers, because they did not know Him, nor even the voices of the Prophets which are read every Sabbath, have fulfilled *them* in condemning *Him*.

Paul warns the people not to follow the example of the Jewish rulers in Jerusalem who rejected the true Messiah. Not only were they unable to discern the Lord Jesus, they were unable to discern the voice of their own prophets from the Old Testament. Each prophet foretold of the coming of Jesus and confirmed that he would be the Messiah, the only means of salvation for both Jew and Gentile.

There was no excuse for not knowing Jesus was the Messiah. The Old Testament prophets were read each Sabbath day in the synagogues around the country. Yet the very scriptures they read each week foretold they would kill the Messiah. The scriptures were fulfilled when they crucified Jesus. Their rejection of Jesus was as much a fulfillment of scriptures as the acceptance of Him by the Jews who received Him as Lord and Savior.

13:28 And though they found no cause for death *in Him*, they asked Pilate that He should be put to death.

The trials held against Jesus were illegal because of the times in which they were held and because they had no legal evidence against Jesus.

13:29 Now when they had fulfilled all that was written concerning Him, they took *Him* down from the tree and laid *Him* in a tomb.

God foretold what the Jewish religious leaders would do to Jesus. Once they had done all they could do to him, God did what only He could do. God raised Jesus from the dead!

10. Jesus Raised from the Dead

13:30 But God raised him from the dead:

In the end, God always wins, whether or not man aligns himself with Him. Jesus was raised by the power of God the Father (Psalm 16:10–11, Acts 2:24, Ephesians 1:19–20) and the Holy Spirit (Romans 8:11, 1 Peter 3:18).

13:31 He was seen for many days by those who came up with Him from Galilee to Jerusalem, who are His witnesses to the people.

Jesus was on the earth for forty days and was seen by men on eleven different occasions (1 Corinthians 15:4–8).

13:32 And we declare to you glad tidings—that promise which was made to the fathers.

The promise is the removal of sins and the barrier of rejection (Genesis 3:15). The debt man was under has been paid in full. The salvation message of Jesus is found throughout the Old Testament. The sacrifices, feasts, temple furniture, priesthood, major and minor prophets all pointed toward Jesus.

11. Fulfillment of Old Testament Prophesy

13:33 God has fulfilled this for us their children, in that He has raised up Jesus. As it is also written in the second Psalm:

> *'You are My Son,*
> *Today I have begotten You.'*

God hath fulfilled (perfect tense) the same unto us their children, in that he hath raised up (brought on the scene) Jesus again; as it is also written in the second psalm (Psalm 2:7), "Thou art my Son, this day have I begotten thee."

The fulfillment of the Old Testament prophecies came to pass in the life-time of those listening to Paul's sermon. The humanity of Jesus was raised up and David prophesied this would occur. "This day" was the day of the virgin birth of Jesus. God was speaking of the deity of Jesus about the form-ing of His human body (Hebrews 10:5–7).

13:34 And that He raised Him from the dead, no more to return to corruption, He has spoken thus:

> *'I will give you the sure mercies of David.'*

And as concerning that he raised him up from the dead, now no more to return to corruption, he said on this wise (Isaiah 55:3), "I will give you the sure (unfailing, absolute, secure) mercies of David."

Not only was Jesus brought into this earth by the power of God the Father, God also raised Him up. The sure mercies of David include a throne, a per-petual kingdom, an everlasting ruler, and seed forever.

13:35 Therefore He also says in another *Psalm*:

> *'You will not allow Your Holy One to see corruption.'*

Wherefore he saith also in another psalm (Psalm 16:10), Thou shalt not suffer thine Holy One to see corruption.

The "Holy One" spoken of in this verse is Jesus, not David, and God would not allow Jesus' human body to reach the point of corruption before He was raised from the dead.

13:36 ¶ "For David, after he had served his own generation by the will of God, fell asleep, was buried with his fathers, and saw corruption;

Psalm 16:10 could not be referring to David because David died, remained buried, and his body decayed in the earth.

13:37 but He whom God raised up saw no corruption.

David was not raised from the dead; therefore, it had to be Jesus Who was raised from the dead and never saw corruption.

G. Introduction to the New Birth

13:38 Therefore let it be known to you, brethren, that through this Man is preached to you the forgiveness of sins;

The message of forgiveness of sins was preached in the Old Testament and it was also preached through the mouth of the One spoken of, Jesus.

13:39 and by Him everyone who believes is justified from all things from which you could not be justified by the law of Moses.

And by him all that believe are justified (aorist passive) from all things, from which ye could not be justified by the law of Moses.

"All things" indicates unlimited atonement. We have been justified from all sins, our position in Adam, spiritual death, and anything else associated with Satan. This is the conclusion of the message.

All the messages preached in the synagogues each week were types and shadows of what was to come. Jesus Christ is the reality of all the prophets, types, and shadows.

H. Closing Admonition

13:40 Beware therefore, lest what has been spoken in the prophets come upon you:

Spoken of in Habakkuk 1:5.

13:41 *'Behold, you despisers,*
Marvel and perish!

> *For I work a work in your days,*
> *A work which you will by no means believe,*
> *Though one were to declare it to you.'"*

Behold, ye despisers, and wonder (be shocked), and perish (die): for I work a work in your days, a work which ye shall in no wise believe, though a man declare it unto you.

"Your days" are the days of the New Testament. Paul is warning these men not to be part of those who will reject Jesus. Habakkuk warned of those who would reject the last day preaching. In God's sight their fate was settled: eternal death.

13:42 ¶ So when the Jews went out of the synagogue, the Gentiles begged that these words might be preached to them the next Sabbath.

After the strictest Jews leave the synagogue, most of the Gentiles remain and want to hear more the following week.

V. God's Grace (43–49)

The next Sabbath, nearly the entire city arrives to hear Paul's message. When the Jews see the multitudes gathered, they become envious, but the Word continues to spread throughout the entire region.

13:43 Now when the congregation had broken up, many of the Jews and devout proselytes followed Paul and Barnabas, who, speaking to them, persuaded them to continue in the grace of God.

The Gentiles and many of the Jews found Paul and Barnabas inside the synagogue and followed them to their room asking questions all the way. Paul and Barnabas admonish them to continue in the grace of God.

Grace covers two main areas: salvation and spirituality. Paul and Barnabas have already observed the destructiveness of legalism in the church at Jerusalem, and so they encourage these men to begin and continue with grace. Apparently, many of them are born again during the service and had-vequestions about how to continue in the Lord.

13:44 ¶ On the next Sabbath almost the whole city came together to hear the word of God.

In the course of one week, the Word taught by Barnabas and Paul brought the entire city out to hear the message of grace. Crowds of people gather to hear more.

A. The Jews Contradict the Message of Grace

13:45 But when the Jews saw the multitudes, they were filled with envy; and contradicting and blaspheming, they opposed the things spoken by Paul.

Legalists are always jealous of grace. People desire to hear messages about freedom and go to great lengths to receive those messages. Legalists retaliate and argue against grace. This is why we are to labor to maintain rest and stand fast in liberty. Legalism contradicts and blasphemes because it attempts to help God through human effort. These legalists are criticizing the Word of God.

B. The Boldness of Paul and Barnabas

13:46 Then Paul and Barnabas grew bold and said, "It was necessary that the word of God should be spoken to you first; but since you reject it, and judge yourselves unworthy of everlasting life, behold, we turn to the Gentiles.

Then Paul and Barnabas waxed bold, and said, "It was necessary that the word of God should first have been spoken to you: but seeing ye put it from you (thrust it from yourselves) and judge (evaluate) yourselves unworthy of everlasting life, lo, we turn to the Gentiles."

God prophesied in the Old Testament that the Jews would be the first to hear the gospel but would reject the message. This is the reason they are without excuse. They turned their will against God. God's will never supersedes man's will except in judgment. Rejecting God's grace will only reap His judgment. Legalists always put God's plans aside and think of themselves as better than God. However, Paul informs them, "If you reject the Lord's plan, we have every right to take God's message to the Gentiles."

C. Ministry to the Gentiles

13:47 For so the Lord has commanded us:

> *'I have set you as a light to the Gentiles,*
> *That you should be for salvation to the ends of the*
> *earth.'"*

For so hath the Lord commanded us, saying (Isaiah 49:6), I have set (appointed) thee to be a light of (to) the Gentiles, that thou (ministers) shouldest be for salvation unto the ends of the earth.

The Old Testament speaks of ministers who will preach to Gentiles. Centuries before this time, God had given Jews permission to turn to the Gentile nations with His message.

13:48 ¶ Now when the Gentiles heard this, they were glad and glorified the word of the Lord. And as many as had been appointed to eternal life believed.

And when the Gentiles heard this, they were glad, and glorified the word of the Lord: and as many as were ordained (*tasso*: perfect tense: assigned) to eternal life believed.

It is amazing how faith is produced with even a minimal amount of the Word. One verse causes these Gentiles to rejoice and receive salvation. The Greek word *tasso* is in the perfect tense. God knew before the foundation of the world who would and would not believe, and assigned everlasting life with Him to those who would(Romans 8:29, Ephesians 1:4).

13:49 ¶ And the word of the Lord was being spread throughout all the region.

As eternal life is received, the converts publish the good news of the Word of God throughout the city and country.

VI. Paul and Barnabas Expelled (50–52)

The religious Jews who are angry with Paul and Barnabas cause prominent men and women to also become angry. Persecution results and they are expelled from the city. Upon leaving, they shake the dust from their feet as instructed by Jesus.

13:50 But the Jews stirred up the devout and prominent women and the chief men of the city, raised up persecution against Paul and Barnabas, and expelled them from their region.

But the Jews stirred up the devout and honourable (religious) women, and the chief men (politicians) of the city, and raised persecution against Paul and Barnabas, and expelled them out of their coasts.

Paul and Barnabas find themselves under religious and political attack and decide to leave the city.

13:51 But they shook off the dust from their feet against them, and came to Iconium.

During His earthly ministry, Jesus instructed His disciples to shake the dust of any city that did not receive them from their feet (Luke 9:5). They did so, then headed for Iconium, a major city in Galatia.

13:52 And the disciples were filled with joy and with the Holy Spirit.

This passage refers to the new converts left behind in Antioch of Pisidia.

Once the enemy can
isolate can bring you down.

14:1–28 Signs, Wonders, and Healings

The Challenge of Chapter Fourteen

Just as Paul and Barnabas preached boldly (even in the face of opposition and persecution) so must we never back down from the message of the gospel. God's Word is alive, powerful, the only message that brings spiritual life and eliminate spiritual death. It brings light and dispels darkness in the hearts and minds of unregenerate men. As long as we are alive on earth, we are to fulfill the great commission to go into all the world and preach the gospel.

I. Preaching in Iconium (1–5) *in in Galaia*

Paul and Barnabas preach in the synagogue in Iconium and many believe. Then unbelieving Jews stir up the Gentiles against those who believe the gospel. Paul and Barnabas continue to speak boldly in the Lord and signs and wonders follow their preaching. The city splits; half side with the Jews and the other half with the apostles. Those against the message determine to stone Paul and Barnabas.

Iconium is located in an area of Galatia. It is a province consisting of four major cities: Antioch of Pisidia, Iconium, Derby, and Lystra. Paul and Barnabas have been removed from Antioch and are traveling further inland into Galatia, and the further they go, the more the persecution will intensify.

A. Many Believe

14:1 ¶ Now it happened in Iconium that they went together to the synagogue of the Jews, and so spoke that a great multitude both of the Jews and of the Greeks believed.

Paul is setting a pattern. In most cities, when available, he goes into the synagogue. Paul knows the customs, manners, and beliefs of the Jews and finds this is a quick platform and audience. He also knows in each city, the gospel was to the Jew first and then to the Greek (Romans 1:16). However, there were exceptions such as Athens and Philippi.

Paul and Barnabas draw large crowds and speak several times. Many more are added each time they speak.

14:2 But the unbelieving Jews stirred up the Gentiles and poisoned their minds against the brethren.

Gentiles run the city of Iconium, and the Jews affect the attitude of the entire city. The city becomes bitter against Paul and Barnabas because of the Jews.

B. Signs and Wonders

> **14:3 Therefore they stayed there a long time, speaking boldly in the Lord, who was bearing witness to the word of His grace, granting signs and wonders to be done by their hands.**

Long time therefore abode (*diatribo*: to remain under pressure) they speaking boldly in the Lord, which gave testimony unto the word of his grace, and granted signs and wonders to be done by their hands.

It took some time for opposition to be stirred up against Paul and Barnabas, so they wasted no time in proclaiming the message of salvation. As they preach the Word, God confirms it with signs and wonders following. God always backs the message of grace with signs and wonders (Galatians 3:5).

Signs and wonders are God's way of making it difficult to say no to the gospel and teaching of the Word. Those in Iconium have to make an effort to ignore the miracles and healings and refuse salvation.

> **14:4 ¶ But the multitude of the city was divided: part sided with the Jews, and part with the apostles.**

Even though there are miracles and healings, many are so hardened they will not believe, even with the display of the supernatural. The city is divided down the middle (Matthew 10:34).

The first four verses of this chapter reveal that the results of the Word are always the same. Some accept the gospel, and others reject it. This was the case in Antioch of Pisidia and now is in Iconium. Verse 3 tells us God performed miracles in Iconium, but in Antioch none were performed (Acts 13). In some cities miracles are performed, and in some they are not. One city does not set a standard. One event does not establish a pattern. God works differently in each city, but the Word is always preached.

Manifestations will always differ. One method of witnessing does not set a precedent. One method for success in life does not set the norm for everyone. How you spend your time in study, prayer, praise, and worship is up to you. How you apply God's principles is up to you. Jesus did not witness or minister healing to any two people the same way. It is important to stay open to the Holy Spirit.

C. Persecution

14:5 And when a violent attempt was made by both the Gentiles and Jews, with their rulers, to abuse and stone them,

Behind the scenes, there is a joint effort by the Jews and Gentiles to kill Paul and Barnabas and make a public example of them.

II. Preaching in Lystra (6–7)

Paul and Barnabas, learning of the plot against them, flee to Lystra and Derbe and preach there and in the surrounding area.

14:6 they became aware of it and fled to Lystra and Derbe, cities of Lycaonia, and to the surrounding region.

The word about the plot to stone them comes to Paul and Barnabas through either the Holy Spirit or through the converts they have made in the city. Paul and Barnabas flee to Lystra and Derbe, the other two cities of Galatia. They arrive in Lystra first.

14:7 And they were preaching the gospel there.

Signs and wonders again accompany the preaching of the gospel. Paul is spared from persecution in Antioch and Iconium. He will be raised out of it in Lystra (2 Timothy 3:12).

Lyconia is a desert area with rugged mountains, and is one of the most desolate areas in the world.

III. Healing of the Cripple (8–10)

There is a man in Lystra who has never walked because he crippled. Paul sees faith in this man and commands him to stand. The man responds and the people witness his healing.

14:8 ¶ And in Lystra a certain man without strength in his feet was sitting, a cripple from his mother's womb, who had never walked.

And there sat a certain man at Lystra, impotent (totally helpless) in his feet, being a cripple from his mother's womb, who never had walked:

The man mentioned in this verse has been a liability on the city of Lystra since his birth. He is well known because for years others have carried him from place to place.

14:9 *This* man heard Paul speaking. Paul, observing him intently and seeing that he had faith to be healed,

The man receives faith when he hears Paul speak (Romans 10:17). While Paul is ministering, the same Holy Spirit who gave the man faith, reveals it to Paul. The Holy Spirit works in both Paul and the crippled man to bring about his healing.

14:10 said with a loud voice, "Stand up straight on your feet!" And he leaped and walked.

Lystra did not have a synagogue, so God used this miracle to draw a crowd. In Iconium, the miracles followed the teaching ministry (verse 3). Here the healing precedes the Word, and a crowd gathers as a result of the healing.

IV. Paul and Barnabas Deemed Gods (11–18)

Because of the miracle, the people cry out in their native tongue that gods have come to visit them in the form of men. A priest of Zeus even brings an ox and garlands with the intention of joining the multitudes in sacrificing to Paul and Barnabas. As soon as Paul and Barnabas realize what is happening, they run out among the people tearing their clothes, declaring they are men just like the people in the crowd. They also attempt to teach the people about the living God they serve.

14:11 Now when the people saw what Paul had done, they raised their voices, saying in the Lycaonian *language,* "The gods have come down to us in the likeness of men!"

The Lycaonian language is a mixture of Greek and Assyrian. Paul does not know what they are saying since it is in their native tongue. He only becomes aware when they begin to sacrifice to him and Barnabas (verse 13).

Maybe it is the Lystran's jealousy of nearby Phyrgia that makes them so quick to label Paul and Barnabas as gods. Two trees stood in Phyrgia as a monument to a supposed visit from Zeus and Hermes. According to legend, the trees had been lovers transformed after requesting from the gods a form that would allow them to be together forever. By worshiping Paul and Barnabas as gods, perhaps the Lystrians hope to have their requests granted as well.

14:12 And Barnabas they called Zeus, and Paul, Hermes, because he was the chief speaker.

A. Sacrifices Brought

14:13 Then the priest of Zeus, whose temple was in front of their city, brought oxen and garlands to the gates, intending to sacrifice with the multitudes.

Oxen were the highest form of sacrifice to the Greeks because they were so expensive. They belonged to the wealthy. Garlands were used in worship to entertain the gods. Paul and Barnabas now begin to understand why the people have made such an uproar. When the people witnessed the miracles, they mistakenly gave credit to Paul and Barnabas rather than the one true God.

B. Paul and Barnabas Cry Out

14:14 ¶ But when the apostles Barnabas and Paul heard this, they tore their clothes and ran in among the multitude, crying out

While the people prepare to make sacrifices, Paul and Barnabas are inside the house where they are staying. When they realize what is happening, they run outside and tear their clothes to prove they are human.

C. An Attempt to Teach the People

14:15 and saying, "Men, why are you doing these things? We also are men with the same nature as you, and preach to you that you should turn from these useless things to the living God, who made the heaven, the earth, the sea, and all things that are in them,

Although the people have cried out in the language of Lyconia, Paul speaks in Greek so everyone understands him. All Galatians worshiped the false gods of the air, land, and sea. Paul explains that there is one true God who made all of these elements as well as them.

14:16 who in bygone generations allowed all nations to walk in their own ways.

Paul explains to the people, "God has allowed you to walk in your foolishness even though He did not like it. That is why He has sent us to reveal Him to you."

14:17 Nevertheless He did not leave Himself without witness, in that He did good, gave us rain from heaven and fruitful seasons, filling our hearts with food and gladness."

The universe and earth are a witness to God's power and existence (Romans 1:20). Because the people Paul address are Gentiles (heathen), they have never known about the manifestations of Jesus revealed in the Old Testament like the angel of the Lord, Jehovah, and the rock. So Paul explains that God sends rain and provides food. Because they live in an agricultural economy, they can understand and appreciate Paul's verbiage. He compares natural food to spiritual food, "filling our hearts with food." God always supplies spiritual nutrition for the new birth.

D. The Crowd Does Not Listen

14:18 And with these sayings they could scarcely restrain the multitudes from sacrificing to them.

The crowd is still in a frenzy and emotionally charged. They are not ready to listen to teaching, and they have not ceased in their attempts to offer sacrifices.

V. Stoning of Paul (19–20)

The Jews from Antioch and Iconium arrive convincing the multitudes to stone Paul and drag him, dead, out of the city. However, the disciples gather around Paul and pray. He is raised from the dead. The very next day, he travels with Barnabas to Derbe.

A. Paul's Message Rejected

14:19 ¶ Then Jews from Antioch and Iconium came there; and having persuaded the multitudes, they stoned Paul *and* dragged *him* out of the city, supposing him to be dead.

And there came thither certain Jews from Antioch and Iconium, who persuaded the people, and, having stoned Paul, drew (dragged) him out of the city, supposing (*nomizo*: concluding him to have died) he had been dead.

The Judaizers from Antioch and Iconium who reject Paul's message attempt to evangelize these Gentiles with the law. They were unable to stone Paul and Barnabas in Iconium because they had fled. They have now followed Paul and Barnabas to Lystra and this time, will see Paul stoned by the people. Believing they have been successful in putting a stop to the gospel, they will leave. These men never cared about Lystra until Paul arrived.

The people in Lystra are fickle and easily persuaded. One minute they are convinced Paul is a god, and the next, they plan to stone him. They are probably disappointed because Paul will not allow them to make sacrifices to him.

This instance of Paul's stoning and death is probably the time he was taken out of his body into the third heaven (2 Corinthians 12:1–4).

B. Paul Raised from the Dead

14:20 However, when the disciples gathered around him, he rose up and went into the city. And the next day he departed with Barnabas to Derbe.

Paul's stoning takes place before a group of his own followers, disciples of the Lord. As they are praying for him, he suddenly comes back to life. Immediately he returns to the city of Lystra.

It must be a shock to the Jews who had just stoned him and a confirmation to the people of the city of the truth of the gospel. After they see Paul has been raised from the dead, they no longer want to offer him sacrifices. Now they are ready to receive the Lord. He only remains in Lystra one day before he continues his journey into Derbe. He will preach again in Lystra on his departure from the region and, like in Antioch, no miracles are performed.

VI. Return to Lystra, Iconium, and Antioch (21–23)

After preaching in Derbe, Paul and Barnabas return to Lystra, Iconium, and Antioch to strengthen and exhort the disciples and to encourage them to continue in the faith. They also appoint elders in every church and, after praying and fasting, commend them to the Lord.

14:21 ¶ And when they had preached the gospel to that city and made many disciples, they returned to Lystra, Iconium, and Antioch,

The word about Paul and the gospel has already spread throughout Galatia, and the people in the next city are ready to receive the gospel and hear the teaching of the Word.

Two words are mentioned in this verse that should be noted: preached and taught. Preaching is for the unbelievers. It is how they hear the gospel. Teaching is for believers, the disciples, and they heard the Word.

Not only have the next cities heard about Paul's resurrection, the word about what happened spreads back to the cities where Paul and Barnabas have received so much persecution. It was probably during this time when people regretted what had happened and would have "plucked out" their eyes and given them to Paul (Galatians 4:15). After having been stoned, Paul probably wasn't a pretty sight!

However, Paul isn't deterred by what has just happened; he continues to preach and teach despite his physical condition. In 2 Corinthians 11:24–27, Paul describes more about his sufferings during this time.

A. Teaching the Word

14:22 strengthening the souls of the disciples, exhorting *them* to continue in the faith, and *saying*, "We must through many tribulations enter the kingdom of God."

Through the teaching of the Word, the souls of the disciples are grounded and established. The soul is stabilized by the Word. Confirmation is for the present. Exhortation is for the future. Paul is unable to remain with them, and he wants them to be spiritually self-sustaining.

The "kingdom of God" is a reference to the spiritual walk of faith God wants all of us to obtain. It is comparable to the land of Canaan in the Old Testament. The life of faith is a goal every believer should attain to and it comes to us through knowledge of the Word of God. It also comes through much tribulation from the religious crowd. This crowd has always opposed the truth from the time of the prophets, to Jesus, and to the apostles of the New Testament. This is true for all believers. Satan will always oppose the deeper walk, but God gives us the strength and power to overcome.

B. Ordaining Elders

14:23 So when they had appointed elders in every church, and prayed with fasting, they commended them to the Lord in whom they had believed.

And when they had ordained them elders in every church, and had prayed with fasting, they commended them to the Lord, on whom they believed.

The Greek word for ordained is *cheirotoneo*. It means to "elect by stretching out the hand." In each of these cities, Paul and Barnabas establish churches as they retrace their steps back through the cities. The believers in each city continue in the Word and in grace, and groups are established. All of the groups need leadership, and Paul and Barnabas make these selections by the laying on of hands. Prayer and fasting accompany each selection to determine whether they have any "checks" in their spirits about any potential leaders. After praying and fasting, their consciences are clear, and they commend the selected leaders to the Lord. This demonstrates Paul and Barnabas have done their part, and what remains to be done is between the new elders and the Lord.

The Greek word for "commended" is *paratithemi* which means "to deposit." This is a banking term. A bank is generally considered a safe place to deposit money. The Lord is the bank, the safe place to deposit the new elders. These elders (*presbuteros*) become the pastors of the churches. The pastor is called an elder in many passages of scripture. A pastor can be called an elder, a bishop, or a deacon. Although not all elders, bishops, and deacons are the pastors, a pastor is each one of these offices as the head of the local church.

VII. Preaching Continues (24–28)

Paul and Barnabas then travel to Perga and Attalia and preach in those places. Finally, they return to Antioch, testify about all God had accomplished during their missionary travels, and report how many Gentiles had received the gospel. They remain in the area to rest and be refreshed.

14:24 And after they had passed through Pisidia, they came to Pamphylia.

Paul and Barnabas now return to the place where Mark deserted them.

A. Perga and Attalia

14:25 Now when they had preached the word in Perga, they went down to Attalia.

Paul does not preach the Word in Perga when he first arrives, but reserves this opportunity for his return trip.

Attalia is the seaport from which Paul will return home.

B. Returning to Antioch

14:26 From there they sailed to Antioch, where they had been commended to the grace of God for the work which they had completed.

They had been sent out from Antioch, and now they had returned. This was the place where they had been commended to God's grace. The Greek word is *paradidomi*, which means to be turned over for safe keeping.

C. Testimony

14:27 ¶ Now when they had come and gathered the church together, they reported all that God had done with them, and that He had opened the door of faith to the Gentiles.

They give God all the glory for what He has done. Not only should missionaries return to the church from which they are sent, they also need to testify of what God has done — signs, wonders, churches established, and people saved.

D. A Time of Rest

14:28 So they stayed there a long time with the disciples.

Paul and Barnabas spend almost eighteen months on the road in Galatia. They deserve a rest, and they take one. Vacation (time off) is a necessity in ministry. It helps ministers prepare for the next journey.

15:1–39 Legalism Versus Grace

The Challenge of Chapter Fifteen

We have been saved by grace (Ephesians 2:8) and are living in the dispensation of grace (Ephesians 3:2). Through Jesus Christ, we have been given an abundance of grace and the gift of righteousness (Romans 5:17), but it is possible for us to frustrate that grace. Romans 11:5 and 6 say, "Even so then, at this present time there is a remnant according to the election of grace. And if by grace, then it is no longer of works; otherwise grace is no longer grace. But if it is of works, it is no longer grace; otherwise work is no longer work."

We must continually be on guard against legalism infiltrating the freedom found in the grace of God. The automatic byproduct of God's grace is works. But often, legalism creeps in, and works become the focus of our Christian walk rather than grace. This is when we begin serving God out of human effort rather than the grace of God. We must always endeavor to remain in the grace of God.

I. Legalism in the Early Church

Since the inception of the local church, legalism has tried to rob believers of the freedom of living by God's grace. The church in Jerusalem is no exception. Since the day of Pentecost, the law has been creeping into the church and criticism has been building against the move of God among the Gentiles.

Legalism versus grace has always been the issue with man. From Adam and his leaves to Cain and his crops, we have fought this battle as long as Satan has been the god of this world.

Until this time, legalism has been brewing under the surface and has even been addressed in part. But in this chapter, it all comes to a head in the Jerusalem church. The church at Antioch has been free to teach and operate in grace and faith. Jealousy in Jerusalem brings this issue to the forefront at the first church council meeting recorded in Acts. Jerusalem has been sliding into the law for many years and is critical of the move of God in Gentile areas of the world (Acts chapter 11).

Many of the legalistic leaders in Jerusalem are truly born again. These are priests who have been saved under the ministry of the disciples (6:7, 13:5). They have not made a smooth transition into the church age and are trying to make a major issue of the law of Moses. These people are called legalists. They do not understand the proper agreement of grace, faith, and works, and are demanding all male Gentile converts be circumcised, and all converts observe the Mosaic law for spirituality.

II. The Triumph of the Policy of Grace (1–29)

While in Antioch, some from Judea have been teaching that circumcision is a requirement of salvation. Paul and Barnabas disagree vehemently with this teaching. The disagreement is so great, the church at Antioch decides to send Paul and Barnabas to discuss the issue with the apostles and elders in the church at Jerusalem.

They are warmly welcomed by the Jerusalem church, but still there is a sect of believers who are teaching that Gentile converts must be circumcised and required to follow the law of Moses.

To resolve the issue, the apostles and elders meet together. Peter argues against putting the yoke of legalism on the Gentile converts and also testifies of the signs and wonders God has performed among the Gentiles. James, a respected leader, then argues that a letter should be written to the Gentile converts to abstain from eating food offered to idols, from eating meat of strangled animals, from consuming blood, and from sexual immorality, again proposing to impose legalism (aside from sexual immorality) upon the Gentile converts.

The apostles, elders, and entire church in Jerusalem choose delegates to travel with Paul and Barnabas back to Antioch to read the letter stating the requirements for the Gentile converts. It does not include circumcision, but still muddies the message of grace.

A. Dissension and Debate in the Early Church

> **15:1 ¶ And certain *men* came down from Judea and taught the brethren, "Unless you are circumcised according to the custom of Moses, you cannot be saved."**

And certain men which came down from Judea (to Antioch) taught the brethren (Gentile believers), and said, Except ye be circumcised after the manner of Moses, ye cannot be saved.

Just as the gospel has been taken to the ends of the world, now the legalistic Jews are also taking the law of Moses to the foreign field. Legalism always persecutes grace (Galatians 2:4, 4:29). We are never born again by observing the law or any system of works (Galatians 2:16, Ephesians 2:8–9), nor are we spiritual because we observe works (Galatians 2:20–21). The purpose of the law is to teach that we are all sinners and need a Savior (Romans 3:20, 5:20, Galatians 3:19). Paul and Barnabas began to resist this teaching to protect the congregation at Antioch. In religious circles, grace must be fought for (Galatians 5:1).

15:2 Therefore, when Paul and Barnabas had no small dissension and dispute with them, they determined that Paul and Barnabas and certain others of them should go up to Jerusalem, to the apostles and elders, about this question.

Paul does not try to "pray and love" the legalists out of Antioch or their false doctrine. Love must stand up to legalism (Galatians 2:11–21, 5:12). On this occasion, when Paul and Barnabas travel to Jerusalem, Titus is with them and will be used by Paul as proof of God's grace (Galatians 2:1). Because Paul is so strong, scriptural, and anointed, he cannot be challenged by the legalistic leaders at Jerusalem. Instead of directly confronting Paul, they retreated and decided on a new tactic. After Paul has taught and is no longer present, they have come in and persuaded the people to follow the law. They discredit Paul after he leaves so he would not be there to defend himself.

B. Paul and Barnabas Sent to Jerusalem by the Church

15:3 ¶ So, being sent on their way by the church, they passed through Phoenicia and Samaria, describing the conversion of the Gentiles; and they caused great joy to all the brethren.

And being brought (*propempo*: sent, accompany, bring on a journey) on their way by the church (at Antioch), they passed through Phenice and Samaria, declaring the conversion of the Gentiles: and they caused great joy unto all the brethren.

Phenice and Samaria are mainly Gentile areas. They are rejoicing as Paul and Barnabas come through telling of their many meetings and conversions in the cities of the Gentile countries. The Gentiles in these cities rejoice when they hear of revivals.

15:4 And when they had come to Jerusalem, they were received by the church and the apostles and the elders; and they reported all things that God had done with them.

And when they were come to Jerusalem, they were received (*apodecheom-ai*: received gladly) of the church, and of the apostles and elders, and they declared all things that God had done with them.

The congregation and church leadership receive Paul and Barnabas gladly. They have not yet been affected by the legalistic group within the church. The lump of leaven in the church at Jerusalem has not yet infected the whole loaf. This will not occur until later chapters when the Holy Spirit will warn Paul to no longer preach in Jerusalem.

The stories that were told to the church at Jerusalem were the missionary trips of Chapters 13 and 14: the Gentiles receiving the new birth, the infilling of the Holy Spirit, divine healing, miracles, and the establishment of churches and pastors. These types of results cannot be disputed by people who love the grace of God.

C. Pharisees Require Circumcision

15:5 But some of the sect of the Pharisees who believed rose up, saying, "It is necessary to circumcise them, and to command *them* to keep the law of Moses."

D. The Jerusalem Council

15:6 ¶ Now the apostles and elders came together to consider this matter.

Within their hearts, the church leadership knew the answer to this question and knew that Jesus Himself had told of the conversion of the Gentiles (1:8). They also knew of Jesus' battles with the religious, legalistic Jewish leaders. The battle Jesus had gone through is the same battle this early church is now facing.

E. Peter Testifies of the Holy Spirit Among the Gentiles

15:7 And when there had been much dispute, Peter rose up and said to them: "Men *and* brethren, you know that a good while ago God chose among us, that by my mouth the Gentiles should hear the word of the gospel and believe.

This is the last time we will hear from Peter in the book of Acts. After this, Peter bounds in and out of legalism and grace. The Pharisees become stronger in the Jerusalem church, and Peter will fight to keep his head above water. He later writes two books and explains how Paul is far more advanced in the Word and understanding of God's grace (2 Peter 3:15–16).

The Jerusalem church is confused like most churches today. They believe in faith for salvation, but they also believe the Christian way of life is a series of dos and don'ts. This same argument continues today: human good versus divine good. Peter recalls for them his housetop vision and the revival among the Gentiles in Caesarea (Chapter 10).

15:8 So God, who knows the heart, acknowledged them by giving them the Holy Spirit, just as *He did* to us,

God gave the Gentiles the gift of salvation and the Holy Spirit without a teaching on the law of Moses. They receive the same experience as those in the upper room in Jerusalem.

15:9 and made no distinction between us and them, purifying their hearts by faith.

Peter is saying that God makes no distinction between Jew and Gentile when he gives the Holy Spirit. These men are making an issue of something God is not making an issue of. So these legalists are now being found to fight God.

15:10 Now therefore, why do you test God by putting a yoke on the neck of the disciples which neither our fathers nor we were able to bear?

Now therefore why tempt ye God, to put a yoke (the law) upon the neck of the disciples, which neither our fathers (Old Testament believers) nor we (New Testament believers) were able to bear?

Tempting God is blasphemy. Legalism is also blasphemy (13:45), a yoke of bondage (Galatians 5:1). It weighs a person down and causes them to slow their pace until they come to a complete standstill. Legalism seeks to attach itself to a believer, especially a disciple. Eventually the entire life is crippled. If the Jews raised under the law could not keep it, why are they trying to put the Gentiles under it (Galatians 6:13)?

15:11 But we believe that through the grace of the Lord Jesus Christ we shall be saved in the same manner as they."

But we believe that through the grace of the Lord Jesus Christ we (Jews) shall be saved, even as they (Gentiles).

It is like Peter is saying, "We Jews, who think we are so smart, should take lessons from these Gentiles. Let's observe how they are saved and become spiritual, and follow their example. If we could not get the law to work for us, why are we trying to put the law on someone who is successful without it? We are failures trying to instruct successes."

F. Paul and Barnabas Testify

15:12 ¶ Then all the multitude kept silent and listened to Barnabas and Paul declaring how many miracles and wonders God had worked through them among the Gentiles.

Then all the multitude kept silence, and gave audience (the floor) to Barnabas and Paul, declaring what miracles and wonders God had wrought among the Gentiles by (through) them.

The multitude keeos silent because they are hearing the truth from Peter and had no answer. In the silence, Paul and Barnabas tell of the missionary journey from which they have just returned. They tell of the salvations, infillings, church plantings, signs, and miracles which have come to the Gentiles. This all had occurred without the preaching of the law. It also had happened to a group of people who have never known the law.

G. James Speaks

James, the pastor of the Jerusalem church, carries a lot of authority with the legalistic Jews who are listening. His words have some effect, but a compromise with legalism will later destroy the Jerusalem church and neutralize the effect of the knowledge gained at this juncture.

15:13–14 And after they had become silent, James answered, saying, "Men *and* brethren, listen to me: 14 Simon has declared how God at the first visited the Gentiles to take out of them a people for His name.

Simeon (Peter) hath declared how God at the first (after Pentecost) did visit the Gentiles (Cornelius' house), to take (receive) out of them a people for his name.

Just as the 120 had been a select group used by Jesus to begin the revival at Jerusalem, the house of Cornelius has also been selected by the same God to bring revival among the Gentiles.

15:15 And with this the words of the prophets agree, just as it is written:

And to this agree (*sumphoneo*: to be harmonious, to concur) the words of the prophets; as it is written,

James will quote from Amos 9:11 and 12. This Old Testament prophet foretold of the church arising out of the Gentile nations.

15:16 *'After this I will return*
And will rebuild the tabernacle of David, which
has fallen down;
I will rebuild its ruins, and I will set it up;

Although the time foretold by Amos was after the second advent, the double meaning also refers to the church age. "After this" is a reference to the day of Pentecost as well as the second advent. Peter also used this when he told of Joel's prophecy (2:17).

The church age is a type of the millennium. Jesus will restore the tabernacle of David, which is open worship of the Lord to all nations. The temple was destroyed in the Babylonian captivity and Roman invasion and will not be physically rebuilt until the second advent. However, it is spiritually rebuilt in our hearts during the church age, a tabernacle built by Jesus. He is the author and finisher of our faith and the one who said, "I will build my church."

The treasure today is in earthen vessels. The church is invisible today, but just as we will have a resurrection body — a physical temple instead of a tent (2 Peter 1:13) — the millennial reign of Jesus will take place and a physical temple will be built.

15:17 *So that the rest of mankind may seek the Lord,*
Even all the Gentiles who are called by My name,
Says the Lord who does all these things.'

That the residue (remnant) of men might seek after the Lord, and all the Gentiles, upon whom my name is called, saith the Lord, who doeth all these things (brings all these things to pass).

The residue of men is born again Jews on the earth. Until Jesus returns, they will always be in the minority when compared to Gentile believers.

15:18 ⸼ "Known to God from eternity are all His works.

The Greek says, "Known from eternity past are all His works."

15:19 Therefore I judge that we should not trouble those from among the Gentiles who are turning to God,

Wherefore my sentence (judgment) is, that we trouble not them, which from among the Gentiles are turned to God:

James now draws his conclusion: legalism always seeks to trouble grace. James is wise to include this phrase in his decision. The statement James makes is also his conclusion, his opinion on the matter. This will become important in the course of events to come (v. 28).

H. James' Compromise with Legalism

15:20 but that we write to them to abstain from things polluted by idols, *from* sexual immorality, *from* things strangled, and *from* blood.

This is a compromise made by James. It shows his weakness toward the legalistic Hebrews in his church. After such a strong introduction and condemnation of legalism, he declares a compromise. This "inch" will become a "mile" in the days to come, and legalism will completely dominate the church. The leaven will destroy the whole lump.

The items mentioned by James are standard procedure for idol worshipers. Although these are offensive to the Jews, they do not need to be mentioned. Gentiles have been saved and become spiritual without these regulations. Paul will take this letter to the churches of Galatia (16:4) but will never mention the different points in any sermon or discuss this letter except with the Thessalonians (1 Thessalonians 4:1–3, 9–11).

James's comments on food and drinks offered to idols are taught in Romans 14. In that passage he tells of expediency and personal conviction. This attempt by James is to draw a compromise between legalism and grace. The two cannot coexist.

There are four things mentioned in this recommendation, only one of which is scriptural. "Pollutions of idols" is actually meat offered to idols (v. 29). This command, along with food strangled and drinking of blood, is not addressed anywhere in the Word as an issue with Gentiles. Only the command to abstain from fornication is scriptural, found in the Old Testament and the New. Legalism elevates its own set of standards to a place equal with the Word of God. With legalism, it is difficult to tell where the Word ends and religion begins.

I. Five Attributes of Legalism

1. Legalism makes mountains out of molehills. Non-issues become major.
2. Legalism is localized. What offends one group in one place is all that is important or presented.
3. Legalism elevates its own set of standards to a place equal with the Word.
4. Legalism desires to bring others into bondage and control their lives.
5. Legalism will use the Holy Spirit for authenticity and validity (v. 28), making anyone who questions them feel they are arguing with God.

This legalism in the Jerusalem church slowly chokes out faith. Finally, the faith of the church is made a shipwreck.

We are to "grow in grace and knowledge." These two work together. What sustains faith is the knowledge of God's grace (Romans 4:16, Ephesians 2:8–9).

Galatians 2:1 through 11 tells us another side of this same meeting. Before the church-wide conference, Paul, Barnabas, and Titus had met with church leadership and the Judaizers in a private meeting (v. 2). Peter and Paul were both vindicated before the leadership and told to preach freely, Peter to the Jews and Paul to the Gentiles. But before the end of the meeting, another issue was introduced, "only they would that we should remember the poor" (v. 10).

The same thing done to the church at Antioch was done to Paul: legalism trying to exercise control over grace. Legalistic people are jealous of grace. Although Paul graciously agrees to do this, it was unnecessary. It had nothing to do with the issue at hand. Paul will never preach about any of these issues after this conference. He will address this subject and meeting in the Thessalonian epistle, but will only mention the one scriptural sin of fornication (1 Thessalonians 4:1–3, 9–11).

15:21 For Moses has had throughout many generations those who preach him in every city, being read in the synagogues every Sabbath."

Most cities in Gentile countries have a Jewish synagogue where many local Jews attend meetings each Sabbath. James is telling the Gentile converts they should refrain from these things so they will not offend their Jewish brothers.

J. New Guidelines Sent with Paul and Barnabas to Antioch

15:22 ⁋ Then it pleased the apostles and elders, with the whole church, to send chosen men of their own company to Antioch with Paul and Barnabas, namely, Judas who was also named Barsabas, and Silas, leading men among the brethren.

Not only do Paul and Barnabas return to Antioch, Jerusalem sends representatives back with them to give the new guidelines. The leaders in Jerusalem want to be in control. Not only does James want to give the edict to the Gentile believers, he wants his own men to be there to read it. Again we see legalism making a mountain out of a molehill.

Although Paul and Barnabas do not say anything, they are probably glad to be getting out of Jerusalem. They have come to resolve a major issue on legalism and have had to settle for a compromise.

Here not only do we see legalism in church doctrines, but also in church politics. Judas (Barsabas) and Silas are both prophets (v. 32) who have risen up in the Jerusalem church since the last mention of leadership (chapter 6). They have been raised up in a legalistic church and are expected to have some influence. However, they are about to be exposed to grace, and Silas will be more influenced by the church at Antioch than the church will be influenced by him. Silas, also called Silvanus (his Roman name, 2 Corinthians 1:19), will go on to accompany Paul on his second missionary journey (v. 40). Later he will work with Peter and carry his first epistle to the churches of Asia Minor.

K. Letter Addressed to Gentiles in Antioch, Syria, and Cilicia

15:23 They wrote this *letter* by them: ⁋ the apostles, the elders, and the brethren, ⁋ to the brethren who are of the Gentiles in Antioch, Syria, and Cilicia: ⁋ Greetings.

And they wrote letters by them after this manner; The apostles and elders and brethren send greeting unto the brethren which are of (*ek*: out from) the Gentiles in Antioch and Syria and Cilicia:

The letter addresses the Gentiles as coming "out from" the nations and also as fellow brothers with the Jews in Jerusalem. This is the recognition of being a member of the family of God, no matter what the nationality of the converts. The Gentiles are addressed in Antioch, Syria, and Cilicia because this is where the Gentile churches have been established.

15:24 Since we have heard that some who went out from us have troubled you with words, unsettling your souls, saying, "*You must* be circumcised and keep the law"—to whom we gave no such commandment—

Forasmuch as we have heard, that certain (legalistic Jews) which went out from us have troubled you with words, subverting (unsettling) your souls, saying, Ye must be circumcised, and keep the law: to whom (legalistic Jews) we gave no such commandment:

Legalism cuts to the foundation of the Christian life. Our entire life is built upon simple faith; faith in Jesus for salvation and faith in His Word for daily living. The law, when taught as a means of salvation and/or spirituality, undermines or subverts the entire Christian way of life. James tells the Gentile believers that the message which has been preached by the legalistic Jews from Jerusalem did not come from him or any church leader.

15:25 it seemed good to us, being assembled with one accord, to send chosen men to you with our beloved Barnabas and Paul,

It is good that James gives such praise and acceptance to Paul and Barnabas. It is the leadership of the Jerusalem church giving their stamp of approval to them before the Gentile believers. (Unfortunately, the legalistic Jewish believers would later attack Paul's calling, character, and reputation.)

15:26 men who have risked their lives for the name of our Lord Jesus Christ.

James also acknowledges that the tribulations faced on missionary journeys are for the furtherance of the gospel.

15:27 We have therefore sent Judas and Silas, who will also report the same things by word of mouth.

Judas and Silas stand with Barnabas and Paul to show the unity between the two churches.

15:28 For it seemed good to the Holy Spirit, and to us, to lay upon you no greater burden than these necessary things:

This is where the letter leaves reality. The Holy Spirit did not inspire these "necessary things." Even though the church leadership and congregation all agree on these guidelines, they do not come from God. When a person puts the Holy Spirit's name on an issue, it is to add validity. So to argue with the decision is to argue with God. However, these things will not be mentioned again in the book of Acts, and Paul will later teach abstinence from food presented to idols as a personal heart issue (Romans 14), not a dictate of the Holy Spirit.

15:29 that you abstain from things offered to idols, from blood, from things strangled, and from sexual immorality. If you keep yourselves from these, you will do well. ¶ Farewell.

Meat offered to idols was then brought to the front of the temple where the finest restaurants were located, and this is the meat being referred to. The Word has nothing to say about eating meat offered to idols; it is just meat. Where the meat has been a few minutes prior to being served has nothing to do with spirituality. Meat is not spiritual and should not be used as a spiritual issue. Again, the only scriptural thing mentioned in this letter is fornication.

III. The Triumph of the Ministry of Grace (30–35)

Judas and Silas, the delegates from Jerusalem, strengthen and encourage the faith of the believers at Antioch and are sent home by the Antioch church with a blessing of peace. Paul and Barnabas remain in Antioch teaching and preaching, along with many others.

A. Reading of the Letter to the Gentiles

15:30 ¶ So when they were sent off, they came to Antioch; and when they had gathered the multitude together, they delivered the letter.

The letter was read out loud.

15:31 When they had read it, they rejoiced over its encouragement.

Which when they (Judas and Silas) had read, they (the congregation) rejoiced for the consolation (comfort).

15:32 Now Judas and Silas, themselves being prophets also, exhorted and strengthened the brethren with many words.

The saints in Antioch have been unsettled by the teachings of the legalistic Jews. Judas and Silas, being prophets, use their spiritual offices and gifts to bring encouragement and stability back to the believers. The saints now know that Paul and Barnabas have taught them correctly from the beginning.

15:33 And after they had stayed *there* for a time, they were sent back with greetings from the brethren to the apostles.

And after they (Judas and Silas) had tarried there a space (while), they were let go in peace from the brethren unto the apostles.

During their time in Antioch, both Judas and Silas experience church services centered on grace and liberty. Even though they come from a church claiming to believe in grace and freedom, they now see what a church truly operating in grace can be like.

15:34 ¶ However, it seemed good to Silas to remain there.

Judas returns to Jerusalem, but Silas is so pleased with the church at Antioch, he stays on and makes Antioch his ministry base. Although this verse is not found in many of the earliest manuscripts, it is still true that Silas remained in Antioch (v. 40).

B. Paul and Barnabas Continue Teaching and Preaching

15:35 Paul and Barnabas also remained in Antioch, teaching and preaching the word of the Lord, with many others also.

Paul and Barnabas continue to work with the church leadership and teach what God wants. The issue of the letter from Jerusalem is not mentioned again in Acts, and is probably not a major point of exposition in the church. The foundation of grace continues in Antioch, and missionary activity is a priority.

IV. The Triumph of the Deeds of Grace (36–39)

Paul speaks with Barnabas about returning to the areas they had first preached to see how the new believers are doing. Before they go, Paul and Barnabas have a major disagreement over taking Mark on the next missionary journey, and they separate from one another as a result. Barnabas travels to Cyprus with Mark and Paul chooses Silas to travel with him to Syria and Cilicia.

A. Paul and Barnabas Agree to Return to Galatia

15:36 ¶ Then after some days Paul said to Barnabas, "Let us now go back and visit our brethren in every city where we have preached the word of the Lord, *and see* how they are doing."

Paul wants to return to Galatia and visit those who are born again. He also wants to see how the churches that had been established on the first missionary journey are doing. Barnabas is in favor of the journey.

B. Dispute over John Mark

15:37 Now Barnabas was determined to take with them John called Mark.

And Barnabas determined (*boulomai*: had intended) to take with them John, whose surname was Mark.

Evidently Barnabas has been waiting for Paul to bring up this subject because he wants to return to Galatia. He also has been keeping up with Mark and knows Mark has recovered from his mistake and wants another chance to prove himself in the ministry. When Barnabas brings up the issue of Mark, Paul probably feels that Barnabas has been planning this for some time. Paul resents this intrusion and will not want to take Mark with them on their journey.

15:38 But Paul insisted that they should not take with them the one who had departed from them in Pamphylia, and had not gone with them to the work.

Paul resists the idea, and the resistance becomes a full blown argument. Paul does not feel Mark is worthy to work in the ministry, and Barnabas is determined to give his cousin another chance.

Paul later repents of his attitude toward Mark and calls him useful for the ministry (2 Timothy 4:11). Mark will also later accompany Peter to Rome (1 Peter 5:13).

C. Paul and Barnabas Separate

15:39 Then the contention became so sharp that they parted from one another. And so Barnabas took Mark and sailed to Cyprus;

Paul and Barnabas have a shouting match between themselves. It is so loud that many in the area probably hear them. Hopefully the people listening realized that ministers are human, giving them an opportunity to walk in forgiveness toward both Paul and Barnabas.

Barnabas takes Mark to Cyprus — the first part of the previous missionary journey — where Mark had been a success. This would be familiar territory to Mark and not a reminder of his failure.

When Paul and Barnabas separate, it is forever. They "parted asunder." This is strong language showing they did not minister together again. Paul's mistake is being legalistic concerning Mark. Mark does deserve another chance, and Barnabas made the right choice. The circumstance of their separation is not good, but both Paul and Barnabas continue on in the ministry. This mistake of Paul's will later become larger, and bring him into a great act of legalism in Jerusalem.

D. Paul Chooses Silas

15:40 but Paul chose Silas and departed, being commended by the brethren to the grace of God.

Silas is still in Antioch and ready to do missionary work. Paul has apparently grown close to Silas during the previous months and recognizes his love for the Lord and ministry calling. The church members at Antioch are champions in grace and love. They do not choose sides in the argument, but commend both Paul and Barnabas to the grace of God as they leave with new ministry partners. This argument does not split the church.

15:41 And he went through Syria and Cilicia, strengthening the churches.

Syria and Cilicia are the other two Gentile areas where prospering churches have been established (v. 23). (The letter from Jerusalem is written to them as well.)

16:1–40 Supernatural Guidance

The Challenge of Chapter Sixteen

Learning to heed the guidance of the Holy Spirit is essential to living a successful, effective Christian life, especially when witnessing to those whose hearts are prepared to receive the gospel message.

Jesus teaches that in this world we would have tribulations and face difficult situations. Some of those circumstances may even seem insurmountable. But Jesus also says He has overcome whatever the world can send our way. God said many are the afflictions of the righteous, but He has delivered us from every difficulty we will ever face. We may never find ourselves chained in an inner prison as Paul and Silas did, but we can learn to handle difficult situations as they did: by confidently singing praises to God knowing our deliverance will surely come.

I. Timothy Accompanies Paul (1–5)

Paul hears of Timothy's reputation from the brethren at Lystra and Iconium. Paul invites Timothy to travel with Silas and him on his second missionary journey to Greece.

16:1 ¶ Then he came to Derbe and Lystra. And behold, a certain disciple was there, named Timothy, *the* son of a certain Jewish woman who believed, but his father *was* Greek.

It is God's desire to continually train new people for the ministry. His plan is to raise up people by having them learn from those presently in the ministry (2 Timothy 2:2). Because of Mark's failure during the previous missionary journey, God will introduce Timothy to Paul's team.

Timothy is born again and young in age. He is probably in his late teens when Paul invites him as a traveling companion. Timothy will be a traveling companion to Paul off and on for the rest of Paul's life. Timothy's mother (Eunice) and grandmother (Lois) are also born again (2 Timothy 1:5).

Timothy has been endowed with the gift to pastor, and in Timothy's early, developmental years, Paul uses him to fill in for churches in need. At Philippi he is very successful, but at Corinth, he is not. (Titus has to come and bail him out.) Later Timothy becomes the pastor at Ephesus and has much difficulty. This is the reason for 1 and 2 Timothy, which are letters of pastoral instruction.

Timothy's mother lives in an isolated part of the world but worships the Lord in the Jewish fashion. She is born again and raises her son Timothy in the scriptures. It appears Timothy's father is an unbeliever who had perhaps left the family in their early years. The term "Greek" is usually used by Paul for an unbeliever. Timothy has been raised by his mother and grandmother and had to be fathered spiritually and physically by Paul.

16:2 He was well spoken of by the brethren who were at Lystra and Iconium.

Apparently Timothy has done some ministering in both Lystra and Iconium before Paul arrives. Paul hears of Timothy from the Christian brothers before he actually meets him.

16:3 Paul wanted to have him go on with him. And he took *him* and circumcised him because of the Jews who were in that region, for they all knew that his father was Greek.

Paul immediately recognizes Timothy's potential. Paul knows Timothy is not a strong person in the Word like Titus was at the Jerusalem conference (Acts 15). Paul has Timothy circumcised because of the pressure he would be spared in the upcoming journey. This is the law of expediency. This type of pressure would not have affected Titus, so Paul had not asked him to be circumcised (Galatians 2:3).

16:4 And as they went through the cities, they delivered to them the decrees to keep, which were determined by the apostles and elders at Jerusalem.

The decrees are delivered at the request of James and the leaders of the Jerusalem church. Paul is obedient to deliver them, but does not preach them. Paul might have had some questions directed to him about the items mentioned in the letter, but he always kept the focus on grace.

16:5 So the churches were strengthened in the faith, and increased in number daily.

An established church increases in numbers. A church is established in faith when the Word is taught. The purpose of a church service is not to preach salvation sermons. The salvation message is to be taken to the world by the congregational members. The church should teach the Word so the members will become strong, go out and win the lost, and bring them into the church to be fed and become disciples. Churches teaching faith will then be established.

II. Paul's Vision to Go to Macedonia (6–10)

Paul has a strong desire to preach in Asia and has been following the small inward voice of the Spirit to lead him. This time, however, Paul receives a vision from God urging him to travel with his companions to Macedonia.

> **16:6 ¶ Now when they had gone through Phrygia and the region of Galatia, they were forbidden by the Holy Spirit to preach the word in Asia.**

Now when they had gone throughout Phrygia and the region of Galatia, and were forbidden (*koluo*: refused) of (by) the Holy Ghost to preach the word in Asia,

Until now, Paul has followed the inward witness and his overwhelming desire to preach the gospel (1 Corinthians 9:16). But he yields to the strong urging of the Holy Spirit who forbids him to go into Asia: the time is not right yet. This will come later in Chapter 19 when he will be released by the Holy Spirit to go to Ephesus.

If God had told Paul at this moment about Macedonia, he would have by-passed many spiritually hungry people in Troas. God will see to it that Paul goes to the right place at the right time on his third missionary journey. These churches will respond positively to the gospel and become the subject of Revelation Chapters 2 and 3, the seven churches of Asia.

> **16:7 After they had come to Mysia, they tried to go into Bithynia, but the Spirit did not permit them.**

After they were come to (up to) Mysia, the assayed (attempted) to go into Bithynia: but the Spirit suffered (*eao*: allowed, permitted), them not.

God wants Paul to go west toward Macedonia, so the Holy Spirit again stops him from going south to Asia or north into Bithynia. He has other ministers planned for these places.

Because Bithynia is very prone to legalism, God has this nation prepared for the preaching of Peter (1 Peter 1:1). First Peter was written to believers in

Bithynia, and the subject is apostasy. Legalism leads to apostasy. God wants Peter to write to them because he is also prone towards legalism.

Since John understood love, God chose him to write to Asia. Paul would have been too rough, and the people probably would not have received God's message through him. Asia and the people of Bithynia will more easily receive rebuke from Peter and John than from Paul.

We are all a team and have individual roles to play. God is preparing Peter to preach to Bithynia and Asia Minor while preparing John to write letters to many of them. God does not call one person or one church to win the whole world.

The Holy Spirit forbids Paul from going to Asia because the time is not right, but also because Paul is not the one God had chosen to take the gospel to them. We also need to be sensitive to the Holy Spirit, whether He speaks to us audibly, through an angel, a vision, a prophecy, with a sense of urgency, through a gentle voice, a still voice, a sense of peace, or a "check" or warning.

16:8 So passing by Mysia, they came down to Troas.

After hearing the Holy Spirit say "no" to Bithynia, Paul and his team bypass Mysia. Apparently the Spirit has told them to forget this city. Paul is now heading in the only direction he has peace about. He does not return in the direction from which he came (east). He cannot go north or south. The only option left is west until he comes to Troy on the Aegean Sea.

Troy is the famous city of the Homeric stories of the Iliad and the Odyssey. It is a center of Greek culture and history. It is the place where Alexander began his world empire and fought many battles. Here at Troas (Troy), Paul will add to the ministry team and take the gospel to Macedonia. Along with Timothy, he will add Luke. He attempts to add Titus, but does not (2 Corinthians 2:12–13). He leaves his coat here and asks Timothy to bring it to him in prison in Rome (2 Timothy 4:13).

16:9 And a vision appeared to Paul in the night. A man of Macedonia stood and pleaded with him, saying, "Come over to Macedonia and help us."

Paul later calls this a "door opened" (2 Corinthians 2:12). Asia and Bithynia are "doors closing." Many times God leads us by closing doors before opening others.

Peter had a vision in Chapter 10, and now Paul has a vision. Visions are a means of God's leading in this age (Joel 2:28). In this vision, Paul recognizes the man who appears to him as being from Macedonia. The man's clothing and speech allows Paul to identify where this man is from. This man represents the readiness of the whole nation of Macedonia. The nation has been evangelized before and is now ready to receive the gospel.

> **16:10 Now after he had seen the vision, immediately we sought to go to Macedonia, concluding that the Lord had called us to preach the gospel to them.**

The narrative is no longer about Paul and his team, but Luke is now a member. The literary style of the book of Acts indicates that Luke is the author. "We" is now added, showing that Luke had joined them.

Paul refers to Luke as "beloved." Luke will leave Paul and rejoin him from time to time (20:15, 21:18, 27:1, 28:16) as do other members of the team. The other members include Silas and Timothy. All of these take Paul's vision as their own. They probably all pray and open their hearts to the will of the Holy Spirit. They do not argue about going to Macedonia, but believe Paul has received direction from the Lord. Once they have agreed to go, they do not argue or criticize but support Paul's decision.

III. First Converts in Europe (11–18)

Paul and his companions travel to Philippi in Macedonia where they remain for several days. On the Sabbath, they speak with some women who have gathered. One woman is Lydia, a businesswoman, who receives the message of salvation and invites Paul and his companions to her home.

A. Paul and His Team Travel to Macedonia

> **16:11 ¶ Therefore, sailing from Troas, we ran a straight course to Samothrace, and the next *day* came to Neapolis,**

After the vision at Troy, Paul and his crew immediately sail straight for the next mission. Samothrace is an island northwest of Troy about halfway to the port of Neopolis. Neopolis is one of two main seaports of Macedonia (the other is Thessalonica). Samothrace can be reached in one day from either Troy or Neapolis depending on the winds. Samothrace had a high peak (5500 feet) that could be seen and used as a navigation point for sailors.

Paul's crew sail the Aegean Sea in two days. Later, when the wind is contrary, this same trip traveling in the opposite direction will take five days (20:6).

16:12 and from there to Philippi, which is the foremost city of that part of Macedonia, a colony. And we were staying in that city for some days.

Philippi is a famous city to the Romans for its history and location. Here Mark Antony and Octavius met Brutus and Cassius and defeated them. As a result of this battle, almost half of Brutus' army committed suicide. Philippi was then known as the city of suicide.

The word "colony" is important because Philippi is under Roman ownership. Anyone in Philippi, regardless of nationality, is given Roman citizenship and protection, and no Roman citizen can be beaten or crucified. "Colony" is the highest Roman honor for a city.

Philippi had been named for Philip Macedon, the father of Alexander the Great; thus the names Philippi and Macedonia. This city is strategically important to Rome because it guarded the Egnatian Way, a road that connected the Adriatic to the Aegean Sea. Philippi, because of its beauty, also became a popular retirement center for Roman military personnel. It has a large Greek population and a small number of Jewish people.

Paul and his crew will have a long stay and a slow beginning. This shows just because events do not happen quickly, it does not mean you are out of God's will. They are making the most of a slow situation. They are praying and waiting on the opening of doors within this city.

16:13 And on the Sabbath day we went out of the city to the riverside, where prayer was customarily made; and we sat down and spoke to the women who met *there*.

The river with many fountains is the Ganges, about a mile outside the city. This is the battle sight of Mark Antony and Brutus. Paul and his team went there to pray on the Sabbath. They want to win the Jews first and it made no difference to them what day they prayed. They became "all things to all men." Paul found some Jewish women who prayed each Sabbath day at this river. The men probably had little going in the way of worship and their wives met to pray at this river. Apparently, the women living in the Gentile countries who were following Jewish customs were more zealous than the men (13:50).

B. Lydia's Conversion

16:14 Now a certain woman named Lydia heard *us*. She was a seller of purple from the city of Thyatira, who worshiped God. The Lord opened her heart to heed the things spoken by Paul.

And a certain woman named Lydia, a seller of purple (purple-dyed robes and garments), of the city of Thyatira, which worshipped (reverenced) God, heard us: whose heart the Lord opened, that she attended (listened intently) unto the things which were spoken of Paul.

Lydia is a businesswoman originally from Thyatira, a city famous for the production of dye. Lydia learned the trade, sold garments died purple, and traveled throughout Europe selling her line of clothing. She moved to Philippi because of the wealth and location of the city. Her heart is open to the Lord. God sends Paul and his team to give her the gospel. The "opening" of her heart is the drawing ministry of the Holy Spirit. Her desire is to know and this is all the Holy Spirit needs. She becomes born again.

16:15 And when she and her household were baptized, she begged *us*, saying, "If you have judged me to be faithful to the Lord, come to my house and stay." So she persuaded us.

And when she was baptized, and her household, she besought (continually questioned) us, saying, If ye have judged (discerned) me to be faithful (committed) to the Lord, come into my house, and abide (base yourself) there. And she constrained (continued to persuade) us.

Lydia lives in Philippi and has a family. Being a key leader of the revival in the city, she runs home and leads her family to the Lord, and they are also all baptized.

Before this time, Paul and his team having stayed to themselves. Once she is baptized and becomes more committed to the Lord, she desires more teaching. There is no church in town, so she invites Paul and the others to move into her large house. Paul and the team accept her invitation and after this, go into the city from time to time to speak, pray, and evangelize. Lydia's house becomes the home of the church at Philippi.

C. Conversion of the Demon Possessed Woman

16:16 ¶ Now it happened, as we went to prayer, that a certain slave girl possessed with a spirit of divination met us, who brought her masters much profit by fortune-telling.

And it came to pass, as we went to prayer, a certain damsel possessed with a spirit of divination (*puthos*: soothsaying) met us, which brought her masters (owners) much gain (profit) by soothsaying (fortune telling):

Paul is probably taking his team to the same place of prayer by the river, when he is confronted by this girl. A "damsel" is a Greek slave. At first, Paul does not perceive her problem and tolerates her presence. What Paul does not immediately realize is that she has been sent by Satan to stop his ministry in the city of Philippi. She is demon-possessed and is being used by her owners to make a great financial profit. They have been using her for fortune-telling, but for many days insists on going to the place where the prayer meeting is being held and speaking out about Paul and his team.

The demon possessing her is called "a spirit of divination." The Greek word here is *puyov*, from which the English word python is derived. In Greek mythology the python was the guard over the oracle of Apollo. The oracle was the hidden knowledge of the gods. The python rose from mud pits and guarded the secret until Apollo slew it in the caves of Mount Parnasus. The oracle of Delphi was also called the Phythian Oracle. A demon controlled this mythological belief and it is now controlling this woman. She gives false prophesies and is harassing Paul and his men.

16:17 This girl followed Paul and us, and cried out, saying, "These men are the servants of the Most High God, who proclaim to us the way of salvation."

The same followed Paul and us, and cried (kept on shouting), saying, These men are the servants of the most high God, which shew unto us the way of salvation.

This verse shows the deception of Satan. Every word she says is true, but the intent is not to lead people into permanent freedom. After Paul and the team are gone, this woman looks like a herald, a forerunner of Paul's ministry like John the Baptist was to Jesus. Everyone knows this girl is a fortune-teller, and Satan wants them to think of her as an ambassador of the gospel.

16:18 And this she did for many days. ¶ But Paul, greatly annoyed, turned and said to the spirit, "I command you in the name of Jesus Christ to come out of her." And he came out that very hour.

Paul is wrestling within himself until he senses the leading of the Holy Spirit. He is grieved, which is a leading of the Holy Spirit. Not only can the Holy Spirit lead us in the right direction, He can also warn us against going in the wrong direction. A warning from the Holy Spirit is not always as strong as it was with Paul's desire to go to Bithynia or Asia; it can be a still small voice, a mild warning, or just a bad feeling. Paul now realizes this is not a woman of God but a messenger of Satan, and he turns and speaks directly to the demon commanding it to come out of the girl. Within a short period of time, the demon comes out. Paul is not angry with the girl but with Satan and the demon.

It is not necessary for Paul to stay with the girl to ensure the demon has come out. He goes on his way, and the demon leaves the girl within a short time. Jesus also cast out demons that tried to announce Him (Mark 1:23–25, 3:11–12).

IV. Paul and Silas in Prison (19–24)

Because Paul cast the demon out of a slave girl who gained money for her owners through divination, Paul and Silas are dragged before the rulers of the city. Magistrates order Paul and Silas beaten with rods and thrown in prison. The jailer is ordered to keep them safe, so he moves them to the inner prison and puts their feet in stocks.

16:19 But when her masters saw that their hope of profit was gone, they seized Paul and Silas and dragged *them* into the marketplace to the authorities.

And when her masters saw that the hope of their gains was gone, they caught (violently) Paul and Silas, and drew (dragged) them into the market-place (*agora*: assembly) unto the rulers (Roman),

The masters soon see that the girl no longer had her powers, and they are angry. They are not interested in the girl's well-being, only in money. They should have rejoiced when she was set free, but instead, they see that a great income is now gone. They find Paul and Silas and drag them (probably via hired men) into the public marketplace before the Roman rulers.

The Greeks held their courts at the city gates. This court scene occurred in the middle of town, before a large crowd. Paul and Silas are falsely accused before a Roman court. The magistrates do not know Paul and Silas are Roman citizens until the next day.

16:20 ¶ And they brought them to the magistrates, and said, "These men, being Jews, exceedingly trouble our city;

And brought them to the magistrates, saying, these men, being (*huparcho*: existing as) Jews, do exceedingly trouble our city (disturb the peace),

The men do not know Paul is a Roman citizen and assume him to be only a Hebrew. To be a Roman was a great privilege, and anyone who was not a Roman citizen existed as any other nationality. The accusation is a very sarcastic remark toward Paul and Silas. The men do not even take time to learn the nationality or citizenship of Paul and Silas.

16:21 and they teach customs which are not lawful for us, being Romans, to receive or observe."

These men are saying, "We have always been Romans and are proud of it." The implication is Paul and Silas are foreigners trying to pollute a pure Roman culture; anything contrary to Roman culture must be wrong. These men are using patriotism to stir up emotions against Paul and Silas.

Roman law was usually very good, but here the lawyers outsmart the ruler. Later, however, Roman law will save Paul at Ephesus and Corinth. These owners are not really patriots but are using any means to gain back their business. They want to be rid of Paul and Silas.

16:22 Then the multitude rose up together against them; and the magistrates tore off their clothes and commanded *them* to be beaten with rods.

And the multitude rose up together against them: and the magistrates rent off their (Paul's and Silas's clothes), and commanded to beat them.

These men struck a nerve with the townspeople. Emotional patriotism is running high, and Paul and Silas are caught between Satan's revenge and the emotions of the people. These leaders never question Paul or they would have discovered he was a Roman citizen. This will be realized later, after Paul is released from prison (37–38). Once the emotions die down, the magistrates repent for this miscarriage of justice the following day.

16:23 And when they had laid many stripes on them, they threw *them* into prison, commanding the jailer to keep them securely.

They put thirty-nine stripes on their backs (2 Corinthians 11:25). They are stripped to the waist and whipped with rods before being put into prison. This is all illegal.

16:24 Having received such a charge, he put them into the inner prison and fastened their feet in the stocks.

Who, having received such a charge, thrust them into the inner (under) prison, and made their feet fast (secure) in the stocks.

The under prison is a pit beneath the prison. It is the most secure place, and the stocks around their feet make them immobile. It is physically impossible to escape. This is torture added to torture.

V. Conversion of the Philippian Jailer (25–34)

Paul and Silas begin praying and singing praises to God while in prison. As a result, the foundations of the prison shake, all the doors in the prison open, and all the prisoner's chains release. When the jailer wakes and sees the situation, he draws his sword to kill himself. Paul and Silas stop him, revealing they have not escaped. The jailer then falls to his knees and asks how he can be saved.

A. Paul and Silas Sing Praises

16:25 ¶ But at midnight Paul and Silas were praying and singing hymns to God, and the prisoners were listening to them.

And at (approaching) midnight Paul and Silas prayed (middle voice), and sang praises (middle voice) unto God: and the prisoners heard (were listening to) them.

Paul and Silas pray and sing praises for their own benefit. They are not trying to witness to the other prisoners but are edifying themselves and ministering faith to their own hearts (Jude 20).

16:26 Suddenly there was a great earthquake, so that the foundations of the prison were shaken; and immediately all the doors were opened and everyone's chains were loosed.

The earthquake is sudden, violent, and local. It only affects the prison. It is strong enough to do internal damage to the cells and open the doors. The day after the quake, the magistrates know nothing of it. The foundations are shaken; this is where Paul and Silas are being held.

This is a unique earthquake; there is no damage, only shaking and freedom for the prisoners. The prisoners receive a message by song and demonstration. They know it must be the Lord who delivers them. They hear the praises of Paul and Silas before the quake hit.

B. The Salvation of the Philippian Jailer

16:27 And the keeper of the prison, awaking from sleep and seeing the prison doors open, supposing the prisoners had fled, drew his sword and was about to kill himself.

This jailer is a very tough man. For years, he has slept through all of the moans and screams of the prisoners. But the earthquake wakes him from his sleep and he sees the open prison doors and the chains, which were no longer bound to the prisoners. He thinks he is too late and that many of the prisoners have escaped. He is fearful for his own life because he knows the Roman leaders will take his life. He wants to commit suicide and possibly make it appear as if the prisoners had killed him in a riot. The Romans would never believe the earthquake story, and would kill him as a traitorous or negligent. However, the power of God is so strong in the jail cells that the prisoners do not leave even though the doors are standing wide open.

16:28 But Paul called with a loud voice, saying, "Do yourself no harm, for we are all here."

The jailer runs into the halls ready to kill himself. He is not in the inner prison, but above the cell of Paul and Silas. Paul sees him, screams out, and stops the jailer from committing suicide.

16:29 ¶ Then he called for a light, ran in, and fell down trembling before Paul and Silas.

Then he called for a light (torch), and sprang in (jumped down in), and came trembling, and fell down (prostrated himself) before Paul and Silas,

16:30 And he brought them out and said, "Sirs, what must I do to be saved?"

He is still fearing the Romans and for his own life. His desire to be saved was not spiritual but physical. He sees no way out of death, but is willing to listen to Paul before he dies. How is he going to explain the opened doors and the loose chains? Paul is the only one who has given him any words of hope. Now he is asking about his life being spared, and Paul will use his own words to witness to him.

16:31 ¶ So they said, "Believe on the Lord Jesus Christ, and you will be saved, you and your household."

This man is also fearful for his family. They might be killed as co-conspirators. Paul and Silas know this because they are Roman citizens. They tell him how he as well as his family can receive salvation.

C. Paul and Silas Invited to the Jailer's Home

The jailer invites Paul and Silas to his house after he is born again because he wants his family to hear the gospel message.

16:32 Then they spoke the word of the Lord to him and to all who were in his house.

The order is first presenting the gospel to the jailer and next, the jailer's conversion. The jailer invites Paul and Silas to his house where the rest of his family hears the gospel are also saved (v. 34). Paul and Silas later return to the jailer's house for a meal and for fellowship.

16:33 And he took them the same hour of the night and washed *their stripes*. And immediately he and all his *family* were baptized.

The new birth immediately fills the man's heart with love for Paul and Silas. He has beaten many prisoners and witnessed many other beatings, but he has never had compassion for anyone who suffered in his prison. Paul and Silas have witnessed to the family, seen all of them saved and they are all baptized together immediately following salvation. Before morning, Paul and Silas are eating at the jailer's home. They have all had an exciting night. Paul and Silas have gone through a beating, been thrown in prison, experienced an earthquake, led a jailer and his family to the Lord, and had a baptismal service!

16:34 Now when he had brought them into his house, he set food before them; and he rejoiced, having believed in God with all his household.

The meal is accompanied with shouts of joy. The family has found true peace, and they are excited. God's desire is always to begin His work in families, the basic unit of society and churches. When stability affects the home, it eventually changes nations. Other examples include Rahab and her family and also Lydia.

VI. Magistrates Release Paul and Silas (35–40)

The rulers then send notice to release Paul and Silas, but Paul demands the rulers personally release them from prison and points out how poorly they have been treated as Roman citizens. The rulers apologize, release Paul and Silas, and ask them to leave the city.

> **16:35 ¶ And when it was day, the magistrates sent the officers, saying, "Let those men go."**

And when it was day, the magistrates sent the sergeants (*lictors*: ancient Roman officers), saying, Let those men go.

It is now the morning after. The magistrates have realized their mistake in beating and condemning men without a fair trial. They are afraid of what might happen if their treatment of Paul and Silas should reach the streets, so they ask Paul and Silas to immediately leave the city.

> **16:36 ¶ So the keeper of the prison reported these words to Paul, saying, "The magistrates have sent to let you go. Now therefore depart, and go in peace."**

The new convert is happy to tell Paul and Silas they are free. He is speaking openly to them in front of the men sent by the city leaders.

> **16:37 ¶ But Paul said to them, "They have beaten us openly, uncondemned Romans, *and* have thrown *us* into prison. And now do they put us out secretly? No indeed! Let them come themselves and get us out."**

But Paul said unto them, They have beaten us openly (before many witnesses) uncondemned, being (*huparcho*: existing as) Romans, and have cast us into prison; and now do they thrust us out privily? Nay verily; but let them come themselves and fetch us out.

Paul speaks right past the jailer to the representatives of the Roman magistrates. Paul and Silas have been beaten in the sight of many in the city. Their beating did not take place in a back alley but in an open area of the city. The people of the city also witnessed that Paul and Silas were beaten without a trial. Added to all this is the fact that they are Roman citizens. This frightens the representatives. They realize this could mean havoc with the Roman government. To beat a Roman citizen is illegal. Not to give a fair hearing is also illegal. Nor can Roman citizens be beaten, put in chains, or crucified. In addition, they can be jailed only if they commit a capital crime, can not be tortured in any way, and if execution is in order, the convicted are decapitated. (History tells us Paul was killed in this way at the end of his life.)

If a colony was guilty of mistreating a Roman citizen, they could lose their charter and Roman protection. Rhodes, an island located eleven miles southwest of Turkey in the Aegean Sea, had their charter revoked under Claudius.

These Roman magistrates have believed a report without giving Paul and Silas a fair trial. They thought of Paul and Silas only as Jews and not Roman citizens. It is possible for their treatment of Paul and Silas to reach all the way to Caesar!

16:38 ¶ And the officers told these words to the magistrates, and they were afraid when they heard that they were Romans.

The magistrates fear Paul and the citizens; they fear for their jobs and their relations with Rome. They also feared for their own lives and for the future of their own city, Philippi.

16:39–40 Then they came and pleaded with them and brought *them* out, and asked *them* to depart from the city. 40 So they went out of the prison and entered *the house of* Lydia; and when they had seen the brethren, they encouraged them and departed.

Paul and Silas encourage the others after being beaten. They come to Lydia and a house full of people. Apparently the people gathered were afraid and discouraged for Paul and Silas.

When Paul and Silas depart, they leave Timothy and Luke in Philippi. Timothy does not rejoin Paul until Berea (Acts 17:14). Luke does not rejoin Paul until the third missionary journey (Acts 20:5–6).

17:1-34 The Macedonian Tour

The Challenge of Chapter Seventeen

Jesus instructs us to "go into all the world" to preach the gospel, and we must not allow opposition to stop us from sharing the gospel. We have opportunities in the world around us daily to share the gospel of Jesus Christ, and like Paul, we should meet people where they are at in their understanding of the true God. As born again believers, we should be living supernaturally in obedience to the guidance of the Holy Spirit and whether that obedience results in thousands or just one finding Jesus Christ as Lord and Savior, obedience is the key. Every life matters to God.

I. Paul Reasons with the Thessalonians (1–4)

Paul and Silas have arrived in Thessalonica, and for three days, Paul reasons from the scriptures with the Jews who are gathered in the temple. Some Jews are persuaded, and many Greeks and leading women of Thessalonica join Paul and Silas, receiving the message of the gospel.

A. The Egnatian Way

17:1 ¶ Now when they had passed through Amphipolis and Apollonia, they came to Thessalonica, where there was a synagogue of the Jews.

Paul and Silas are now traveling on the Egnatian Way and will travel from Philippi to Thessalonica through Amphipolis and Apollonia. They will leave the highway and go on to Berea. The Egnatian Way is a five hundred mile highway joining the Adriatic Sea at Dyrrhachium to the Aegean Sea at Neapolis.

Thessalonica is a gulf city. Today it is the modern city of Salonica. It was the largest and most important city in Macedonia, and was the name of a very famous woman: a sister of Alexander the Great. Since a Jewish population has existed in Thessalonica for some time, there is a synagogue where the Jews gather for worship.

B. Paul's Ministry to the Jews at Thessalonica

17:2 Then Paul, as his custom was, went in to them, and for three Sabbaths reasoned with them from the Scriptures,

And Paul, as his manner (custom) was, went in unto them, and three Sabbath days reasoned (*dialegomai*: dispute) with them out of the scriptures,

Paul's usual custom in a city is to first find a synagogue (if there is one) and minister to the Jews (Romans 1:16). Because Paul has so many credentials from the Jewish religion, they quickly give him the floor the first time or two. In Thessalonica, Paul is able to preach three times before he is recognized as a Jewish rebel. In Thessalonica, Paul not only teaches, he answers questions. This demonstrates the vast amount of knowledge and confidence Paul possesses. Later, word spreads from the Jewish headquarters in Jerusalem not to allow him to speak in the synagogue. This will all catch up with him in chapter 21 in Jerusalem at the temple.

17:3 explaining and demonstrating that the Christ had to suffer and rise again from the dead, and *saying*, "This Jesus whom I preach to you is the Christ."

Opening (revealing form scriptures) and alleging (proving), that Christ must needs (*deo*: had an obligation) have suffered (died), and risen again from the dead; and that this Jesus, whom I preach unto you, is Christ.

Paul takes familiar Old Testament scriptures and pulls the revelation out of them. He teaches whom the sacrifices were speaking of, not only the ritual. Jesus is the Messiah they have been waiting for. The Old Testament prophesied of His coming, and Jesus fulfilled it. Jesus Christ is clearly revealed in the Old Testament.

17:4 And some of them were persuaded; and a great multitude of the devout Greeks, and not a few of the leading women, joined Paul and Silas.

This is a usual pattern in the Gentile areas Paul has traveled to. Some of the Jews receive, many of the Gentiles become born again, and many of the chief leaders in the city accept Jesus. Persecution then arises from the Jews who do not believe Paul's message.

II. Uprising and Attack on Jason's House (5–9)

Some of the Jews become jealous of Paul and Silas, form a mob, and inflame the people to the point of attacking the house of Jason, thinking they will find Paul and Silas. They drag Jason and his brothers from his home and accuse them of being against the decrees of Caesar. The authorities take money from Jason and those with him and then release them.

A. Unjust Accusations

17:5 ¶ But the Jews who were not persuaded, becoming envious, took some of the evil men from the marketplace, and gathering a mob, set all the city in an uproar and attacked the house of Jason, and sought to bring them out to the people.

But the Jews which believed not, moved with envy (jealousy), took unto them (*proslambano*: hired, received) certain lewd fellows (*poneros*: evil men, wicked, malicious) of the baser sort (*agoraios*: from the market place, vulgar), and gathered a company (mob), and set (incited) all the city on an uproar (into a riot), and assaulted the house of Jason, and sought to bring them out to the people.

When we reject the Word, we fall back on our emotions. When logic and reasoning are exhausted, many resort to shouting and making unfounded accusations. This is true in liberal politics and religion. When a person is controlled by emotions, sin is the result. The evil men from the market place are paid by the religious leaders to speak against Paul and Silas. These evil men are hucksters, petty thieves, and traffickers. These vagrants hang around the marketplace each day looking for ways to make a quick dollar by petty crimes and pick-pocketing. They are good contacts for what was happening in the streets and know of ways to get a person into trouble. These men began a riot against Paul and Silas, and the entire city is pulled into it. After hearing about Paul and Silas staying in the home of Jason, the crowd then commits breaking and entering. Paul and Silas are not in Jason's home at the time of the crime, and Jason receives the brunt of the attack.

B. Ensuing Riot

17:6 But when they did not find them, they dragged Jason and some brethren to the rulers of the city, crying out, "These who have turned the world upside down have come here too.

And when they found them (Paul and Silas) not, they drew (dragged) Jason and certain brethren (recent converts) unto the rulers (judges) of the city, crying, These that have turned the world upside down are come hither also;

This mob is yelling exactly what they have been told. They accuse Paul of causing the riot. They also claim Paul and his team have caused riots in other cities and are now trying to do the same thing in Thessalonica.

17:7 Jason has harbored them, and these are all acting contrary to the decrees of Caesar, saying there is another king—Jesus."

Whom Jason hath received; and these all do (*prasso*: practice, repeatedly, habitually) contrary to the decrees of Caesar, saying that there is another (*heteros*: other, different) king, one Jesus.

They are saying, "It's Jason who is hiding these rebels. He is their contact here." They are accusing Paul and his team of teaching practices contrary to the law. What a fine group of hypocrites to call Paul and his followers lawbreakers!

17:8 And they troubled the crowd and the rulers of the city when they heard these things.

These government leaders are being influenced by an emotional mob, not by due process of law and fair trial. They are overlooking the usual procedure of evidence, witnesses, and examination. They are committing the same mistake as the leaders in Philippi (16:22–23).

17:9 So when they had taken security from Jason and the rest, they let them go.

And when they had taken security (bond) of Jason, and of the others, they let them go (released them).

The bond was taken so Jason and the new converts would not escape.

III. Paul and Silas Sent to Berea (10–15)

For the protection of Paul and Silas, the Thessalonian brothers send them to Berea in the night. The Jews in Berea more readily receive God's Word and examine the scriptures daily. Many receive the message of salvation. When the Jews in Thessalonica hear about Paul preaching to the Bereans, they travel to Berea to once again stir up the crowds against them. Paul is then sent by the brethren out to sea, and they take him as far as Athens.

A. Paul Preaches to the Bereans

> **17:10 ¶ Then the brethren immediately sent Paul and Silas away by night to Berea. When they arrived, they went into the synagogue of the Jews.**

Berea is south of Thessalonica, approximately fifty miles off of the Egnatian highway.

> **17:11 These were more fair-minded than those in Thessalonica, in that they received the word with all readiness, and searched the Scriptures daily *to find out* whether these things were so.**

These were more noble (*eugenes*: well born, high in rank) than those in Thessalonica, in that they received the word with all readiness (eagerness) of mind, and searched the scriptures (Old Testament) daily, whether those things were so.

Those in the synagogue in Berea include both Jews and Gentiles. They are of a different attitude than those in the other cities. Cities within a short distance of each other can be totally different in attitude and personality. This city is more receptive to the Word and willing to check out Paul and his message. They do not search to prove him wrong but to honestly evaluate his teaching.

> **17:12 Therefore many of them believed, and also not a few of the Greeks, prominent women as well as men.**

Therefore (because of this [studying of the Word]) many of them believed; also of honourable (noble) women which were Greeks, and of men, not a few.

This revival is also unique because many men are saved as well as the women. In many of the cities in which Paul speaks, women received the Word and only a few of the men.

B. Thessalonian Jews Stir Up Trouble in Berea

> **17:13 But when the Jews from Thessalonica learned that the word of God was preached by Paul at Berea, they came there also and stirred up the crowds.**

The new believers and unbelievers are quickly stirred up by the legalistic Jews from Thessalonica. These who have never come to give good news are quick to spread bad news and divisive words about Paul and his message.

17:14 Then immediately the brethren sent Paul away, to go to the sea; but both Silas and Timothy remained there.

The disciples make it look like Paul went to the sea when in fact he continued on land and goes to Athens. Paul goes to Athens alone, leaving Timothy and Silas behind in Berea. Timothy has come down to Berea to join Paul and ends up staying with Silas. Every person Paul leaves behind is like a seed. Their results cannot be immediately seen, but eventually there is a crop. The crop for Paul will come in a time of desperation while he is in Corinth.

C. Paul Escorted to Athens

17:15 So those who conducted Paul brought him to Athens; and receiving a command for Silas and Timothy to come to him with all speed, they departed.

Paul is protected and escorted to Athens by many new converts from Berea. Once they arrive in Athens, they leave Paul and return home.

IV. Paul Encounters Greek Philosophers (16–21)

As Paul waits at Athens for the arrival of Silas and Timothy, his spirit is provoked within him because the city is filled with idols. Paul reasons daily with the Jews in the synagogue and in the marketplace with anyone present. Some of the Greek philosophers converse with Paul, and bring him to the Areopagus, a place where philosophical debates take place, to hear about Paul's "new teaching."

A. Paul's Spirit is Stirred

17:16 ¶ Now while Paul waited for them at Athens, his spirit was provoked within him when he saw that the city was given over to idols.

Paul wanders around in Athens while he waits for Silas and Timothy. His spirit becomes angry and resentful toward the heathenism in Athens. Paul now devises a plan to put himself before the people in Athens. He will discuss the Word in the synagogue and on the streets.

17:17 Therefore he reasoned in the synagogue with the Jews and with the *Gentile* worshipers, and in the marketplace daily with those who happened to be there.

Therefore disputed (*dialegomai*: discussed, reasoned with) he in the synagogue with the Jews, and with the devout persons, and in the market daily with them that met with him.

Paul begins by answering questions and discussing the Old Testament scriptures with Jews and Gentile proselytes. He also begins to draw a crowd in the streets as he tells them of Jesus. His teaching also draws many of the philosophers.

B. The Epicureans and Stoics

17:18 Then certain Epicurean and Stoic philosophers encountered him. And some said, "What does this babbler want to say?" ¶ Others said, "He seems to be a proclaimer of foreign gods," because he preached to them Jesus and the resurrection.

Then certain philosophers of the Epicureans, and of the Stoics, encountered (confronted) him. And some said, What will this babbler (*spermologos*: seed picker, loafer) says? Other some, He seemeth to be a setter forth of strange gods: because he preached unto them Jesus, and the resurrection.

In Athens, philosophy began with Aristotle and Plato. By the time Paul comesto Athens, two schools of philosophy have developed: the Epicureans and the Stoics. Both take offense to Paul because he teaches absolute right and wrong. They called Paul a "babbler," which comes from the Greek word *spermologos,* meaning a "seed picker." This is a term of derision. Crows and other unclean birds would wait for someone to plant seeds and then come steal them. They are accusing Paul of picking up seeds of other teachings and putting them together to make his own doctrine. They are accusing him of looking for an audience and making up a new religion.

Jesus and the resurrection Paul preaches is contrary to all Greek philosophy, especially the fact that Jesus took our sins with His death. This was in direct opposition to the Epicureans who taught there was no sin, no right or wrong.

C. Opposition to the Teaching of the Resurrection

The resurrection was contrary to both the Epicureans and Stoics (1 Corinthians 15).

1. Epicureans

Founded by Epicurus who taught happiness is found in pleasure. There is no standard of right or wrong, but whatever gives you pleasure is right. Pleasure is an instinct; therefore, it cannot be wrong and should be cultivated. Materialism was the next step in that line of thought, and then atheism. They believed God was whatever you made Him to be. All the emphasis was on the body. They believed in the soul but believed it was so integrated with the feelings and emotions of the body; they were actually one. Death was the final pleasure, and there was nothing following death.

2. Stoics

Founded by Zeno who taught from the porches (*stoikos*) of the temples in Athens. His followers were called "porch people" or "Stoics." Zeno believed the Epicureans were too emotional and needed to be more reasonable. Reason is the foundation of the Stoics. The mind could conquer anything, and virtue was the most important attribute. To Stoics, God was the spirit of reason in the universe, and the gods of the Pantheon were each concepts of reason.

D. Paul at Mars Hill

Verses 19 through 21 are the background for Paul's sermon on Mars Hill. He has taught in the synagogue and market just to get to a place of public audience.

17:19 ¶ And they took him and brought him to the Areopagus, saying, "May we know what this new doctrine *is* of which you speak?

And they took (seized) him, and brought him unto Areopagus (Court of Ares), saying, May we know what this new doctrine, thereof thou speakest, is?

The Court of Ares (the god of war) is the supreme court of Athens. It has six judges who make final decisions on philosophy. This court meets on Mars Hill near the Acropolis, by the Parthenon.

Another temple, located at the bottom of the hill, is the Temple of the Furies. This is the place where Socrates had been condemned and then gave his famous last speech, "The Apologia." Paul is now being asked about his doctrine before the six judges. Thousands of people on the hill are listening and want to understand Paul's teaching.

17:20 For you are bringing some strange things to our ears. Therefore we want to know what these things mean."

The judges speak for the philosophers and the people.

17:21 For all the Athenians and the foreigners who were there spent their time in nothing else but either to tell or to hear some new thing.

(For all the Athenians [citizens] and strangers [tourists] which were there spent their time in nothing else, but either to tell, or to hear some new thing.)

This is an indication of their intellectual snobbery. They continually wait to hear the latest philosophical ideas. They are novelty seekers, changing philosophies as often as some people change clothing.

V. Paul Reasons with Greek Philosophers (22–34)

Paul meets the Greek philosophers where they are by explaining that the "unknown god" they worship is the true and living God. He shares the gospel message, including the resurrection of the dead. Some mock, others want to hear more, and some receive the gospel.

A. False "Gods"

17:22 ¶ Then Paul stood in the midst of the Areopagus and said, "Men of Athens, I perceive that in all things you are very religious;

Then Paul stood in the midst of Mars' hill and said, Ye men of Athens, I perceive that in all things ye are too superstitious (*deisidaimoneros*: more religious)

This is the most shocking thing they have ever heard. They expect to be approached with dignity, respect, and fear. But Paul tells them they have too much religion. They think the more religions, the safer. They believe if they have many forms of religion, they are bound to hit the right one at some point. Paul tells them their religion and form of life is a façade. These men are stupid but think they are the intellectuals, yet Paul is the true intellectual. He sees the truth of life and has the best grasp on right and wrong. These men have over thirty thousand statues in Athens dedicated to different gods, and Paul is the only one in the city who knows the true God.

17:23 for as I was passing through and considering the objects of your worship, I even found an altar with this inscription: ⸹ TO THE UNKNOWN GOD. ⸹ Therefore, the One whom you worship without knowing, Him I proclaim to you:

Paul has been casually observing their forms of worship while waiting to have an audience. His first observation is their over-devotion to many religions. When no statue could be built for a particular concept, an altar would be built instead with a plaque and an inscription to that god. To ensure no god was overlooked, an altar was built to the unknown god where people could place their offerings to satisfy him. Paul calls this "ignorant" because they worship the true God without knowing Him.

B. The True God

17:24 "God, who made the world and everything in it, since He is Lord of heaven and earth, does not dwell in temples made with hands.

He is telling them, in essence, that Zeus, Apollo, and Athena are all myths; they did not create the world, God did. The true Lord does not live in hand-made buildings. Imperfect men cannot make a house or plan for God, but perfect God can make a house and plan for man.

17:25 Nor is He worshiped with men's hands, as though He needed anything, since He gives to all life, breath, and all things.

False religions think their gods need their works to fulfill their missions. God does not nor ever will need man's help. It is quite the opposite. Man needs God's help. This concept is that man is necessary to make God happy. God was happy before man ever came along. God is happy for Himself and needs no one to fulfill Him or to make Him happy. However, God is necessary to make man happy in salvation, physical life, and all things afterward.

17:26 And He has made from one blood every nation of men to dwell on all the face of the earth, and has determined their preappointed times and the boundaries of their dwellings,

And hath made of (from) one blood all nations of men for to dwell on all the face of the earth, and hath determined (predetermined) the times (*kairos*: dispensations, set or proper time) before appointed, and the bounds of their habitation (nations);

God predetermined dispensations and national boundaries to protect man. Paul is actually telling these men God determined countries (including their own), yet they are turning away from Him by looking for other gods.

17:27 so that they should seek the Lord, in the hope that they might grope for Him and find Him, though He is not far from each one of us;

That they should seek the Lord, if haply they might feel (*pselaphao*: feel, handle, touch) . . .

C. Offspring of God

17:28 for in Him we live and move and have our being, as also some of your own poets have said, 'For we are also His offspring.'

We "live." We have spiritual as well as future physical life with the Lord. Only in Christ are we truly alive. We also "move." All of our functions in life are now accomplished in Him who (currently) cares for every part of our daily lives. We finally "have our being." This is our entire existence. Our existence (spiritual, soulish, and natural) are wrapped up in Him. He is our entire life.

Paul quotes two Stoic writers, Aratus and Cleanthes, who admitted there was a God who created them, not vice versa. We find the same thing even in our atheistic society; our founding fathers told us that our "Creator gave us certain inalienable rights."

17:29 Therefore, since we are the offspring of God, we ought not to think that the Divine Nature is like gold or silver or stone, something shaped by art and man's devising.

We do not create God with our imaginations and with tools. Even those are created by God.

17:30 Truly, these times of ignorance God overlooked, but now commands all men everywhere to repent,

Paul is telling them that God has overlooked their ignorance in the past, but no more. Now that the gospel is presented to them, they are responsible. God does not wink at sin but will overlook the ignorance of it. "All men" is referring to those who are questioning Paul in this meeting in Athens on Mars Hill. They are no longer ignorant.

D. The World Will be Judged by Righteousness

17:31 because He has appointed a day on which He will judge the world in righteousness by the Man whom He has ordained. He has given assurance of this to all by raising Him from the dead."

Because he (God) hath appointed a day, in the which he will judge the world in righteousness by that man (Jesus) whom he hath ordained (chosen); whereof he hath given assurance (proof) unto all men, in that he hath raised him from the dead.

Righteousness is the standard by which the whole world will be judged (John 16:8, 10). The "proof" Paul is referring to is the miracles, signs, and wonders Jesus performed on the earth and the continued miracles of the disciples. Paul is showing he is as much chosen by God as Jesus was. Anyone who is born again becomes one of the chosen of God and can also move into a life of the supernatural.

When Paul mentions the resurrection, the Athenians fall apart. They have no teaching or belief in the resurrection. Of all the gods they give credence to in Athens, none taught of resurrection, so they have no frame of reference.

E. Reaction to Paul's Message

17:32 And when they heard of the resurrection of the dead, some mocked, while others said, "We will hear you again on this *matter*."

When others had spoken from Mars Hill, some listening could understand and some could not. When Paul speaks, no one can understand. It is only by the Holy Spirit that some can believe in Paul's message and become born again.

17:33–34 So Paul departed from among them. [34] However, some men joined him and believed, among them Dionysius the Areopagite, a woman named Damaris, and others with them.

Paul was sent by the Holy Spirit to Athens for these few people. Just as in Philippi, Thessalonica, and Berea, Paul is obedient even when only a few accept the Lord. We do not know exactly how many believe at the time, but Athens goes on to have a revival through the converts in Greece.

18:1–28 Paul's Third Missionary Journey

The Challenge of Chapter Eighteen

There are people all around hungering for the truth, and God will send us to those crying out to know Him. We must always be ready to respond to God in boldness and resist fear of the opinions of others. Our motive for ministry must never be for personal gain but for the gaining of souls into the kingdom of God. We must also determine to continually be renewed in our minds by the Word of God so we can share the truth in love with those God brings across our paths.

I. Paul Ministers in Corinth (1–17)

After Paul leaves Athens, he arrives in Corinth where he meets Aquila and Priscilla who have also recently arrived in Corinth from Rome. Like Paul, they are tent makers by occupation. Although Paul works as a tent maker for a time, he still reasons with those present in the synagogue every Sabbath. When the Jews oppose Paul, he departs to minister to the Gentiles. The Lord then appears to Paul in a night vision, encouraging him not to fear and to continue sharing the gospel message.

A. Paul Makes Tents

18:1 ¶ After these things Paul departed from Athens and went to Corinth.

To the natural mind, Athens would be a nice place to stay because of the beauty of the country. But overall, the people are against the message of Paul, and he departs to other areas to evangelize. His next stop is Corinth.

Corinth is a strategic city in the Roman Empire, built by Julius Caesar. It is a convention town: a pleasure city. The temple of Aphrodite housed over one thousand prostitutes, priestesses to the Roman goddess of love. It was also a great sports city, and during the writing of the New Testament, the greatest games were the Isthmus games of Corinth, not the Olympic or Pythian games of Greece.

Claudius is the Roman emperor at this time. His stepson, Nero, will be next in line for the throne. Claudius is a very gracious man but becomes intolerant of the Jews for their religious arguing. He eventually commands all Jews to be cast out of Rome. One of the Jews who had to leave was Aquila, a very prosperous tent maker in Rome who made tents both for individuals and the military. He was married to a Roman aristocrat, Priscilla. Both of them traveled to Corinth and continued their tent making business.

18:2 And he found a certain Jew named Aquila, born in Pontus, who had recently come from Italy with his wife Priscilla (because Claudius had commanded all the Jews to depart from Rome); and he came to them.

Pontus was a city on the southernmost end of the Black Sea. Both Aquila and Priscilla are believers and have a very successful marriage. They are a monument to God's call on a married couple. They are involved in business, but are also instructors in the Word (v. 26). The church meets in their home (Romans 16:5, 1 Corinthians 16:19). Paul enters Corinth at the perfect time. He will meet Aquila and Priscilla (believers) and Gallio (an unbeliever) in the Corinthian court. All of these greatly impact the history of the church.

Many factors are critical in God's timing for a nation. When a person obeys God's command to go, God knows the state of the government leaders, the attitude of the people toward the gospel, the laws of the land, and the hearts of the believers in the area.

18:3 So, because he was of the same trade, he stayed with them and worked; for by occupation they were tentmakers.

And because he was of the same craft, he abode with them, and wrought: (*ergozomai*: worked) for by their occupation they were tent makers.

Paul had been a tent maker at one time and so helps in the business. First, he works because he is low on money. He has left his team in Macedonia, and Paul is now alone. He spent what money he had to live on and is now forced to work for an income; he preaches whenever he has the opportunity.

He does not send word back to Antioch to ask for more money and does not itinerate to request offerings. He goes to work. In the natural, this looks like a setback, and Paul becomes discouraged (vv. 9–10). Discouragement is the great offender in the ministry (Hebrews 12:1, 3). Paul works during the day and teaches each Sabbath. He continues to do this until a large amount of money arrives from Macedonia (v. 5).

Not only does Paul work because he needs money to live, he also works because he is led to do so. At the moment, he does not understand, but the reason becomes apparent to him. The people at Corinth will accuse

Paul of being in the ministry for the money. His willingness to work completely stops that argument (1 Corinthians 9:18–19, 2 Corinthians 8:20–23, 11:7– 8).

18:4 And he reasoned in the synagogue every Sabbath, and persuaded both Jews and Greeks.

And he reasoned (*dialegomai*: say thoroughly) in the synagogue every Sabbath, and persuaded (*peitho*: influenced over) the Jews and Greeks.

Paul's only free day to minister is Saturday, and he goes to the synagogue. Since Aquila and Priscilla are also Jews, it makes it possible for Paul to minister. He wins many of the Jews and Greeks over with the teaching of the Word. Many of the converts become established in the Word of God.

B. Jews Oppose Paul

18:5 ¶ When Silas and Timothy had come from Macedonia, Paul was compelled by the Spirit, and testified to the Jews *that* Jesus *is* the Christ.

And when Silas and Timotheus were come from Macedonia, Paul was pressed in the spirit (by the Word), and testified to the Jews that Jesus was Christ.

Silas and Timothy had been left in Berea when Paul went to Athens. Paul waits for them in Athens (17:15–16), but is only there a short time before going on to Corinth alone(1 Thessalonians 3:1). Silas and Timothy must have known in their spirits of Paul's financial need and received an offering for him from the believers of Macedonia. They bring this large offering to Paul in Corinth (2 Corinthians 11:9, Philippians 4:15, 1 Thessalonians 3:6) so he can quit tentmaking and preach full-time.

When Paul receives the offering, it relieves his affliction (tribulation) and distress (necessity) (1 Thessalonians 3:7). Paul then writes 1 Thessalonians to thank them for the gift and to correct some mistakes about the rapture, he had learned of through Silas and Timothy. Now Paul has money, and he can be pressed by the Word alone and not the need for money or the necessity to work.

18:6 But when they opposed him and blasphemed, he shook *his* **garments and said to them, "Your blood** *be* **upon your** *own* **heads; I** *am* **clean. From now on I will go to the Gentiles."**

And when they opposed themselves (set themselves in opposition), and blasphemed (maligned Paul), he shook his raiment (Matthew 10:14: shook off the dust), and said unto them, Your blood be upon your own heads; I am clean: from henceforth (now on) I will go unto the Gentiles.

Paul is declaring that he has done all he can do. He has given them the Word, and now their blood is on their own heads. Paul stands clean. These men will now stand accountable before God.

C. Salvations

18:7 And he departed from there and entered the house of a certain *man* **named Justus,** *one* **who worshiped God, whose house was next door to the synagogue.**

Titus Justus, "a man of the potters," is well known. His house was built on the same property as the synagogue. Paul has just moved next door to the church and typically would not have done this, but God allows him to. Paul does not do this for any vindictive reason.

18:8 Then Crispus, the ruler of the synagogue, believed on the Lord with all his household. And many of the Corinthians, hearing, believed and were baptized.

Paul took the chief ruler with him. Crispus is one of the two most influential people to be born again in Corinth. The other is Sosthenes (v. 17). The Corinthians "hearing, believed." You must hear to believe (Romans 10:13–15). Paul baptize Crispus and Gaius, but the rest of the converts are baptized by others (1 Corinthians 1:14).

D. Paul's Vision

18:9 ¶ Now the Lord spoke to Paul in the night by a vision, "Do not be afraid, but speak, and do not keep silent;

This verse emphasizes the tremendous pressure Paul faces in Corinth. He is being criticized by the Jewish leaders, and the people are being told that

Paul is only there for money, which they believe. Even though there are great victories each day, Paul has become discouraged.

Often during or after a great victory, times of discouragement come. It is an occupational hazard in the ministry. But the word of the Lord is always there to deliver us. Usually God will minister to us through someone (maybe receiving a nice letter from a congregational member or from someone outside the church). In this particular instance, the Lord Himself comforts Paul. The ministry of the Holy Spirit comes to Paul by a vision of Jesus and assures him he is not alone. Jesus is with him and so are many believers in Corinth. Paul is apparently disturbed and upset with his recent time of discouragement and cannot sleep. The Lord comes to him by night in a vision to tell him of the great victories he will see in the next eighteen months.

Paul has also become fearful (Isaiah 41:10). Apparently some of the converts are accusing Paul of being in the ministry for money, and he becomes hesitant to speak about money or to receive an offering for fear of the opinions of people. He is probably overly cautious because of fear. God assures Paul the Word would go forth without fear of man. The book of 2 Corinthians becomes a defense for the arguments made against Paul.

E. Accusations Against Paul

1. Walks according to the flesh (2 Corinthians 10:2).

2. Writes powerful letters, but is a coward in person (2 Corinthians 10:2).

3. In the ministry for money (2 Corinthians 8:20–23, 11:7–8).

4. Not one of the original apostles, no credentials (2 Corinthians 3:1, 11:5, 12:11–12).

5. Is boastful (2 Corinthians 10:8, 15).

6. Is deceitful (2 Corinthians 12:16).

18:10 for I am with you, and no one will attack you to hurt you; for I have many people in this city."

Paul thinks no one appreciates him. He is probably discouraged because of poor results (in numbers) and opposition in Philippi, Thessalonica, Berea, and Athens. When he arrives in Corinth, he has to make tents because support runs low and he is rejected by the Jews.

But the Lord confirms Paul is in His will and will not be forsaken. God also promises no one will assault him (threats had already been made against his life). The Lord also knows that many will be born again and Spirit-filled. Satan does not know the future but can predict with great accuracy. When he knows a city is ripe for the gospel because the people are hungry, he will oppose God's man through criticism and discouragement.

18:11 And he continued *there* a year and six months, teaching the word of God among them.

This verse is the introduction to the rest of the chapter. During the eighteen months Paul is in Corinth, a religious mob rises up against him and tries to use violence and Roman law to get rid of Paul.

E. Paul Brought Before Gallio

18:12 ¶ When Gallio was proconsul of Achaia, the Jews with one accord rose up against Paul and brought him to the judgment seat,

And when Gallio was the deputy (procounsel) of Achaia, the Jews made insurrection (withstood, assaulted) with one accord against Paul, and brought him to the judgment seat,

A deputy is the same as the governor. Pontius Pilate was a governor. Gallio was an excellent administrator and one of the greatest proponents of Roman law of his day, along with his brother, Seneca. Because of his strong stand for Roman law, he will later be executed by Nero who defies Roman law. (Gallio and Paul die within two years of each other.) Gallio is a man of excellent manners, and these Jews think it will be easy to intimidate him and use him against Paul.

18:13 saying, "This *fellow* persuades men to worship God contrary to the law."

They try to stir up Gallio by accusing Paul of persuading people to go against Roman law. Paul is about to defend himself, but Gallio beats him to the point.

18:14 ¶ And when Paul was about to open *his* mouth, Gallio said to the Jews, "If it were a matter of wrongdoing or wicked crimes, O Jews, there would be reason why I should bear with you.

And when Paul was now about to open his mouth, Gallio said unto the Jews, If it were a matter of wrong (civil indictment) or wicked lewdness (criminal acts), O ye Jews, reason would (it would be right) that I should bear (put up) with you:

Gallio immediately recognizes that Roman law is being practiced by the Jews. Even though there was a state religion in Rome, people are allowed to worship as they please. Gallio observed a man being wronged by a religious group trying to use Roman law to settle a religious argument. Because of Gallio's excellent interpretation and use of Roman law, Paul is free to teach the Word of God in Corinth for the next eighteen months.

18:15 But if it is a question of words and names and your own law, look *to it* yourselves; for I do not want to be a judge of such *matters.*"

But if it be a question of words (teachings) and names (of gods), and of your law (Jewish religion), look ye to it; for I will be no judge of such matters.

Gallio is saying, "If it is a religious question, you handle it. If it is a criminal act, I'll handle it." The state has no right to solve a religious controversy, only to protect the people involved.

18:16 And he drove them from the judgment seat.

And he drave them (threw them out) from the judgment seat.

18:17 Then all the Greeks took Sosthenes, the ruler of the synagogue, and beat *him* before the judgment seat. But Gallio took no notice of these things.

Then all the Greeks took Sosthenes, the chief ruler of the synagogue, and beat him before (in front of) the judgment seat. And Gallio cared for none (was not concerned) of those things.

Apparently Sosthenes is with the religious mob who has tried to get rid of Paul. The Greeks in the courtroom are impressed and ecstatic over the way Gallio handled the case, so after Gallio leaves the bench, the mob apprehends Sosthenes and beats him before leaving the courtroom. They are determined there will be no more religious mobs in Corinth.

Somehow, in spite of what happens, Sosthenes receives the Lord. In 1 Corinthians 1:1, Paul refers to him as a brother in the Lord. Gallio knew what
occurred after he left, but did not become involved. It was still a religious
matter, the Christian religion against the Jewish.

II. Paul's Return to Antioch (18–23)

Paul is released and remains in Corinth for an extended time. He eventually travels with Aquila and Priscilla to Syria and then departs to Ephesus
leaving his traveling companions behind. Upon arriving in Ephesus, Paul
reasons with the Jews in the synagogue and finally returns to Antioch, then
to the regions of Galatia and Phyrgia to encourage the disciples.

A. Paul Stops in Ephesus

Verses 18 through 28 are transitional verses ("meanwhile, back at the
ranch"). They actually lead up to the Ephesus revival of chapter 19. Paul
will spend more time in Ephesus than any other place in his ministry: three
years.

Chapter 18 describes Paul as just passing through Ephesus because it was
not the time to remain in Ephesus, but to prepare. Paul leaves Aquila and
Priscilla in Ephesus and travels alone to Jerusalem. He will then travel to
Antioch and begin his third missionary journey.

While in Ephesus, Aquila and Priscilla meet Apollos and train him in New
Testament doctrine. Apollos then travels to Corinth. These few verses
demonstrate how far God goes to prepare a city for the Word. God takes
time for every small detail!

> **18:18 ¶ So Paul still remained a good while. Then he took leave
> of the brethren and sailed for Syria, and Priscilla and Aquila
> *were* with him. He had *his* hair cut off at Cenchrea, for he had
> taken a vow.**

And Paul after this (trial) tarried there yet a good while, and then took his
leave of (departed from) the brethren, and sailed thence into Syria, and
with him Priscilla and Aquila; having shorn his head in Cenchrea: for he had
a vow.

The "good while" Paul stays in Corinth is eighteen months (v. 11). When he
departs, he stops in Ephesus first, but Syria is the final destination. Aquila
and Priscilla lay down their lives for Paul, and Aquila takes a vow to save
Paul's life (Romans 16:3–4). This is a carryover of Jewish tradition. This is

not legalistic, but a personal vow Aquila makes to God on Paul's behalf. Paul later does the same in Jerusalem (21:22–26) but with the wrong motive. He is pressured by legalistic Jews to keep a religious vow in order to preach the gospel. We do not have the details of Aquila's vow, but they all face a great danger when he takes this memorial vow to save Paul.

18:19 And he came to Ephesus, and left them there; but he himself entered the synagogue and reasoned with the Jews.

And he came to Ephesus, and left them (Aquila and Priscilla) there: but he himself (alone) entered into the synagogue, and reasoned with the Jews.

Ephesus is the capital of the Roman province of Asia. The population is around three hundred thousand and has a large temple for the worship of Diana.

18:20 When they asked *him* to stay a longer time with them, he did not consent,

Paul had a good response, and many are born again, but Paul is only there to plant seeds for the new church. He will return later for an excellent ministry, a good harvest.

18:21 but took leave of them, saying, "I must by all means keep this coming feast in Jerusalem; but I will return again to you, God willing." And he sailed from Ephesus.

The "feast that cometh in Jerusalem" is the feast of Pentecost. Paul wants to be in Jerusalem during the feast to see many of his friends and visit the church at Jerusalem. This will be the last time he will be able to visit the church in the Lord's will. The next time he visits, he will be out of God's will. He tells the saints at Ephesus he will return if it is the Lord's will. It will be the Lord's will, and he will return after a number of months to witness the harvest which has been sown and watered for quite awhile.

B. Paul Strengthens the Disciples

18:22 ¶ And when he had landed at Caesarea, and gone up and greeted the church, he went down to Antioch.

Paul docks at Caesarea and goes to Jerusalem. He visits the church and the many saints who were his friends. When the feast of Pentecost concludes, Paul returns to his home church of Antioch and rests for an extended time.

18:23 After he had spent some time *there*, he departed and went over the region of Galatia and Phrygia in order, strengthening all the disciples.

Beginning his third missionary journey, Paul visits the same churches he has established on his first and second trips. He goes to encourage the pastors and saints in Galatia. Since they have a tendency toward legalism, he reminds them of their position in Christ and the walk of faith which remains throughout the Christian life.

III. Ministry of Apollos (24–28)

Apollos is strong in the scriptures and fervent in spirit but knows nothing beyond the baptism of John. Aquila and Priscilla hear him speak boldly in the synagogue and afterward take him aside to teach him "more accurately" about following the way of God in Jesus Christ.

18:24 ¶ Now a certain Jew named Apollos, born at Alexandria, an eloquent man *and* mighty in the Scriptures, came to Ephesus.

The plan of God does not stop when the main minister leaves a city. God always has a plan and never leaves a group of hungry people without a minister. Alexandria was a university city and apparently Apollos is a language or speech major. He is eloquent in speech but an unbeliever until some of John the Baptist's followers come to the city and lead him to the Lord. He grew in the Scriptures, which he had known since childhood, and became powerful in revealing salvation in the Old Testament to his listeners.

He is now called by the Holy Spirit to go to Ephesus to instruct the believers and sinners in the plans of God. He not only leads many to the Lord, but is also instructed himself by Aquila and Priscilla.

18:25 This man had been instructed in the way of the Lord; and being fervent in spirit, he spoke and taught accurately the things of the Lord, though he knew only the baptism of John.

Since he has been led to the Lord by the disciples of John the Baptist, he only knows of the plan of God up to the baptism of John. He knows nothing of New Testament doctrine, his position in Christ, the new birth, the indwelling Holy Spirit, the gifts of the Spirit, the body of Christ, the church, the bride of Christ, and many other areas of the age of grace.

18:26 So he began to speak boldly in the synagogue. When Aquila and Priscilla heard him, they took him aside and explained to him the way of God more accurately.

Aquila and Priscilla hear Apollos speak in the temple and know immediately he has no knowledge of the new covenant. After having spent much time with Paul, they are capable to lead him into the deeper truths of the dispensation of the church.

18:27 And when he desired to cross to Achaia, the brethren wrote, exhorting the disciples to receive him; and when he arrived, he greatly helped those who had believed through grace;

Achaia is southern Greece. He goes there with letters of recommendation and is able to help the new believers who have recently been saved by grace.

18:28 for he vigorously refuted the Jews publicly, showing from the Scriptures that Jesus is the Christ.

The strength of Apollos is leading Jews to the Lord Jesus through Old Testament scriptures.

19:1–41 Paul at Ephesus

The Challenge of Chapter Nineteen

Paul never preaches against the worship of the goddess Diana. Instead, he preaches the Word of God, and the Word prevails. So many lives are transformed, businesses which previously had been very prosperous begin to suffer. As long as we are in the world, there will always be opposition to the effects of the gospel. In spite of the opposition, Paul never backs down from the purity and power of the gospel message.

Once again, Paul serves as an example to us. We never need to water down the message of God's Word simply because the world is demanding a different, "more acceptable" message. We must continue to speak the truth by the direction of the Holy Spirit because only the truth sets people free.

I. The Infilling of the Holy Spirit in Ephesus (1–7)

When Paul arrives in Ephesus, he finds disciples who have not yet heard of the Holy Spirit but have been baptized through the ministry of John the Baptist. Paul instructs them and then baptizes them in the name of Jesus Christ, and all are filled with the Holy Spirit and begin to speak in tongues when Paul lays hands on them. After this, Paul enters the synagogue and boldly shares the gospel for three months. When Paul's listeners become hardened against the gospel message, Paul departs and spends two years teaching in the school of Tyrannus.

A. Paul Finds Disciples Ignorant of the Holy Spirit

19:1 ¶ And it happened, while Apollos was at Corinth, that Paul, having passed through the upper regions, came to Ephesus. And finding some disciples

The disciples Paul meet will play a major role the revival in Ephesus. Paul has been gone for a number of months and is now refreshed in his soul and body. He is now ready to give himself completely to the revival that will occur in this key city of Asia Minor. The men he meets are disciples who are born again and will become filled with the Holy Spirit. This revival will be one of the supernatural. Great signs and wonders will accompany the teaching of the Word of God.

19:2 he said to them, "Did you receive the Holy Spirit when you believed?" ¶ So they said to him, "We have not so much as heard whether there is a Holy Spirit."

The Holy Spirit can be received at the point of the new birth. Paul asks the believers he met if this has happened to them. Paul must have recognized a deficiency in their Christian lives much the same way Aquila and Priscilla recognized a spiritual deficiency in the life of Apollos. These twelve men had been born again only and not instructed in the infilling of the Holy Spirit.

19:3 ¶ And he said to them, "Into what then were you baptized?" ¶ So they said, "Into John's baptism."

These men had been born again under the ministry of Apollos when he remained in Ephesus for a brief time (18:25).

19:4 ¶ Then Paul said, "John indeed baptized with a baptism of repentance, saying to the people that they should believe on Him who would come after him, that is, on Christ Jesus."

The ministry of John the Baptist brought people to the new birth and water baptism (Matthew 3:1–3, 11). However, the infilling of the Holy Spirit is their doorway into the church age, the dispensation of grace. They will learn, as did Apollos, of the specialized dispensation we live in today.

19:5 ¶ When they heard *this*, they were baptized in the name of the Lord Jesus.

Although they have already been water baptized, they do not understand its New Testament significance. So Paul has them baptized again, this time in the name of Jesus. Now they can apply the act of baptism to the new birth.

19:6 And when Paul had laid hands on them, the Holy Spirit came upon them, and they spoke with tongues and prophesied.

These men speak with tongues and then move into one of the utterance gifts: prophesy. This also occurs in the house of Cornelius in Acts 10:46. In both cases, the people speak with tongues before they move into the gift of the Holy Spirit. Speaking with tongues is the manifestation of being filled with the Holy Spirit.

19:7 Now the men were about twelve in all.

The Ephesian revival begins with a core of twelve men.

II. The Revival in Ephesus (8–22)

God begins to work special miracles through Paul's hands, and handkerchiefs and aprons that have lain on Paul's body, bring healing and deliverance on those on whom the cloths are placed.

In an attempt to mimic Paul, Jewish exorcists, specifically the seven sons of Sceva, use the name of Jesus to cast an evil spirit out of a man. To their great surprise, the demon speaks and then leaps on them, leaving the seven sons wounded and naked. As a result of this incident, fear falls on the people. Many come to know Jesus Christ as Lord and Savior, and many bring their books about magic to be burned. The Word continues to grow and prevail.

19:8 ¶ And he went into the synagogue and spoke boldly for three months, reasoning and persuading concerning the things of the kingdom of God.

The time is now right. Paul had told the new converts in Ephesus that he would return if it was the will of God (18:19–21). This will of God is "yes," and Paul does return with a confidence he did not possess the first time. His words are more anointed and his audience more receptive. Paul has never shared the gospel in any synagogue for a three-month period of time. This is evidence of the degree of success he is having among the Jews.

19:9 But when some were hardened and did not believe, but spoke evil of the Way before the multitude, he departed from them and withdrew the disciples, reasoning daily in the school of Tyrannus.

Not everyone receives Paul's message. Some harden their hearts the more they hear. Not only do some not receive, they set themselves in opposition to the Word. David calls this type of person a "scorner" in Psalm 1:1. Paul went to the Jews first but left them when they rejected the message. He now sets his sights on the Gentiles.

The School of Tyrannus is a medical school. The medical students learn in the mornings, and the building is empty during the day. Paul uses this building during the afternoons and evenings. For two years, this will be one of Paul's most successful bases of operation.

19:10 And this continued for two years, so that all who dwelt in Asia heard the word of the Lord Jesus, both Jews and Greeks.

The two-year revival spreads throughout the Roman province of Asia. This area includes six other cities which later established churches. Together these make up the seven churches of Asia found in the first three books of Revelation. All seven churches begin from the Ephesian revival. The revival began with the Word of God. Both Jews and Greeks hear the Word. Paul speaks and God accompanies the Word with signs following (Mark 16:20, Hebrews 2:3–4).

A. Miracles Through Paul's Hands

19:11 ¶ Now God worked unusual miracles by the hands of Paul,

Again, these miracles are performed in response to the Word of God being preached. This revival begins with the Word. Signs and wonders follow the Word. The revival ends with the Word increasing (v. 20). These miracles, signs, and wonders are not the "usual" miracles. They are exceptional and out of the ordinary.

Special miracles only occurred once in Paul's ministry. The Holy Spirit can minister in a unique way from time to time, but it will be rare. The idea of a "special anointing" for only one area is not true. The anointing will break every yoke of bondage. Jesus declared the Spirit of the Lord was upon him (Luke 4:18) and the end result was the preaching of the gospel to the poor, the recovering of sight to the blind, healing of the brokenhearted, and setting at liberty those who were bruised. One anointing covers all of these needs.

Like Jesus, God's power worked through the hands of Paul. He laid hands on sick people and special miracles occurred. Prayer cloths were taken to the sick and demon possessed, and they were delivered.

19:12 so that even handkerchiefs or aprons were brought from his body to the sick, and the diseases left them and the evil spirits went out of them.

The handkerchiefs and aprons carry God's anointing to both heal and deliver (Mark 5:30, Luke 6:19). The handkerchiefs come from the women who attend the meetings during the day. The aprons are work aprons the men wore to their jobs. Most of the employment available in the city is for craftsmen who make statues of Diana (v. 24). These men come to the meetings in the evening to join their wives. When the anointing of God moves strongly in the meeting, handkerchiefs and aprons are taken from Paul's body and delivered to the sick and demon possessed in the city. Great healings and deliverance take place. The same anointing that delivers people from sickness also delivers people from demons.

A greater anointing is not necessary for people to be delivered from demons than from healing. The smaller handkerchiefs are not exclusively for healing and the larger aprons exclusively for deliverance from demons. It is not necessary to use a larger piece of cloth for a person to be delivered from a demon; the anointing breaks the yoke.

B. Seven Sons of Sceva

19:13 Then some of the itinerant Jewish exorcists took it upon themselves to call the name of the Lord Jesus over those who had evil spirits, saying, "We exorcise you by the Jesus whom Paul preaches."

Then certain of the vagabond Jews, exorcists (*exorkistes*: enchanters), took upon them to call over them which had evil spirits the name of the Lord Jesus, saying, We adjure (*horchizo*: put on oath, make swear) you by Jesus whom Paul preacheth.

These "vagabonds" are traveling Jews who cast devils out for money. They have become quite rich by temporarily ridding people of demons. These men are revered in the city and thought to be holy men. People do not know they are working in league with Satan himself.

The word for exorcist means "one who casts out devils by magic formulas and incantations." These men virtually have a monopoly on their trade until Paul comes to town with real power over demons. Apparently, the men attend one of Paul's meetings and notice he uses the name of "Jesus" over each person. They decided to add the name of Jesus to their formula in an attempt to get their business back. In the past, when these men cast out devils, the results were never permanent. These men knows Paul has the greater power and are trying to duplicate or increase it.

19:14 Also there were seven sons of Sceva, a Jewish chief priest, who did so.

Sceva is one of the twenty-four ruling priests in the Sanhedrin of Jerusalem. This passage refers to his seven sons who are using their family name and religious affiliation to bring in money. Luke has seen and met Sceva and remembers the address Jesus had given him (Luke 11:14–20). This verse reveals the demonic control that can be attached to religion. Even those practicing the Jewish religion and quoting Old Testament scriptures, including the chief priests, do not believe in Jesus Christ and open themselves up to demonic activity.

19:15 ¶ And the evil spirit answered and said, "Jesus I know, and Paul I know; but who are you?"

The seven sons do not expect this response. They have never experienced a demon speaking to them, especially in an insulting way. The demon knew Jesus and Paul because both were new creations. When Paul was born again, he instantly became a citizen of God's kingdom and was no longer part of Satan's kingdom. Every demon knew it.

What is most amazing about this verse is the demon did not know or recognize the seven sons of Sceva, and they worked for the demon! Satan does not know his own, but he does know God's. The only way to be known in the kingdom of Satan is to become born again. You are then on Satan's hate-list and God's love-list (the Book of Life). God knows His own but does not know Satan's. One day, the seven sons of Sceva will stand before the Lord in judgment and ask "Didn't we cast out devils in your name?" Jesus will answer them "Depart from me ye workers of iniquity, I never knew you" (Matthew 7:22).

19:16 ¶ Then the man in whom the evil spirit was leaped on them, overpowered them, and prevailed against them, so that they fled out of that house naked and wounded.

And the man in whom the evil spirit was leaped on them, and overcame them, and prevailed (*ischuo*: be of strength) against them, so that they fled out of that house naked and wounded.

This is the supernatural power of one demon. One man leaped on seven. One man overcame the strength of seven. One man prevailed against seven and tore their clothes off before they could reach the front door of the house.

C. Reverence for the Lord Jesus Increases

19:17 This became known both to all Jews and Greeks dwelling in Ephesus; and fear fell on them all, and the name of the Lord Jesus was magnified.

The sons of Sceva are exposed, and now everyone know they are working for Satan himself. Great reverence for the true God falls on the entire city and the name of Jesus is magnified. Many unsaved people and backslidden Christians come to the Lord. The ripples of this event spread throughout Asia.

19:18 And many who had believed came confessing and telling their deeds.

Believers who are out of fellowship with the Lord come and repent of their fear and apathy toward the things of God. They also begin to tell of their involvement with witchcraft and sorcery.

19:19 Also, many of those who had practiced magic brought their books together and burned *them* in the sight of all. And they counted up the value of them, and it totaled fifty thousand *pieces* of silver.

These books taught witchcraft, demon worship, séances, and occult operations. This burning is a monument to their renewed life. There were no printing presses then, so these were handwritten on scrolls.

19:20 So the word of the Lord grew mightily and prevailed.

So (*houto kata*: thus, by the same standard) mightily (*kratos*: power, strength) grew the word of God and prevailed (*ischuo*: gained strength).

The Word of God began far behind the power and might of Diana and the religion of Ephesus. But during a three-year period of time, the Word continues to grow until it overcomes and prevails. Here Luke is making an analogy to the demon who overcame odds seven times worse than himself. He first jumped on the seven, overcame them, and prevailed. The Word of

God also began against incredible odds, but over a period of time becomes dominant in Asia. Because of the power accompanying the signs and wonders, the Word spreads. The purpose of signs and wonders is to confirm the Word.

D. Paul Purposes to Go to Jerusalem

19:21 ¶ When these things were accomplished, Paul purposed in the Spirit, when he had passed through Macedonia and Achaia, to go to Jerusalem, saying, "After I have been there, I must also see Rome."

Paul's ministry does not end in Ephesus. In chapter 20, we see he returns after a few months to admonish the pastors of the churches in this city. What has been fulfilled are the signs and wonders. These all have done their job by promoting the Word to the place of overcoming the opposition of religion, demons, and Satan.

Although the miracles, signs, and wonders have been fulfilled, they are not completely over. Many more miracles and signs are performed in the days to come, but they are being accomplished by the individual saints in the churches. God's best is for believers to perform the miracles, not just the evangelist or prophet.

God's best is for the people to receive their healings by standing on the Word for themselves. This is taught by the local churches who instruct the people in the Word.

Paul knows his own time is coming to an end, and it will be necessary for him to leave for a time. He now purposes by the Holy Spirit to go to Jerusalem and then to Rome. It will be God's will for him to go to Rome but not to Jerusalem. This will sidetrack Paul for over five years as he will be thrown in jail in Caesarea and Rome before he is released. God will confirm to Paul that Rome is in His will (23:11) as will an angel of the Lord (27:23, 24). God will also try to warn Paul that going to Jerusalem is not in His will (21:3, 4, 8–13).

19:22 So he sent into Macedonia two of those who ministered to him, Timothy and Erastus, but he himself stayed in Asia for a time.

So he sent into Macedonia two of them that ministered (*diakoneo*: serve, wait upon) unto him, Timotheus and Erastus; but he himself stayed in Asia (Ephesus) for a season.

Erastus is a Corinthian believer. He came to investigate the Corinthian situation and report back to Paul, resulting in the letters sent to Corinth. Romans 16:23 records Erastus as being a chamberlain, a member of the city council in Corinth. Paul will stay in Ephesus for a short time to bring a brief period of comfort to the saints who will be experiencing opposition and tribulation for the sake of the gospel.

III. A Riot in Ephesus (23–41)

A silversmith named Demetrius is unhappy about how all of the conversions are affecting his business, which is predominantly comprised of making silver shrines for Diana. He calls together other workers and businesses that have been adversely affected by the conversions. Demetrius stirs them up until the entire city is filled with confusion and wrath against Paul and his followers. Paul wants to quiet the crowd, but the disciples will not allow him to. Alexander, a Jewish lawyer, is pushed forward by the crowd to quiet them, but when they realize he is a Jew, they loudly cry out to their goddess Diana. The mayor of the city finally silences the mob, pointing out that Paul and his disciples have done nothing unlawful and warns that if the crowd takes the law into their own hands, they will be guilty of violating the law.

A. Demetrius Stirs Unrest

19:23 ¶ And about that time there arose a great commotion about the Way.

During this "same time," the Word is increasing, but the opposition of Satan is also increasing (Mark 4:17). The Word is always attacked in the life of a believer, a church, or a city.

19:24 For a certain man named Demetrius, a silversmith, who made silver shrines of Diana, brought no small profit to the craftsmen.

Demetrius is the head of the crafts union in Ephesus. This is a huge organization comprised of miners, craftsmen, distributors, wholesalers, and retailers who handle the statues.

19:25 He called them together with the workers of similar occupation, and said: "Men, you know that we have our prosperity by this trade.

A massive union meeting is called, and Demetrius tells them their jobs, income, homes, and families are in jeopardy because of Paul's gospel. When a business of this size is in trouble, many smaller businesses whose existences depend on it are also jeopardized. When it is announced that sales are way off and layoffs and firings will occur, a riot breaks out, and Paul will be blamed.

19:26 Moreover you see and hear that not only at Ephesus, but throughout almost all Asia, this Paul has persuaded and turned away many people, saying that they are not gods which are made with hands.

Paul is well-known throughout all of Asia. To many, he has brought the message of salvation. To others, he is one who has broken the back of a thriving business which employ tens of thousands of people. To them, Paul is responsible for an economic downturn in the city because his teaching has turned many people away from idolatry and Diana worship to Jesus Christ. Instead of seeing this as a blessing to many people who have been in religious bondage, they take it personally because their income is threatened. Paul has faced this previously with the owners of the girl possessed by a spirit of divination (16:19).

19:27 So not only is this trade of ours in danger of falling into disrepute, but also the temple of the great goddess Diana may be despised and her magnificence destroyed, whom all Asia and the world worship."

"We are just the 'little guy' to this Paul. He is out to destroy our entire religion! He is not only after Ephesus but the whole world!"

B. The Three Elements of Diana Worship

1. The Priesthood

These men are eunuchs. They are castrated to keep them from participating in the worship of Diana. They can keep their minds focused on the stories and tell of the exploits of Jupiter, Bacchus, and other gods.

2. The Virgins

These girls handle the rituals of the temple. The forms of worship outside sex are conducted by the virgins.

3. The Dancers

These women dance to arouse the men and at the end of their dance, give themselves to the nearest man for sex.

C. People Filled With Wrath and Confusion

19:28 ¶ Now when they heard *this*, they were full of wrath and cried out, saying, "Great *is* Diana of the Ephesians!"

This anger and emotion will spread from these few men into the crowds in the street. Demetrius knows exactly what he is doing. He will work the people up into a senseless rage so Paul is either killed or driven out of the city.

19:29 So the whole city was filled with confusion, and rushed into the theater with one accord, having seized Gaius and Aristarchus, Macedonians, Paul's travel companions.

Apparently, Demetrius leads the crowd to the house of Aquila and Priscilla where Paul is staying. They protect Paul and will not allow the crowd to have him (Romans 16:2–3). Instead, the crowd grabs two from Paul's team to flush him out, and it almost works. Paul makes mention of fighting with "beasts at Ephesus" (1 Corinthians 15:32), and this may be what he was referring to.

Gaius is mentioned in Romans 16:23 and 1 Corinthians 1:14. Aristarchus is mentioned in several places (Acts 20:4, 27:2; Colossians 4:10, Philemon 1:24). When they take the two men into the amphitheater, the mob has reached fever pitch. A mob always has an organizer behind it who uses the mob as a weapon. The people are always the pawns. They react quickly and then forget why they are rioting (v. 32).

D. Paul Desires an Audience with the Mob

19:30 And when Paul wanted to go in to the people, the disciples would not allow him.

Paul wants to speak to the crowd, but the disciples see the frenzy and know Paul would be killed before he could speak.

19:31 Then some of the officials of Asia, who were his friends, sent to him pleading that he would not venture into the theater.

Paul has friends in high places. These are born again, Spirit-filled aristocrats who are powerful in the government of Ephesus. They have been saved under Paul's ministry and are protecting him from the mob. They also know this is not a matter for Paul but for the authorities.

> **19:32 Some therefore cried one thing and some another, for the assembly was confused, and most of them did not know why they had come together.**

Meanwhile, back at the theatre, the mob has gained many followers and everyone is confused as to what is happening. They are all shouting different things because they are being controlled and ruled by their emotions. Most of them do not even know why they are there. They shout along with the rest of the mob, but do not know about Demetrius or Paul.

E. Alexander Fails to Quiet the Crowd

> **19:33 And they drew Alexander out of the multitude, the Jews putting him forward. And Alexander motioned with his hand, and wanted to make his defense to the people.**

Religion is always afraid of mobs but will use them if necessary. Alexander is an excellent lawyer. The Jews hope he can still the mob. He fails when the crowd recognizes he is a Jew. He had previously been a coppersmith and a brilliantly evil man. Paul warned Timothy about him (2 Timothy 4:14). Alexander tries to quiet the people with his hand, but the people cry even more loudly and longer.

> **19:34 But when they found out that he was a Jew, all with one voice cried out for about two hours, "Great *is* Diana of the Ephesians!"**

At the moment, national pride is high and their goddess, Diana, is in question. A Jew is not who they want to hear from. A mob will often shout and use noise to cover the real issue.

F. The Town Clerk Speaks

> **19:35 And when the city clerk had quieted the crowd, he said: "Men of Ephesus, what man is there who does not know that**

the city of the Ephesians is temple guardian of the great goddess Diana, and of the *image* which fell down from Zeus?

And when the townclerk (mayor) had appeased (silenced) the people, he said, Ye men (*aner*: noble men) of Ephesus, what man is there that knoweth not how that the city of the Ephesians is a worshipper of the great goddess Diana, and of the image which fell down from Jupiter?

The town mayor uses the issue of the law to disperse the mob. This man is the highest in office in Ephesus, knows Roman law very well, and uses it. He waits for the people to shout themselves hoarse and then speaks.

He appeals to their ego in three ways:

1. He calls them noble men (*anhr*).
2. He reminds them of Ephesus' worldwide reputation for the worship of Diana.
3. He tells them the statue was given to them as a gift from the chief god Jupiter.

19:36 Therefore, since these things cannot be denied, you ought to be quiet and do nothing rashly.

Seeing then that these things cannot be spoken against (contradicted), ye ought to be quiet, and to do nothing rashly.

He reminds them that if they are well aware of the facts, this type of action is unnecessary and below their dignity.

19:37 For you have brought these men here who are neither robbers of temples nor blasphemers of your goddess.

The banks are in the temples. Paul and his team never ran down the false religion and evils of Ephesus. Paul only preaches Christ, and then the people change their own minds about Diana. Most ministers today run down other religions. If there was nothing to run down, they would have no message. They know nothing about the Word.

19:38 Therefore, if Demetrius and his fellow craftsmen have a case against anyone, the courts are open and there are proconsuls. Let them bring charges against one another.

Gamaliel is advising the council to remove the pressure and opposition they have against the disciples.

19:39 But if you have any other inquiry to make, it shall be determined in the lawful assembly.

In other words, "If you have any other charges against Paul and his men, bring it before a lawful assembly. You are about to take the law into your own hands and become the criminals."

19:40 For we are in danger of being called in question for today's uproar, there being no reason which we may give to account for this disorderly gathering."

Basically, the mayor reminds them, "Rome will call us about this and can pull our city rights. We will have no legal leg to stand on."

19:41 And when he had said these things, he dismissed the assembly.

20:1–38 Greece, Troas, Miletus

The Challenge of Chapter Twenty

Paul warns the pastors to "take heed" of themselves and of the "flock" God has made them overseers for. We may not be called to pastor, but the principle still applies to our daily lives. If we do not keep ourselves built up in the Word and in the Spirit, how can we be an influence over those God has entrusted to us, whether they are family members, friends, coworkers, or neighbors?

Each of us has been called to be an ambassador of the Lord, and to be a successful representative of His kingdom, we must not neglect our personal relationship with the Lord.

I. Journeys in Greece (1–6)

Once the mob in Ephesus has been dispersed, Paul departs for Macedonia. After exhorting the Macedonians, Paul travels to Greece and remains for three months until a plot against him is revealed. He then travels through Macedonia and arrives in Troas.

This chapter begins the closing section of the book of Acts. It begins with Paul's pastor's conference, and the remainder of the book recounts Paul's great failure in Jerusalem. He will begin to chart his own course and disregard the leading of the Holy Spirit. His desire to return to Jerusalem will become an emotional issue rather than a principle of the Word of God.

After the revival in Ephesus, Paul possibly develops an attitude of independence. He acts as if he has "arrived." He will repent of this attitude while in prison in Caesarea, and he eventually meets up with the geographical will of God in Rome.

A. Macedonia

20:1 ¶ After the uproar had ceased, Paul called the disciples to *himself*, embraced *them*, and departed to go to Macedonia.

The "uproar" is the mob of chapter 19. Paul calls together the converts and church leaders who have come to know the Lord and have become disciples during the previous three years. Paul embraces them and heads for the northern part of Greece. He will be there for almost one entire year.

On this trip, Paul travels to Troy where he will meet Titus (2 Corinthians 2:13, 7:13–14) and train him as a troubleshooter. Paul will then send him to Corinth. He will later bring back word that the trouble in the church has been solved (2 Corinthians 7:13–16). Paul writes 2 Corinthians and Romans during his year in Macedonia.

It is Paul's desire to visit Macedonia again because of the faithful brothers who have stood with him financially during his hardships in Corinth. Paul has become great friends with them and they are close to his heart.

B. Greece

> **20:2 Now when he had gone over that region and encouraged them with many words, he came to Greece**

Paul travels again the path through Berea, Thessalonica, and Philippi. He exhorts the disciples this time because he had been unable to do so the first time he preached; he had been run out of town before he was able to. Now that the trouble has settled down, Paul returns to build up the members of the congregations he had helped begin. He is also able to thank them for their tremendous financial gifts brought to him by Timothy and Silas (18:5). After Paul leaves Macedonia, he heads to Achaia.

C. Return to Macedonia

> **20:3 and stayed three months. And when the Jews plotted against him as he was about to sail to Syria, he decided to return through Macedonia.**

During the three months Paul is in Achaia, he writes the epistle to the Romans. Also during this time, the Jews make an assassination attempt on his life. The Jews are on board a ship Paul is to take to Syria. While on board, the Jews plot to kill him. Instead, Paul determines to go to Macedonia. Paul is being directed by the Spirit without his knowledge. Paul may have thought he was determining to do this himself, but he is being prompted by the Holy Spirit.

We will never know until we get to heaven how many times the Holy Spirit led us without our understanding. We have been protected and guided by angels and the Holy Spirit numerous times. This is all part of the walk of faith.

D. Paul's Traveling Team to Macedonia

> **20:4 And Sopater of Berea accompanied him to Asia—also Aristarchus and Secundus of the Thessalonians, and Gaius of Derbe, and Timothy, and Tychicus and Trophimus of Asia.**

This verse lists Paul's traveling team and seminary into Macedonia. They will receive "on the job training." The calling and operation of the apostle will be both taught and demonstrated. Many will be left to establish churches along the way. Berea was where the Word was received with "readiness of mind" (7:4). This is the place where the believers were commended for searching out the scriptures to verify the teaching of Paul.

Sopater came from Berea and must have been a wonderful and strong believer. Aristarchus and Secundus were from Thessalonica. Aristarchus was almost killed in Ephesus (19:29) and will be with Paul in prison (Acts 27:2, Colossians 4:10, Philemon 24). Gaius, from Derbe, was with Aristarchus in the Ephesian uprising against Paul (19:29). Tychicus is mentioned as being on Paul's team. He delivered the letters to Ephesus and Philippi from Paul who was in prison (Ephesians 6:21, Colossians 4:7, 2 Timothy 4:12, Titus 3:12). Trophimus will be the innocent party in a riot in Jerusalem (21:29). He later has an attack from Satan and cannot resist it. His faith becomes weak, and Paul leaves him sick at Miletus (2 Timothy 4:20).

E. Seven Days in Troas

20:5 These men, going ahead, waited for us at Troas.

Paul's team goes ahead and waits for Paul and Luke in Troas. Luke has rejoined the team and writes of "us," Paul and Luke.

20:6 But we sailed away from Philippi after the Days of Unleavened Bread, and in five days joined them at Troas, where we stayed seven days.

And we sailed away from Philippi after the days of unleavened bread, and came unto them (via Samathrocia [16:11]) to Troas in five days; where we abode seven days.

The Feast of Unleavened Bread is a full week long. Paul desires to be in Jerusalem on Pentecost (v. 16) which will be fifty days later. The trip to Troas is usually two days. On the way, Paul apparently preaches for awhile in Samathrocia.

II. Paul in Troas (7–12)

Paul meets with disciples to break bread and speaks with them until midnight. A man sitting on a windowsill falls into a deep sleep and plummets from a third story window to the ground, and is "taken up dead." Paul falls on the man, embracing him and quiets the crowd by telling them the man is alive. Paul continues sharing with the disciples until daybreak.

A. Paul Preaches Until Midnight

20:7 ¶ Now on the first *day* of the week, when the disciples came together to break bread, Paul, ready to depart the next day, spoke to them and continued his message until midnight.

The early disciples meet together for worship and fellowship on ~~Sunday, not Saturday. This was to celebrate the resurrection~~. On this day, it is their custom to celebrate communion. Communion is followed by the breaking of the bread of life, God's Word.

20:8 There were many lamps in the upper room where they were gathered together.

Paul is preaching in an upper room as Jesus did. Upper rooms are located above restaurants or taverns and used for public meetings. They have many windows and oil lamps by each one for light at night. The windows are open onto the streets, three floors below.

B. Eutychus's Fall

20:9 And in a window sat a certain young man named Eutychus, who was sinking into a deep sleep. He was overcome by sleep; and as Paul continued speaking, he fell down from the third story and was taken up dead.

This is a teenaged boy. While sitting in the room with the lamps, he becomes warm. He probably fights off sleep for a while but is finally overcome by slumber. He falls from the window and dies on the pavement below. When the disciples rush to the boy, Paul is right behind them.

20:10 But Paul went down, fell on him, and embracing *him* said, "Do not trouble yourselves, for his life is in him."

And Paul went down, and fell on him, and embracing him said, Trouble not yourselves (Wuest Translation: stop wailing); for his life is in him.

Paul falls on the boy as Elijah and Elisha had in their ministries. In Elijah's case, he had fallen three times on the son of a widow woman who had fallen ill and died. Afterwards, the boy had come back to life (1 Kings 17:21).

Similarly, Elisha had brought a boy back to life whose head began to hurt while reaping in a field with his father. The boy had been carried home and died. After Elisha had lain on the on the boy, life returned to boy's body (2 Kings 4:34). This is a type of intercession, an exchange of life. Paul assures the crowd the boy who fell to the ground will live. The people around the young boy are in hysterics, so Paul quiets them.

C. Paul Continues His Sermon

20:11 Now when he had come up, had broken bread and eaten, and talked a long while, even till daybreak, he departed.

When Paul goes back upstairs, he dines with the disciples and continues his sermon until dawn.

20:12 And they brought the young man in alive, and they were not a little comforted.

Apparently, the boy is well-known. The crowd was not only ecstatic over the miracle, but also relieved.

III. Paul in Miletus (13–16)

Paul and his companions continue their travels to Assos, Samos, and Miletus.

20:13 ¶ Then we went ahead to the ship and sailed to Assos, there intending to take Paul on board; for so he had given orders, intending himself to go on foot.

Luke travels with the team by ship. Paul has decided to walk to Assos (about twenty miles south of Troas). Apparently Paul wants to be alone to pray for direction. He sends the disciples ahead and will meet them later.

During that time of solitude, the Lord will instruct Paul to have a pastors' conference for all the "shepherds" of Ephesus. Paul is also making up his mind to go to Jerusalem and preach to believers who have become legalistic. He had seen the condition of the church there (18:22) and has desired to return for some time. He had visited previously and was a blessing to the believers. He will go again, but this time it will be against the will of God.

Verses 14 and 15 describe Paul's voyage down the coast of Miletus. Paul will spend some time relaxing at some of the most famous resort spots of the Mediterranean.

20:14 And when he met us at Assos, we took him on board and came to Mitylene.

Mitylene is the capital of the island of Lesbos, which is a short distance from Assos. Lesbos is a famous Roman resort island. The English word "lesbian" is derived from the name of this island.

20:15 We sailed from there, and the next *day* came opposite Chios. The following *day* we arrived at Samos and stayed at Trogyllium. The next *day* we came to Miletus.

At this time, Chios is famous for wine, and Samos is located in the Aegean region further down from Chios. It is also a famous resort for the Romans, especially the military. It is close to Ephesus and a free state under Rome. It is also the location of the temple of Hera, and the worship of this goddess is similar to that of Diana.

Paul and his team stay at Trogyllium, a major city on Samos. Paul and his men rest at each of these cities. They do not preach, witness, or evangelize. These cities have great need, but Paul and his team know they need the rest to complete what God has called them to do.

They finally arrive in Miletus, the place where God instructed them to hold a conference for the pastors of Ephesus. This will be Paul's first contact with the ministers since the disassembling of the rioting mob at Ephesus and Paul's departure.

20:16 For Paul had decided to sail past Ephesus, so that he would not have to spend time in Asia; for he was hurrying to be at Jerusalem, if possible, on the Day of Pentecost.

Paul is trying to "fit in" the will of God by speaking in Ephesus before departing for Jerusalem. Miletus is in the will of God, and Jerusalem is out of God's will. Paul has determined he will be in Jerusalem for the feast of Pentecost and will squeeze Miletus in as quickly as he can. He has reasoned that if he did go to Ephesus, he would have to remain longer than he wants to. Miletus will make it easier for Paul to leave quickly. Paul is in a hurry.

This is always an indication you are not on solid ground. When you feel pressured by time, this is Satan's trap; "Act now or you will miss God's will." Until this moment, Paul has been thinking about going to Jerusalem and has been casually traveling from city to city and relaxing. Now he is in a hurry. Verse 16 is an extreme contrast to the preceding verses. At Miletus, Paul is in a hurry because he has now determined to go to Jerusalem.

IV. Paul's Pastors Conference (17–31)

From Miletus, Paul invites the elders from the church at Ephesus to Miletus where he makes a deposit into their lives. He holds his first "pastors conference." While the elders are with Paul, he expresses his determination to travel to Jerusalem and assures them he has not kept back anything from them concerning the gospel.

In verses 17 through 30, Paul calls the pastors from Ephesus to join him thirty miles away at the seaside town of Miletus. The pastors are called elders. This particular word is frequently used when referring to the office of the pastor.

A. Greek Words Referring to the Office of the Pastor

1. *Presbuteros*: elder, the one or ones in authority
2. *Episcopov*: bishop, overseer, superintendent
3. *Diakonov*: minister
4. *Poimhn*: pastor, shepherd

20:17 ¶ From Miletus he sent to Ephesus and called for the elders of the church.

And from Miletus he sent to Ephesus, and called the elders (*presbuteros*: elder; the one or ones in authority) of the church.

Paul calls for the elders (plural) because there is more than one local church in Ephesus. There are many churches meeting in homes throughout the city. The word "elder" here refers to the pastors of those churches.

The Greek word *presbuteros*, shows the authority of the pastor. His authority lies in his teaching ministry. He does not rule lives, he rules the teaching of "the whole counsel of God." A minister cannot teach without authority. The authority is not given by men, but by the Holy Spirit (v. 28).

The Greek word *episkopov* emphasizes the work of the minister. He is an overseer, a bishop. He observes and watches over God's heritage, the congregation.

The Greek word for pastor, *poimhn* is his title, shepherd. There are functions within a local church of administration called *diakonov*, or deacons. They are taken from the congregation and carry out authority in their own realm of service to the people.

B. Paul's Message

20:18 And when they had come to him, he said to them: "You know, from the first day that I came to Asia, in what manner I always lived among you,

Paul begins his message to the ministers, the pastors of Ephesus. They have seen Paul's lifestyle since the day he had arrived over three years before. He has been with them through "all seasons." They have watched Paul handle struggles and turmoil. They have watched him rise above troubles he knew about and others he did not. The seasons of the ministry range from good to bad, pleasant to difficult, and calm to stormy. There are times when people are for you and your message and other times when you are opposed.

20:19 serving the Lord with all humility, with many tears and trials which happened to me by the plotting of the Jews;

Serving the Lord with all humility of mind (*tapeiphrosune*: grace thinking), and with many tears, and temptation, which befell me by the lying in wait of the Jews:

The first attribute any minister needs is grace thinking. This is freedom from arrogance. The first step into greatness in God's kingdom is to realize you are nothing, and God is everything. This way, God can build your ministry and not you.

Paul points out that many sufferings are found in the Christian life, especially in the ministry. A minister is a special target to the devil. When a minister falls, the rest of the congregation will probably not be far behind. With humility comes true godly exaltation (Proverbs 3:34, Philippians 2:8–9, James 4:10, 1 Peter 5:6). God's protection also comes (Isaiah 54:17). Often there are tears when you discover what people are really like. Temptation comes from the religious, legalistic people. The worst type of persecution comes from the religious crowd.

20:20 how I kept back nothing that was helpful, but proclaimed it to you, and taught you publicly and from house to house,

And how I kept back (*hupostello*: did not furl the sails, cower, shrink, conceal) nothing that was profitable unto you, but have shewed (*anaggello*: announce or teach again and again) you, and have taught you publickly, and from house to house.

The revival at Ephesus meets in the school of Tyrannus, a public building. Then as churches begin to form, they move into houses. Paul has been with them from the early days of the revival to the later days when they are meeting from house-to-house or church-to-church. Churches met in homes in many of the cities where Paul preaches (Acts 12:17, Romans 16:5, 1 Corinthians 16:19, Colossians 4:15).

Paul teaches by example three principles of ministry. These are important areas pastors need to know about:

1. Paul holds nothing back.
2. What he teaches is profitable.
3. He repeats the teaching again and again.

20:21 testifying to Jews, and also to Greeks, repentance toward God and faith toward our Lord Jesus Christ.

Testifying both to the Jews, and also to the Greeks, repentance (*metanoeo*: reversal of decision, to change the mind) toward God, and faith toward our Lord Jesus Christ.

Repentance and faith are two sides of the same coin. When you exercise faith toward Jesus Christ, you are automatically repenting to God for your attitude toward His Son. Repent means to change the mind (*metanoeo*). You do not change your mind about sin, although that is part of it. You change your mind (your attitude) about Jesus Christ. You have been rejecting Him, and now you are accepting Him.

C. Paul's Prophecy of Future Events

20:22 And see, now I go bound in the spirit to Jerusalem, not knowing the things that will happen to me there,

And now, behold, I go bound in the spirit unto Jerusalem, not knowing the things that shall befall (confront) me there:

In his own heart, Paul senses the warning of the Holy Spirit. He feels bound in his own spirit because he will be bound in his own body when he arrives in Jerusalem. The Holy Spirit says "no," but Paul will rationalize it into "yes." Paul probably thinks since he will face suffering in Jerusalem, it must be God's will. Some people think if they are not suffering, they are out of God's will. Paul even says in this verse that he does not know what will happen there. Paul is usually "confident," "always confident," "knowing," etc. (2 Corinthians 5:1, 6, 8, 11).

20:23 except that the Holy Spirit testifies in every city, saying that chains and tribulations await me.

Save (except) that the Holy Ghost witnesseth (*diamarturomai*: makes a solemn warning, protest earnestly) in every city, saying that bonds (imprisonment) and afflictions abide (await) me.

Paul has been visiting many places on the way to Miletus trying to relax. Since that time he has been determined to go to Jerusalem, yet he has been warned by the Holy Spirit and believers in every city not to go.

20:24 ¶ But none of these things move me; nor do I count my life dear to myself, so that I may finish my race with joy, and the ministry which I received from the Lord Jesus, to testify to the gospel of the grace of God.

Paul is simply saying, "I am hard-headed!" Although he knows he will ultimately be thrown in prison, he is stating he is willing to die for the gospel. This is noble but stupid. All of the things Paul is saying he is willing to do are right and commendable, but if you are out of God's will, you can have all the right attitudes and still be wrong.

Paul is prepared to go to jail and suffer persecution yet still plans to preach the gospel. He will go to jail, and he will be persecuted, but he will be unable to preach the gospel in Jerusalem. Specifically, he will be unable to preach the gospel of grace. He will take a legalistic vow to preach the gospel of grace. In essence, he will sin that grace may abound.

D. Paul Fulfills His Responsibility

20:25–26 ¶ "And indeed, now I know that you all, among whom I have gone preaching the kingdom of God, will see my face no

more. 26 Therefore I testify to you this day that I *am* innocent of the blood of all *men*.

Paul is pure from their blood. He is free from responsibility. Their blood is now on their own hands because Paul has done with them what God has commanded.

20:27 For I have not shunned to declare to you the whole counsel of God.

For I have not shunned (*hupostello*: did not furl the sails, cower, shrink, conceal [v. 20]) to declare (*anaggello*: announce or teach again and again) unto you all the counsel (*boule*: plan, will, purpose) of God.

Paul's responsibility is to teach the Word to these men. He is free from their blood (responsibility for them); if they fail, they are responsible, not Paul. He has given them the Word. They are now responsible for their own decisions and the consequences of those decisions.

When a minister gives his people the Word of God and leaves nothing out, he is free from responsibility over them. The pastor can walk away from the pulpit knowing he has delivered all God has required him to share. When a minister finally leaves this earth and enters into heaven, he can do so with the assurance that he has preached all the Word of God and left nothing out (Colossians 4:12).

Paul walks away from these ministers knowing he has given them everything God has told him to share. Paul has a free conscience toward God and these ministers. When the congregation opens their hearts to the teaching of the Word, this makes a pastor's job even easier. Not only is the pastor free from responsibility, so are the people (see 2 Corinthians 6:11–13).

E. Paul Encourages Pastors

20:28 Therefore take heed to yourselves and to all the flock, among which the Holy Spirit has made you overseers, to shepherd the church of God which He purchased with His own blood.

Take heed (beware) therefore unto yourselves, and to all the flock, over the which the Holy Ghost (not men) hath made (*tithemi*: appointed) you overseers (*episkopos*: bishops), to feed (*poimaino*: pastor or feed the flock;

pastor the older sheep) the church of God, which he hath purchased with his own blood.

Paul tells pastors to first take heed to themselves before they take heed to the flock. If a minister does not take care of himself and his own personal life, he will not be in any condition to take care of the flock of God. He must spend time with his family, take days off and holidays. Without these things, he will not live long enough to take the congregation to the level they need to go. Moses also faces this issue, and his father-in-law tells him to delegate the responsibilities so he will live long (Exodus 18:17–23).

Paul then tells these men they have been placed into their positions by the Holy Spirit. The office of pastor is God-given and not man-appointed (Galatians 1:1, Ephesians 1:1). The Holy Spirit put these men into the positions of bishops (overseers). Peter reminds the pastors to "take the oversight (bishopric)" (1 Peter 5:2). Once the position has been given by God, it is up to the minister to fully accept the responsibility and boldly exercise the authority given.

Paul then confirms that the main responsibility of a pastor is to "feed the flock." Peter tells the pastors under his authority to do the same thing (1 Peter 5:2). The word for "feed" in this passage (*poimaino*) means to pastor the flock. Peter knew these words well because the Lord Jesus Christ spoke them to him (John 21:15–17). It is the pastor's responsibility to hand feed (*basko*) the newborn sheep and feed (*poimaino*) the older sheep. The mature sheep need only to be led to the grass, and they will eat what is before them. The pastor is to prepare sermons and lead the sheep to the finest food available. The sermons should be prepared days or weeks in advance.

Finally, Paul reminds them the sheep (the congregation) belong to the Lord Jesus. He purchased them with His own blood; therefore He owns them. Whoever purchases is the owner. The sheep actually belong to God. The pastor does not own the sheep. He is tending another man's flock. Moses watched over Jethro's sheep and David watched over Jesse's sheep. The shepherd is hired by the owner to watch over the sheep. The responsibility for food and finances is not the shepherd's, but the owner's. The pastor does not provide for the sheep, God does.

The pastor is not to force the sheep to do anything. He can only teach them. Where they go to church and how often they attend is between them and God, not the pastor. The pastor can instruct, but not force. Peter tells the pastors not to be "lords" (dictators), but "examples to the flock" (1 Peter 5:3). Paul told Timothy to "exhort with patience and teaching" (2 Timothy 4:2).

When people leave to go to another church, the pastor cannot demand they stay or pronounce curses over them for leaving. If they are going to a church that is wrong or filled with false doctrine, the pastor can warn and leave an open door for return. If they are attending a good church, the pastor must release them as seed sown. The sheep are God's property.

F. Paul Warns Pastors

20:29 For I know this, that after my departure savage wolves will come in among you, not sparing the flock.

For I know (*eido*: perceive, understand) this, that after my departing shall grievous (*barous*: vicious) wolves enter in among you, not sparing the flock.

Wolves represent unbelievers (Matthew 7:15, 10:16; Luke 10:3). They come from the outside (Colossians 4:5) and desire to destroy the work of God. They do not seek people to follow after them, they only desire to destroy God's work in the earth.

20:30 Also from among yourselves men will rise up, speaking perverse things, to draw away the disciples after themselves.

Also of (*ek*: out from) your own selves shall men arise, speaking perverse (*diastrepho*: distorted, twisted, corrupt) things, to draw away disciples after them.

This is the worst group. They "rise up" in arrogance from within the church. They know correct teaching, but twist and pervert it to draw people away and after themselves. They are looking for an audience, a congregation they do not have to raise up for themselves. They prefer taking an existing congregation, dividing it, and drawing their own followers from that existing congregation. They are looking for a unique teaching to create their ministry from. They take good doctrine (a sound teaching) and confuse people with perversions.

These same men are sitting before Paul as he speaks. Paul prophesies they will rise up and split congregations for their own selfish desires. Peter also mentions these types of ministers in 2 Peter 2:10.

20:31 Therefore watch, and remember that for three years I did not cease to warn everyone night and day with tears.

Therefore watch (be alert), and remember, that by the space of three years I ceased not to warn (admonish) every one night and day with tears.

Paul is concluding his teaching and instruction to the pastors at Ephesus. He wants them to remember his own teaching and examples from the previous three years. They must also use the Word for themselves and set an example before their own people. They have seen Paul at his best and worst and know of his love for the Lord and for people.

V. Paul Commends the Pastors to God (32–38)

Paul exhorts the pastors to take care of themselves and the flock which has been entrusted to them. He warns them about "wolves" in their midst and those who would pervert the truth. Paul prays with the elders gathered and then bids them farewell.

> **20:32 ¶ "So now, brethren, I commend you to God and to the word of His grace, which is able to build you up and give you an inheritance among all those who are sanctified.**

And now, brethren, I commend (*paratithemi*: deposit, commit) you to God, and to the word of his grace, which is able to build you up (*epoikodomeo*: build upon), and to give you an inheritance among all them which are sanctified.

Paul deposits these men with the Lord and His grace after he holds back nothing. Their blood is not on his hands, and he can trust them with God (v. 26). The keeping of these men also lies in the Word of God as well as the grace of God. The Word alone does not build you up; faith is necessary for this to occur. Paul is like a father turning his sons over to God before they go into the world or into marriage (Proverbs 1:8, 9, 6:20–23).

A. Seven Deposits of the New Testament
1. Salvation, life deposited with the Lord (2 Timothy 1:12).
2. The Word in us (2 Timothy 1:14).
3. Our cares and problems with the Lord (1 Peter 4:19, 5:7; Psalm 55:22).
4. The gospel with unbelievers (Romans 1:14).
5. The Word with other believers by the pastor (2 Timothy 2:2).
6. Finances with God (Philippians 4:15–19).
7. The results of your labors in others lives (Acts 20:32).

By studying and applying the Word, these pastors will receive an inheritance from the saints. The main function of a pastor is to study the Word. Pastors not only have rewards from God in heaven (1 Peter 5:4), but also from the changed lives of believers on earth.

B. Paul's Motivation for the Ministry

20:33 I have coveted no one's silver or gold or apparel.

Paul has received many offerings during his travels. He has often received gold, silver (money), and clothing (1 Thessalonians 2:3–6). However, Paul is not in the ministry for money. If money is his motivation, he would have quit in Corinth when it was necessary for him to make tents to support himself. Paul covets souls, maturity, and spiritual blessings.

Pastors should not covet the riches of those in their congregation. No matter how much you may own, there is always someone who will possess more.

20:34 Yes, you yourselves know that these hands have provided for my necessities, and for those who were with me.

The money Paul made in ministry and during the time of tent making went toward supporting him and his team.

20:35 I have shown you in every way, by laboring like this, that you must support the weak. And remember the words of the Lord Jesus, that He said, 'It is more blessed to give than to receive.'"

I have shewed (revealed) you all things, how that so laboring ye ought to support the weak (astheneo: spiritually and physically impotent, sick weak [James 5:14]), and to remember the words of the Lord Jesus, how he said, It is more blessed to give than to receive.

Paul has given everything he knows to these pastors. Paul makes an issue of the Word, not money. He is telling the ministers that if the church does not bring in enough financially to support them as pastors, they should go to work. Even if you are a pastor just beginning in the ministry, it is not wrong to work with your hands to give to the poor. The last phrase about being more blessed to give was not recorded in the four gospels but handed down by Paul's followers (John 21:25).

20:36 ⸏ And when he had said these things, he knelt down and prayed with them all.

This is Paul's final prayer with these pastors, many of whom he has personally instructed and watched move into spiritual maturity. They feel close to Paul like he is their own earthly father.

20:37 Then they all wept freely, and fell on Paul's neck and kissed him,

This is the weeping of gratitude, love, and respect. They know they will not see him again. He has been close to them for three years and will now go on to Jerusalem.

20:38 sorrowing most of all for the words which he spoke, that they would see his face no more. And they accompanied him to the ship.

21:1–40 Paul Is Warned

The Challenge of Chapter Twenty-One

When we are warned by the Holy Spirit, it is important to obey regardless of our own personal desires, even when our desires appear to be good. The Holy Spirit is sent to lead us, guide us, and show us things to come. He will help us avoid problems in our lives if we are willing to listen, even if His guidance is contrary to our own set agenda.

We must also guard against serving God by the law rather than grace. Religion will always attempt to blind us to the freedom of living by the grace of God, emphasizing self-effort rather than God's enabling power.

I. Several Warnings About Jerusalem (1–14)

During their journeys, Paul and his companions land in Tyre where they remain for seven days. The disciples in Tyre warn Paul, by the Holy Spirit, not to travel to Jerusalem. Paul and his team then voyage to Ptolemais and Caesarea. They enter the home of an evangelist named Philip who has four daughters who prophesy to Paul. Then a prophet named Agabus comes from Judea and prophesies to Paul, warning him of what awaits him if he travels to Jerusalem. Finally, everyone present pleads with Paul not to go to Jerusalem, but he is determined, his mind is made up, and he will not be persuaded.

A. Disciples in Tyre Warn Paul

21:1 ¶ Now it came to pass, that when we had departed from them and set sail, running a straight course we came to Cos, the following *day* to Rhodes, and from there to Patara.

This chapter begins the account of Paul's great failure. From this time on, Paul is a prisoner. His prison time begins in Jerusalem (21–23), moves to Caesarea (24–26), and ends in Rome (27–28). While Paul is bound, the gospel is never bound because the Word can never be stopped. The message continues even when the messenger is in chains.

Paul has been warned in many cities not to go to Jerusalem (20:23); he will be warned by the saints in Tyre (21:3–4), by Philip's daughters (8–9), by Agabus (10–11), and his own companions (12). Paul rejects their guidance. He becomes hardheaded by rejecting the guidance of the Holy Spirit and accepting the guidance of carnal men. He will take a vow in the streets of Jerusalem (24).

As Paul leaves the pastors of Ephesus, it is an emotional departure. It is difficult on Paul and the elders to separate and for Paul to go on his way. He and his team will revisit a few resort islands on their way to Jerusalem. They first come to Coos, the birthplace of Hippocrates, a beautiful island famous for its medical schools. Next, they sail to Rhodes, a large island northeast of Crete, famous for its navy, located in a strategic point between the Aegean and Mediterranean seas. They then travel to Patara, a pleasure city on the coast between the West and Middle East. Here they board a ship to Phoenicia.

21:2 And finding a ship sailing over to Phoenicia, we went aboard and set sail.

Phoenicia is an early seafaring nation famous for its navy and worldwide commerce. The Phoenicians sailed to America long before anyone else. It was a large country located south of Syria. Tyre is a chief city in Phoenicia. It was quite a task to sail from Patara to Phoenicia. The distance was about 340 miles.

21:3 When we had sighted Cyprus, we passed it on the left, sailed to Syria, and landed at Tyre; for there the ship was to unload her cargo.

They do not stop at Cyprus but sail by and dock in Tyre, a free city of Roman Syria. It had been destroyed by Alexander and partially rebuilt by Herod. Along with its sister city, Sidon, it was always popular for its heathenism. It was the object of many Biblical prophesies (Isaiah 23:1–17, Joel 3:4, Matthew 11:22). While the ship is unloading its cargo, Paul finds some believers, strong disciples.

21:4 And finding disciples, we stayed there seven days. They told Paul through the Spirit not to go up to Jerusalem.

There are not many disciples in the city of Tyre, so it takes some searching to find Christians, much less disciples filled with the Word and sensitive to the Holy Spirit. Paul and his team remain in Tyre for one week. He ministers to the believers and they to him. Paul must have mentioned to them about his upcoming trip to Jerusalem. He probably told them in wonderful terms of his plans to preach the gospel and what he thought was the leading of the Holy Spirit to go, even though he would face bonds. While he spoke, the same Holy Spirit revealed and warned the disciples that Paul should not go to Jerusalem. God will move from disciples in Tyre giving warning to a prophet in Caesarea, but Paul will still not listen.

> **21:5–6 When we had come to the end of those days, we departed and went on our way; and they all accompanied us, with wives and children, till *we were* out of the city. And we knelt down on the shore and prayed. 6 When we had taken our leave of one another, we boarded the ship, and they returned home.**

These people are so thankful for Paul coming to minister to them, they follow him and his team to the dock and pray with him before he boards the next ship.

> **21:7 ¶ And when we had finished *our* voyage from Tyre, we came to Ptolemais, greeted the brethren, and stayed with them one day.**

And when we had finished our course (completed our mission) from Tyre, we came to Ptolemais (Tol-o-mais), and saluted (greeted) the brethren, and abode with them one day.

Ptolemais is a very old and famous city in the ancient world. In Judges 1:31, it is the city of Accho. When Alexander sailed into its natural harbor, he named it Ptolemais for his famous general Ptolemy, who later became the ruler of Egypt. Today it is the famous seaport of Haifa. Word had already spread about Paul coming, and the disciples in Ptolemais came out to greet him.

B. Paul Warned by Philip's Daughters

> **21:8 On the next *day* we who were Paul's companions departed and came to Caesarea, and entered the house of Philip the evangelist, who was *one* of the seven, and stayed with him.**

And the next day we that were of Paul's company departed, and came unto Caesarea (cf. 10:1): and we entered into the house of Philip the evangelist, which was one of the seven (original deacons, 6:5); and abode with him.

Philip had been used by the Lord to fulfill the prophecy of Jesus "into Samaria" (1:8) in Acts 8 where he held the Samaritan revival. He also led the Ethiopian eunuch to the Lord (8:26–39) and based himself in Caesarea after being translated by the Spirit to Azotus (8:40).

For some time, Paul remains in Caesarea and receives two warnings about continuing to Jerusalem.

21:9 Now this man had four virgin daughters who prophesied.

Philip's daughters are not prophets like Agabus, but they are known to move in the Holy Spirit and prophecy. They fulfill Joel 2:28. They are proficient in the ways of the Holy Spirit, coming from the home of an evangelist. The phrase "did prophesy" in this passage indicates that Philip's daughters were not new to operating in prophecy; it also indicates they prophesied at that very moment over Paul.

Since Paul has been warned against going to Jerusalem, it can be assumed from the context that these daughters also prophesied to Paul not to go to Jerusalem.

C. Paul Warned by Agubus

21:10 And as we stayed many days, a certain prophet named Agabus came down from Judea.

Paul is now running into another pioneer of the early church. Paul had met Agabus in the early days of the church at Antioch. Agabus had first prophesied to the entire church of an upcoming drought headed to Jerusalem (11:28). Here Agabus will prophesy again, but this time to an individual, Paul, about his upcoming imprisonment.

21:11 When he had come to us, he took Paul's belt, bound his *own* hands and feet, and said, "Thus says the Holy Spirit, 'So shall the Jews at Jerusalem bind the man who owns this belt, and deliver *him* into the hands of the Gentiles.'"

The "girdle" is a money belt wrapped around Paul's waist. Paul has received an offering from Macedonia and is taking it to the saints at Jerusalem (Romans 15:24–28). Paul usually delegates this responsibility, but this time he convinces others (and himself) that it would be better accomplished by himself personally. In other words, Paul takes the money himself as an excuse to go to Jerusalem. God intends for Paul to go to Spain and then to

Rome. Paul has decided to do this after he has accomplished his mission at Jerusalem.

The money belt is used as an illustrated sermon. The money will be a blessing to those in Jerusalem but a curse to Paul.

Agabus does not correctly prophesy to Paul. He tells Paul the Jews will bind him and turn him over to the Romans. However, it is the Jews who try to kill Paul, and the Romans rescue him (vv. 27–33).

The New Testament prophets are not like those of the Old Testament. They are not stoned for missing the voice of the Holy Spirit. The anointing on the office of prophet was stronger in the Old Testament than in the New. The Old Testament prophets wrote scripture. The New Testament prophets did not. The Old Testament prophet was replaced by the New Testament apostle. This is why New Testament prophets were to be judged in church by the other prophets (1 Corinthians 14:29–32).

D. Paul's Team Pleads with Paul

21:12 ¶ Now when we heard these things, both we and those from that place pleaded with him not to go up to Jerusalem.

Those pleading with Paul are Paul's team and the group present who hear the message by Agabus. Apparently, Agabus gives this message in the presence of many people from the church. Paul is called forward for a demonstration of the Holy Spirit's message. Paul has now had three warnings by the Holy Spirit; the saints at Tyre, the daughters of Philip, and now Agabus. Paul's team and the Caesarean congregation are smarter than Paul. He will not listen. God will now quit striving with Paul and let him do what he is determined to do.

21:13 Then Paul answered, "What do you mean by weeping and breaking my heart? For I am ready not only to be bound, but also to die at Jerusalem for the name of the Lord Jesus."

These friends and disciples are crying because they fear for Paul's life. They know he is going to Jerusalem out of God's will. They have seen it confirmed many times. Their crying got to Paul, and he knew they feared for his life. But he had already made up his mind to go and die if need be.

Here Paul is being stubborn. Paul's attitude is commendable, but his reasons for going are wrong. If he were to die, it would not be in the name of Jesus, but because of stupidity. He is being noble but stupid.

21:14 ¶ So when he would not be persuaded, we ceased, saying, "The will of the Lord be done."

They continue reasoning with Paul after his answer, but he will not change. They leave Paul alone and turn him (and their frustration) over to the Lord. They can no longer take the care of Paul upon themselves; it will cause them to sin. They know they have gone as far as they could.

II. Paul and His Team Gladly Received (15–30)

Once Paul and his companions arrive in Jerusalem, the brethren warmly greet Paul and his team. The next day, Paul greets James and the elders present and begins to testify about what God has been doing among the Gentiles through his ministry. The elders Paul address tell him to take a vow to demonstrate brotherly love in preaching the message of grace. Paul takes a Nazarite vow because of the influence of the elders in Jerusalem. Seven days after his arrival in Jerusalem, Jews from Asia who have seen Paul in the temple stir up the people against him. A mob is formed and they grab Paul and drag him from the temple.

A. Paul and His Team Gladly Received

21:15 ¶ And after those days we packed and went up to Jerusalem.

Among the baggage is the offering for the saints at Jerusalem from the believers of Macedonia (Romans 15:25–26). They go "up" to Jerusalem because it is an ascent from Caesarea to Jerusalem.

21:16 Also some of the disciples from Caesarea went with us and brought with them a certain Mnason of Cyprus, an early disciple, with whom we were to lodge.

A group of disciples went with Paul and his team to Jerusalem. Mnason was a Greek Cypriot like Barnabas. The group spends their last night in his home before they leave Caesarea.

21:17 ¶ And when we had come to Jerusalem, the brethren received us gladly.

Paul is now out of God's will. God has been warning Paul not to go, and Paul has not heeded. At the gates of Jerusalem, Paul is disobedient and officially out of God's protection. Money came with Paul, and this is one reason he is gladly received. This offering has been received over a period of time from Greece and Asia. In verse 17, Paul meets the brethren. In verse 18, he will meet the church leadership.

B. Paul Meets with the Elders

21:18 On the following *day* Paul went in with us to James, and all the elders were present.

Jerusalem has weak leadership. They do not stand up for the Word, and legalism has entered in. Instead of defending grace, they have allowed born-again Pharisees to run the church, and they have put these Jewish believers under the law of Moses for salvation and spirituality. These legalistic leaders were truly born again as the church was growing (6:7), but they are not correctly taught and so bring the law of Moses into the church. Because of their knowledge of the Old Testament, few withstand them and they become the church leaders.

21:19 When he had greeted them, he told in detail those things which God had done among the Gentiles through his ministry.

And when he (Paul) had saluted (greeted) them, he declared particularly (in detail) what things God had wrought among the Gentiles by his ministry.

In the past, this has always worked (11:18, 15:6–19). Peter and Paul have told the church at Jerusalem about the miracles, signs, and wonders God has performed among the Gentiles. They have also been saved and filled with the Holy Spirit and spoken with tongues just as the saints at Jerusalem. This has always caused a great amount of praise and admission of grace.

21:20 And when they heard *it*, they glorified the Lord. And they said to him, "You see, brother, how many myriads of Jews there are who have believed, and they are all zealous for the law;

The church leadership admits Paul is right, but they are faced with many Jews who have received Jesus and are still clinging to the law of Moses. James is simply saying they are afraid of the Jews. They do not want to lose people from the church or lose their offerings. They have become the very people they broke away from.

They should have stood for the Word and not allowed these Jews to have influence over the beliefs and government of the church.

They call Paul "brother." They begin with religious talk, but Paul is wiser than this. He recognizes manipulation, but he so wants to speak to his own people, he tolerates their religious talk. They tell Paul the Jewish converts want the law. "What can we do when so many thousands want to keep the law of Moses?" Weak leadership produces a weak congregation. These converts are zealous for the law because the leaders are. The leaders have given up on the good fight of faith. They have yielded to the pressure, and so will Paul. The church has become legalistic, and the city will soon go under.

21:21 but they have been informed about you that you teach all the Jews who are among the Gentiles to forsake Moses, saying that they ought not to circumcise *their* children nor to walk according to the customs.

And they are informed of (concerning) thee, that thou teachest all the Jews which are among the Gentiles to forsake (*apostasia*: falling away) Moses, saying that they ought not to circumcise their children, neither to walk after the customs.

These Jewish leaders have been running Paul down from the pulpits. Paul has a bad reputation in Jerusalem. He cannot be argued with face to face, so they have chosen to run him down when he is not present. Paul is too brilliant with the Word to be challenged publicly.

They have done this before and lost. Paul has Jewish converts in each city of his missionary journeys. He usually preaches to the Jews in the synagogues first. Those who did not receive his message sent warnings back to Jerusalem, distorting his message. Paul has not taught the Jews not to circumcise their young boys; he has taught them not circumcise them for spiritual reasons. He has truly taught them to forsake the law of Moses because it has been fulfilled in Jesus. He has taught them to turn from the shadows to the substance (Colossians 2:17).

21:22 What then? The assembly must certainly meet, for they will hear that you have come.

Paul is a very controversial figure. They will not come together to reason but to argue and malign Paul. They will want to kill him (vv. 27–31). Paul is now beginning to understand how far this city has fallen into legalism and how liberal the leadership has become toward them. James and the church leaders are more concerned about not offending people than standing up for the truth. Paul is now slipping into their way of thinking, "Let's do anything that allows us to preach to them."

C. The Strategy of the Elders to Weaken Paul

21:23 Therefore do what we tell you: We have four men who have taken a vow.

Do therefore this (imperative mood) that we say to thee: We have four men which have a vow on them:

These men have switched from the defensive to the offensive. They are now commanding Paul to become legalistic in order to preach grace. They are saying to Paul, "Be like us. We have four leaders from our church who have taken a seven-day vow and shaved their heads. Join with them Paul, shave your head and show the people you are one of us and there is no division. Show them brotherly love."

21:24 Take them and be purified with them, and pay their expenses so that they may shave *their* heads, and that all may know that those things of which they were informed concerning you are nothing, but *that* you yourself also walk orderly and keep the law.

James is minimizing grace while magnifying unity around the law, legalism. This is blasphemous. These men have not unified around grace. Why should they now want Paul to unify around religion? Why must Paul stand with them? Paul should now be telling these men to stand with him around the truth of God's Word. Paul has never considered grace to be nothing. He does believe in walking orderly, but by the Holy Spirit and grace, not by keeping the law.

This argument, that Paul does not believe in walking orderly, is a tactic used by weak people. Because you do not believe the way they do, they accuse you of not believing in holiness, the move of the Spirit, grace, etc. Anything can be taken to an extreme by the excessive Christian and used against the balanced believer.

21:25 But concerning the Gentiles who believe, we have written *and* decided that they should observe no such thing, except that

they should keep themselves from *things* offered to idols, from blood, from things strangled, and from sexual immorality."

They are appealing to Paul's Jewish heritage. They are making the gospel different by race. "It is alright for your converts not to keep the law, Paul, because they are Gentiles. But you are a Jew. You above everyone should know how important keeping the law is to a Jew. This is cultural, part of our heritage. You are different than the Gentiles you preach to."

At this point, Paul should have seen the spiritual and religious arrogance coming from the church leaders and should have left Jerusalem and told his team he had been wrong to come in the first place. He should have asked God to forgive him and headed for Rome.

D. Paul Takes a Jewish Vow

21:26 ⁋ Then Paul took the men, and the next day, having been purified with them, entered the temple to announce the expiration of the days of purification, at which time an offering should be made for each one of them.

Then Paul took the men, and the next day purifying himself (passive voice) with them entered (having entered) into the temple, to signify (give public testimony) the accomplishment of the days of purification, until that an offering should be offered for every one of them.

Paul swallows their hypocrisy. He will now do something he teaches against in the book of Romans. He is about to "sin that grace may abound." He will take a Jewish vow in order to preach grace to the Jews. Paul goes through the purification rights of the temple, something that was totally abolished at the cross. Paul knows this and has even taught it (Colossians 2:16–17).

This purification right is when Paul enters the temple, stands before the leaders, and vows to abstain from a number of items for thirty days. Vows could include abstinence from certain foods, shaving, sex, etc. This vow is describe in Numbers 6:1–21 as the Nazarite vow.

21:27 ⁋ Now when the seven days were almost ended, the Jews from Asia, seeing him in the temple, stirred up the whole crowd and laid hands on him,

And when the seven days were almost ended, the Jews which were of Asia, when they saw him in the temple, stirred up all the people, and laid (*epiballo*: threw themselves, attacked), hands on him,

When the week was almost ended, all hell breaks loose. Paul has stood publicly each day in the temple with four church elders and made this vow before the multitudes. Each day he announces he will not eat certain foods and that he is shaving his head, etc.

Just before the seventh day, certain men in the multitude recognize Paul and begin a riot. Asian Jews in Jerusalem for Pentecost recognize Paul from Ephesus. They see him make the vow and begin to stir up a riot against him. They throw themselves at Paul, attacking him and then cry out to the people for help.

> **21:28 crying out, "Men of Israel, help! This is the man who teaches all *men* everywhere against the people, the law, and this place; and furthermore he also brought Greeks into the temple and has defiled this holy place."**

Crying out (shouting), Men of Israel, help (*boetheo*: come running, aid, relieve): This is the man, that teacheth all men (Jews and Gentiles) every where (Asia, Macedonia, Achai) against the people (Jews), and the law (Mosaic) and this place (the temple): and further brought Greeks (Gentiles) also into the temple, and hath polluted this holy place.

The "Greeks" referred to are Trophimus (v. 29). Places are not holy and nationalities do not pollute. This is religious and national pride, jealousy, and prejudice.

These people do notshout all their accusations in unison, but instead say one thing and another. This verse lumps together everything that was said.

> **21:29 (For they had previously seen Trophimus the Ephesian with him in the city, whom they supposed that Paul had brought into the temple.)**

These people are jealous of Paul's success in Ephesus. When they are in Jerusalem, they see Paul with Trophimus and assume wrongly that Paul has taken him, a Gentile, into the temple. They use this to incite the Jews with the belief that Paul is weakening their religion by bringing Gentiles into their system and holy place.

These people are more zealous for tradition than they are truth and the accompanying signs from God (cf. 2 Peter 2:19). Here, Peter gives a description of religious teachers. They make promises they cannot keep. They are slaves themselves. How can a slave give you liberty? They tell you of freedom from sin when they are steeped in sin themselves. The one seeking freedom is bound, overcome, and brought to bondage by the very one promising liberty. The result is being brought into worse sin than what the individual began with.

III. A Riot in Jerusalem (31–40)

As the mob attempts to kill Paul, a chief captain of the Roman army and his soldiers run toward the rioting crowd. When the mob sees the soldiers, they stop beating Paul. The chief captain has Paul bound in chains and send him to prison while they try to determine who he is and what he has done. Paul is led into the Roman fort where he explains to the chief captain who he is and asks to speak to the people. He is granted permission.

A. Mob Determines to Kill Paul

21:30 ¶ And all the city was disturbed; and the people ran together, seized Paul, and dragged him out of the temple; and immediately the doors were shut.

And all the city was moved (*kineo*: kinetic, to stir), and the people ran together (rioted): and they took (seized) Paul, and drew (dragged) him out of the temple: and forthwith (immediately) the doors were shut.

In the temple, they observe the law of no killing. Outside, however, they are overlooking the law of murder. Religion only observes the convenient laws and disregards those that slow down its cause.

21:31 Now as they were seeking to kill him, news came to the commander of the garrison that all Jerusalem was in an uproar.

And as they went about (sought) to kill him, tidings (news) came unto the chief captain of the band (Roman army, 1000 men), that all Jerusalem was in an uproar.

Mob violence is running the city. They are using religion to disobey the law and murder someone without a trial. There will only be an execution. They can never trap Paul by legal means in Corinth (Chapter 18) or Ephesus (Chapter 19), so they are breaking the law themselves. This is why the Romans have every right to come in and seize and protect Paul. The chief captain (*tribune*) is a leader of one thousand soldiers in the Roman garrison. This represents the extent of law in the church. When the religious person violates civil law, he must face the system. The Romans represent law and order, especially in the midst of chaos.

> **21:32 He immediately took soldiers and centurions, and ran down to them. And when they saw the commander and the soldiers, they stopped beating Paul.**

Who (commander) immediately took (grabbed the nearest) soldiers (foot soldiers) and centurions (captains over 100), and ran down unto them (the rioting Jews): and when they saw the chief captain and the soldiers, they left beating Paul.

This commander is such a contrast to Pontius Pilate who catered to the people. This ruler knows the law, order, and the destructive potential of mobs. Since those beating Paul fear the death sentence for murder, they stop. They then stand back and scream accusations to justify themselves. Their intent is to convince the Roman government to kill Paul since they can't without suffering the consequences.

> **21:33 Then the commander came near and took him, and commanded *him* to be bound with two chains; and he asked who he was and what he had done.**

Then the chief captain came near, and took him (Paul), and commanded him to be bound with two chains; and demanded (investigated) who he was, and what he had done.

Paul is taken for his own protection until he can be tried. He is bound with two chains, which is the way the Romans bound their prisoners (12:6). The military leader remains calm and reacts smoothly in an emotional event. He now demands information after putting the mob and Paul in their proper places.

B. Confusion in the Mob

> **21:34 And some among the multitude cried one thing and some another. ¶ So when he could not ascertain the truth because of the tumult, he commanded him to be taken into the barracks.**

And some cried one thing, some another, among the multitude: and when he (the officer) could not know the certainty (get the straight facts) for the tumult (riot), he commanded him (Paul) to be carried into the castle.

The Roman officer inquires of the mob about who Paul is and what he had done, but he cannot get a straight answer. There are as many opinions as people in the mob. Paul is taken into the Antonio Fort named for Mark Antony, a close friend of Herod. Herod had this castle built in Jerusalem in honor of his friend.

C. The Reaction of the Mob

21:35 When he reached the stairs, he had to be carried by the soldiers because of the violence of the mob.

As the soldiers come to the steps of the fort, they are forced to carry Paul in the air over their heads to prevent him from being killed by the mob running after them. Paul is rushed by the mob on the stairs. The Jews know the accuracy of Roman law, and that there is little chance of seeing Paul sentenced since he has done nothing illegal. Paul has simply offended their religious, traditional thinking. They now decide to kill Paul on the steps and forget whether it is legal or illegal, or whether or not the Romans witness the killing. They feel it is worth losing their own lives to see Paul dead. The Roman soldiers have risked their own lives to uphold the law and protect a man who has yet to be tried.

21:36 For the multitude of the people followed after, crying out, "Away with him!"

The Jews go up the stairs right behind the Roman soldiers. They are shouting the same thing the mob was crying before they crucified Jesus. However, this time the group is comprised predominantly of believers.

Legalism causes believers to act just like or even worse than unbelievers.

D. Paul and the Chief Captain

21:37 ¶ Then as Paul was about to be led into the barracks, he said to the commander, ¶ "May I speak to you?" ¶ He replied, "Can you speak Greek?

And as Paul was to be led into the castle, he said unto the chief captain, May I speak unto thee? Who (the tribune) said, Canst thou speak Greek?

This is the fort where Herod lived for a time. It was more than 100 yards wide and long. It had four towers, each seventy-five feet high. Inside was a small city with a parade route around called Gabbatha. This is where the mob stood when Jesus was brought before Pilate.

The tribune does not know Paul is an aristocrat. He had been beaten and looks like a common criminal. When Paul speaks aristocratic Greek, it surprises the soldier.

21:38 Are you not the Egyptian who some time ago stirred up a rebellion and led the four thousand assassins out into the wilderness?"

Art not thou that Egyptian, which before these days madest an uproar (revolution), and leddest out into the wilderness (desert) four thousand men (his syndicate organization) that were murderers (*sikarios*: assassin)?

Paul appears to be a common criminal, and the officer thinks he is an Egyptian crime figure of a syndicate called the *Sikari*, the name taken from their weapon of choice, a dagger called a *sikari*. This leader was from Egypt and had baffled Roman law for some time. In 54 AD, this gangster had organized a revolution by calling himself a prophet and swaying many of the Jews to follow him. He had actually been hired by Jewish leaders to draw followers against the government and had managed to arouse 30,000 people in Jerusalem to revolt and overthrow Rome. The Romans had attacked the mob, killed 400, and taken many prisoners. But the Egyptian criminal escaped with 4000 men into the Negev and operated from there for the next forty years. They were still in operation when Rome destroyed Jerusalem in 70 AD.

Once the officer discovers Paul is not this Egyptian criminal, he gives him great protection.

21:39 ¶But Paul said, "I am a Jew from Tarsus, in Cilicia, a citizen of no mean city; and I implore you, permit me to speak to the people."

But Paul said, I am a man which am a Jew of Tarsus, a city in Cilicia, a citizen of no mean (insignificant) city: and, I beseech thee, suffer (allow) me to speak unto the people.

Paul is telling him, "I'm not an Egyptian. I am from Tarsus."

Tarsus has been made a free city by Rome. It has a mountain range nearby called the Tarsus range, which had one pass running through it called the Cilician Gates. Alexander used it in his conquests. The pass runs into Cilicia where Tarsus is located. Tarsus is a university city, which immediately explains Paul's education to the officer. Since Tarsus is a free city, they are considered Roman citizens. Paul was born a Roman citizen. He is submissive to the Roman leader and asks for permission to speak.

This leader (Claudius Lucius [23:26]), born an aristocrat who purchased his citizenship, represents all that is great in Rome. Felix, the leader in Caesarea, will later represent all that is rotten.

21:40 ¶ So when he had given him permission, Paul stood on the stairs and motioned with his hand to the people. And when there was a great silence, he spoke to *them* in the Hebrew language, saying,

Paul is now speaking under the protection of the Roman Empire. He will use this protection to teach the Jews and give his testimony.

22:1–30 Paul's Defense Before the Sanhedrin

The Challenge of Chapter Twenty-Two

Sometimes there is a tendency to equate spirituality and effectiveness in ministry with the degree of visibility we have before men. However, God equates our success with the degree of our willing obedience to His Word and the Holy Spirit. Ananias who had heard of Saul's reputation for persecuting and killing Christians, still chose to obey God's direction rather than disobey because of fear of who Saul had been.

We must endeavor to have hearts willing to obey God by the direction of the Holy Spirit even if His guidance is contrary to our own human reasoning.

I. Beginning of Paul's Defense (1–3)

Paul begins his defense speaking in Hebrew, explaining he is a Jew born in Tarsus, educated as a Jew, and taught and zealous for the law.

22:1 "Brethren and fathers, hear my defense before you now."

This is the same opening Stephen used in 7:2 to address the Jews. "Brethren" refers to physical Jews, not just believers. "Fathers" refers to Jewish religious leaders, those encouraging and leading the mob.

22:2 And when they heard that he spoke to them in the Hebrew language, they kept all the more silent. ¶ Then he said:

"The more silence" means for the moment they had a desire to hear him. In 21:40 they were silent because they felt a necessity. Now they actually want to hear Paul. These few words in their dialect turn a mob into an audience. This will all end in verse 22 as Paul tells them of his call to the Gentiles.

A. Paul's Credentials

22:3 "I am indeed a Jew, born in Tarsus of Cilicia, but brought up in this city at the feet of Gamaliel, taught according to the strictness of our fathers' law, and was zealous toward God as you all are today.

I am verily a man which am a Jew, born in Tarsus, a city in Cilicia, yet brought up (raised) in this city at the feet of Gamaliel, and taught (trained) according to the perfect (accurate) manner of the law of the fathers, and was zealous toward (for) God, as ye all are this day.

Paul uses his own testimony as a Jew and a believer. He comes from a famous university town and was educated in the Jewish religion under the best known teacher of that day.

His purpose in starting this way is to pique their interest. If Paul was born and educated a Jew, there must be some reason why he changed. Paul had clearly been taught the law and its content. Paul had been religiously zealous, legalistic for God and for the law. He had known the law but not its revelation and application. These people are willing to kill for the Jewish law and tradition.

Paul is pointing out that he had been the same as these other Jews, no better. He is not being arrogant, but has been chosen and used by God. God chooses ordinary people.

Satan also uses ordinary believers, as he is using these born-again but religious Jewish leaders.

B. Enemy's weapons in an Ordinary Life (Proverbs 27:1–6)
- Pride (vv. 1–2): To boast in yourself
- Wrath (vv. 3–4): Explosive temper
- Anger (vv. 3–4): Progressive hostility
- Facades of love (vv. 5–6): Expressions of love covering hate

II. Paul's Testimony of the Road to Damascus (4–11)

Paul tells of his conversion on the road to Damascus. He explains he once persecuted and put to death those who followed "the way." He continues by explaining that he was on his way to Damascus to arrest Christians and bring them back to Jerusalem to be punished, a light shone from heaven, and he heard a voice cry out to him. After being blinded by the light, Paul explains how he was led into Damascus by those traveling with him.

> **22:4–11 I persecuted this Way to the death, binding and delivering into prisons both men and women, 5 as also the high priest bears me witness, and all the council of the elders, from whom I also received letters to the brethren, and went to Damascus**

to bring in chains even those who were there to Jerusalem to be punished.

6 ¶ "Now it happened, as I journeyed and came near Damascus at about noon, suddenly a great light from heaven shone around me. 7 And I fell to the ground and heard a voice saying to me, 'Saul, Saul, why are you persecuting Me?' 8 So I answered, 'Who are You, Lord?' And He said to me, 'I am Jesus of Nazareth, whom you are persecuting.'

9 ¶ "And those who were with me indeed saw the light and were afraid, but they did not hear the voice of Him who spoke to me. 10 So I said, 'What shall I do, Lord?' And the Lord said to me, 'Arise and go into Damascus, and there you will be told all things which are appointed for you to do.' 11 And since I could not see for the glory of that light, being led by the hand of those who were with me, I came into Damascus.

Paul explains to those listening how, at one time, he was zealous against the Christians, throwing both men and women in prison and even killing some with his persecution, as was the case with Stephen. He continues by explaining how he was on his way to Damascus to bring prisoners involved in "the way" to Jerusalem to be punished. On the way, a supernatural light shone from heaven and he heard a voice instructing him to continue to Damascus. Paul tells them how he was blinded by the light and had to be led by his hand into Damascus with his traveling companions.

III. Ananias (12–16)

An ordinary believer named Ananias receives a word from God for Saul and explains to Saul that he has been chosen by God. He also encourages Saul to call upon the name of the Lord to be saved.

A. The Obedience of Ananias

Ananias received a word from God and in response, he helped Paul. He was an ordinary believer who knew the Word of God, which should be an encouragement to all believers who are diligent in the Word. Ananias's actions in helping Paul had a worldwide impact. Full-time Christian service is not just for those in fivefold ministry; it is for all believers.

22:12 ¶ "Then a certain Ananias, a devout man according to the law, having a good testimony with all the Jews who dwelt *there*,

Ananias studied and obeyed the law. He was favored by God and men.

22:13 came to me; and he stood and said to me, 'Brother Saul, receive your sight.' And at that same hour I looked up at him.

Came unto me, and stood, and said unto me, Brother Saul, receive thy sight (*anablepo*: look up, receive sight). And the same hour I looked up upon him.

Ananias knew from God that Paul was born again. He was used by God for Paul to receive a miracle. But that is not all.

B. The Result of Ananias's Obedience

22:14 Then he said, 'The God of our fathers has chosen you that you should know His will, and see the Just One, and hear the voice of His mouth.

And he said, The God of our fathers hath chosen (*procheirizomai*: to take by the hand before time; preappointed) thee, that thou shouldest know his will, and see (*eido*: view, know, perceive) that Just One, and shouldest hear the voice of his mouth.

Because of Ananias's obedience, not only did Paul receive his sight, Paul also received three areas of revelation:
1. Knowing God's Will: Preaching the gospel to the Gentiles (20:24, 26:17)
2. Seeing Jesus: Appearances to Paul (Acts 9:3–6, 23:11, Galatians 1:12)
3. Knowing the Revelation of the New Testament (Ephesians 3:2–7, Colossians 1:25–27).

22:15 For you will be His witness to all men of what you have seen and heard.

You cannot be an effective witness (v. 15) without revelation (v. 14). Part of Paul's witness was his testimony. He will also give this again in chapter 27.

22:16 And now why are you waiting? Arise and be baptized, and wash away your sins, calling on the name of the Lord.'

This verse is poorly translated. The action of the aorist participle precedes the action of the main verb. The aorist participle is "calling on the name of the Lord" (Romans 10:13), being saved. The main verb is "wash away." Sins are washed away by calling on the name of the Lord. Ananias told Paul to quit delaying and head for the water to be baptized. His sins would be washed away by calling on the name of the Lord.

IV. God Prepares Paul for Ministry in Arabia (17–18)

Paul shares about Jesus appearing to him in a trance and telling him to leave Jerusalem quickly.

> **22:17 ¶ "Now it happened, when I returned to Jerusalem and was praying in the temple, that I was in a trance**

And it came to pass, that, when I was come again to Jerusalem, even while I prayed in the temple, I was in a trance (*ekstasis*: ecstatic, astonishment);

Paul skips over much time in his testimony and brings up the supernatural, his experience of being in a trance.

> **22:18 and saw Him saying to me, 'Make haste and get out of Jerusalem quickly, for they will not receive your testimony concerning Me.'**

And saw him (Jesus) saying unto me, Make haste, and get thee quickly out of Jerusalem: for they (legalistic believers) will not receive thy testimony concerning me.

Paul informs them that Jesus had previously told him in a trance that they would not listen to him.

V. Paul's Defense to the People (19–21)

Paul continues explaining how the Lord has instructed him to leave Jerusalem to take the gospel to the Gentiles.

> **22:19 So I said, 'Lord, they know that in every synagogue I imprisoned and beat those who believe on You. 20 And when the blood of Your martyr Stephen was shed, I also was standing by consenting to his death, and guarding the clothes of those who were killing him.'**

"Lord, they know I've been on both sides of the fence." Paul is rationalizing and arguing with the Lord to stay in Jerusalem. He loves Jerusalem and even argues with the Lord over it.

22:21 Then He said to me, 'Depart, for I will send you far from here to the Gentiles.'"

The Lord said, "Depart." The entire ministry of Paul was "Move, move." At this point, Paul is telling the people that God instructed him to turn his attention from the Jews to the Gentiles, and the mob reacts. Legalism has so perverted their thinking they now react to a racial issue. These same leaders, a few years earlier, were thankful and desirous for Gentiles to be evangelized (Acts 15:13–19, 11:15–18, Galatians 2:9). Now they will throw a temper tantrum. They are beyond repentance, and Paul clearly sees it. This is why God did not want Paul to go to Jerusalem.

VI. Mob Calls for Paul's Life (22–23)

The crowd listens to Paul's testimony and they become enraged at the mention of Gentiles. They want Paul's life.

22:22 ¶ And they listened to him until this word, and *then* they raised their voices and said, "Away with such a *fellow* from the earth, for he is not fit to live!"

The word that sends them into a rage is "Gentiles." They now want to kill Paul. They are calling for capital punishment. They are pressuring the Romans for the full extent of the law.

22:23 Then, as they cried out and tore off *their* clothes and threw dust into the air,

They cannot get to Paul, so they vent their anger by throwing temper tantrums. They are typical of legalistic people who hear the truth of grace. When Paul tells them grace is available to all (Romans 4:16, Titus 2:11), including the Gentiles, they begin to scream.

VII. Paul Is Scourged (24–25)

The Roman chief captain commands Paul be taken into the fortress and scourged.

22:24 the commander ordered him to be brought into the barracks, and said that he should be examined under scourging, so that he might know why they shouted so against him.

Paul looks and talks like a Jew, and the officer has no reason to assume he is a Roman. Non-Roman citizens are beaten, but it is illegal to beat a Roman citizen. (This is the Roman system of law called *Lex*. *Lex* is the plural of *Leges*, where we get "legislature," a body of people making laws.)

The officer thinks Paul must be hiding something to cause such a riot and gives an ordinary command to pull this information from him. The military beats a man then question him. If he still does not speak, he is beaten again until he gives an answer or dies.

22:25 And as they bound him with thongs, Paul said to the centurion who stood by, "Is it lawful for you to scourge a man who is a Roman, and uncondemned?"

And as they bound him with thongs (for the leather straps), Paul said unto the centurion that stood by, Is it lawful for you to scourge a man that is a Roman (citizen), and uncondemned?

The chief captain has left and turns Paul over to a centurion. This scourging is an illegal act and could get the whole platoon court-martialed.

VIII. Paul's Roman Citizenship Realized (26–30)

The centurion hears Paul say he is a Roman citizen, and the chief captain fears upon hearing this because they have bound and thrown Paul in prison without following lawful procedures. The chief captain brings Paul before his accusers to learn what he is being accused of by the mob.

22:26 ¶ When the centurion heard *that*, he went and told the commander, saying, "Take care what you do, for this man is a Roman."

This man cares for his commander and wants law to be administered correctly.

22:27–28 ¶ Then the commander came and said to him, "Tell me, are you a Roman?" ¶ He said, "Yes." 28 ¶ The commander

answered, "With a large sum I obtained this citizenship." ¶ And
Paul said, "But I was born *a citizen*."

Then the chief captain came, and said unto him, Tell me, art thou a Roman?
He said, Yea. And the chief captain answered, With a great sum obtained I
this freedom (*politeia*: politics, citizenship, commonwealth). And Paul said,
But I was free born.

This captain was not born a Roman citizen; he was a different nationality
and had paid for his Roman citizenship papers. But Paul's family are well-
known Roman citizens, and Paul is a citizen by birth. Paul is also from Tarsus
(a free Roman city). Because of this citizenship, Paul's nephew will later
have easy access to visit Paul and warn him of an assassination attempt
(23:16). Paul will also have free access to speak with the Roman dignitaries
Felix and Agrippa.

**22:29 ¶ Then immediately those who were about to examine
him withdrew from him; and the commander was also afraid
after he found out that he was a Roman, and because he had
bound him.**

The Roman leader is in a dilemma. He has the mob on one side and a Roman citizen on the other. He has to retreat to think the situation through.

**22:30 ¶ The next day, because he wanted to know for certain why
he was accused by the Jews, he released him from *his* bonds, and
commanded the chief priests and all their council to appear,
and brought Paul down and set him before them.**

Roman law is without religious prejudice. This man needs facts. To get to
the bottom of things, he brings the accusers to the accused. This man will
spot the religious prejudice during the interrogation, and Judaism will have
a setback as Paul is rescued from the courtroom.

23:1-35 The Conspiracy Against Paul

The Challenge of Chapter Twenty-Three

God has a plan and purpose for each one of our lives. He has specific people he intends our lives to reach with the gospel message. Just as Joseph was sold into slavery, Daniel thrown into the lion's den, and Paul taken prisoner, yet each fulfilled God's plan. The adversities we face in life cannot stop God's ultimate plan and purpose for our lives.

I. Dissension Between the Pharisees and Sadducees (1–10)

Paul addresses the council in an attempt to defend himself. Ananias, the high priest, commands that Paul be struck in the mouth, which is illegal. This angers Paul, and he challenges the high priest without realizing the office the man holds. When Paul is informed that Ananias is the high priest, he immediately becomes submissive to the office in which Ananias stands. At the same time, Paul perceives that both Sadducees and Pharisees are present. He cries out that he is a Pharisee who believes in the resurrection knowing this will cause a stir between the Pharisees and Sadducees in the room. The Pharisees in the crowd suddenly want Paul acquitted and the Roman captain who is standing at the back of the room recognizes Paul's innocence. He then commands his soldiers to take Paul by force and take him into the fort.

A. Paul Stuck

23:1 Then Paul, looking earnestly at the council, said, "Men *and* brethren, I have lived in all good conscience before God until this day."

And Paul, earnestly beholding (eye to eye) the council (Sanhedrin), said, Men and brethren, I have lived (*politeuomai*: been a citizen [politics]) in all good conscience before God until this day.

The Jewish council is comprised of the lawmakers and supreme court of the land. Jewish law is excellent but has been corrupted by religion. The lawmakers are also the religious leaders and are religiously prejudice. Paul tries to defend himself by Jewish law, but is immediately met with their prejudice. It will be Roman law that will save him again. Paul thinks these men represent Jewish law, not religion. Paul has broken no civil law and begins by telling of his innocence as a free citizen.

23:2 And the high priest Ananias commanded those who stood by him to strike him on the mouth.

And the high priest Ananias commanded them that stood by him (officers, bailiffs) to smite (beat) him on the mouth.

This is illegal. They cannot legally sentence and execute punishment in the courtroom. This was done with Jesus (Matthew 26:67) and was also illegal (Leviticus 19:35, Deuteronomy 25:1, John 7:51). Paul knows Jewish law, and this shocks Ananias. Paul loses his temper.

23:3 Then Paul said to him, "God will strike you, *you* white-washed wall! For you sit to judge me according to the law, and do you command me to be struck contrary to the law?"

Paul charges, "You gave a command to smite me, and God will smite you! God gave you the law you are using to try me, and you are abusing it." Paul calls the judge a whitewashed wall. Whitewash was used to hide stains. This man is using his office to cover corruption and prejudice. This is a term for being a hypocrite (Matthew 23:27).

No one has ever called the chief priest a phony, a hypocrite. A judge is supposed to presume a person innocent until proof has been presented to confirm or contradict this ruling. This judge has already passed a sentence without evidence.

23:4 ¶ And those who stood by said, "Do you revile God's high priest?"

This is a shock to Paul. He now realizes how corrupt the Jews have become. This man represents the highest office a man can have in the nation of Israel. This man is ordering the corruption of the law. Paul knows that God demands respect for the office even though it may be filled by a corrupted and evil person (Romans 13:1–7, 1 Peter 2:13–17).

23:5 ¶ Then Paul said, "I did not know, brethren, that he was the high priest; for it is written, 'You shall not speak evil of a ruler of your people.'"

Then said Paul, I wist (knew) not, brethren, that he was the high priest: for it is written (Exodus 22:28), Thou shalt not speak evil of the ruler of thy people.

Paul understands where he now stands and who he spoke against. The word of God comes into the scene now. Paul will be submissive and respectful of the office although the man Ananias is corrupt. This also occurred to the disciples in 5:27–42. They respected the office, but disobeyed their commands against preaching the Word of God.

23:6 ⸿ But when Paul perceived that one part were Sadducees and the other Pharisees, he cried out in the council, "Men *and* brethren, I am a Pharisee, the son of a Pharisee; concerning the hope and resurrection of the dead I am being judged!"

But when Paul perceived that the one part were Sadducees, and the other Pharisees, he cried out in the council, Men and brethren, I am a Pharisee, the son of a Pharisee: of (concerning) the hope and resurrection of the dead I am called in question (*krino*: judge, decree, determine).

B. Dissension Over the Resurrection

23:7 And when he had said this, a dissension arose between the Pharisees and the Sadducees; and the assembly was divided.

And when he had so said, there arose a dissension (*stativ*: static, uproar, uprising) between the Pharisees and the Sadducees: and the multitude was divided (*schizo*: schizophrenia, split).

This one phrase hit the major area of disagreement between the two sides: the resurrection of the dead.

23:8 For Sadducees say that there is no resurrection—and no angel or spirit; but the Pharisees confess both.

For the Sadducees say that there is no resurrection, neither angel, nor spirit: but the Pharisees confess (*homologeo*: acknowledge) both.

The Sadducees do not believe in the supernatural. They are rationalists (Matthew 22:23–32) and dismiss the spirit world and its existence. The

Pharisees are the scholars who pour over the letters of the Word of God. They are legalistic about salvation and spirituality and thus reject Jesus for righteousness. But they do believe in the future resurrection of the dead and the past resurrections recorded in the Old Testament.

> **23:9 Then there arose a loud outcry. And the scribes of the Pharisees' party arose and protested, saying, "We find no evil in this man; but if a spirit or an angel has spoken to him, let us not fight against God."**

The Pharisees are the great students of the Mosaic Law and Old Testament prophets. It is no longer Paul on trial, but the Pharisees and their doctrine. They are now fighting to protect one of their own. They even change their charge against Paul from guilty to innocent. They wanted to kill Paul earlier and now they have acquitted Paul without a trial since they have found him to be a Pharisee. They even go on to admit that condemning Paul is fighting against God. God taught Paul. Angels can also teach. In the Old Testament, many prophets were taught by angels.

> **23:10 ¶ Now when there arose a great dissension, the commander, fearing lest Paul might be pulled to pieces by them, commanded the soldiers to go down and take him by force from among them, and bring *him* into the barracks.**

The Romans are standing in the back of the courtroom, observing this mockery of justice. Now the Sadducees probably hate Paul even more for using his background to divide the courtroom. The Roman captain sees Paul is innocent and is now required to protect him. Paul is taken away by the Romans and left alone.

Paul now becomes very discouraged. His ministry is stopped, and he is fighting for his life. After this mockery of justice, he realizes how far the Jews have degenerated. He also realizes what a great mistake he has made and the arrogance with which he has been involved.

II. The Lord Jesus Encourages Paul (11–16)

Paul becomes discouraged, and the next night Jesus appears to him and tells him he will share the gospel in Rome. A group of Jews join together and express their determination to kill Paul. This group of more than forty, ask the Sanhedrin to call for Paul as if they need to question him more, but instead they plan to kill him.

A. Paul Is Discouraged

23:11 ¶ But the following night the Lord stood by him and said, "Be of good cheer, Paul; for as you have testified for Me in Jerusalem, so you must also bear witness at Rome."

And the night following the Lord (Jesus) stood by him, and said, Be of good cheer, Paul: for as thou hast testified (*diamartureomai*: stood up, witnessed) of (concerning) me in Jerusalem, so must thou bear witness (*martureo*: speak out for me) also at Rome.

Jesus encourages Paul: "Be of good cheer! Don't be discouraged!" Why was Paul discouraged?

1. He missed God's will because of his personal legalism.

2. He is frustrated by his lack of progress in Jerusalem.

3. He is being kept alive by the Roman military, yet they are also detaining him.

Jesus now appears in a vision to encourage Paul. This is the third time Paul has been encouraged by a vision from the Lord (16:9, 18:9–10). In prison, Paul begins to condemn himself. He is probably feeling as if God can never use him again and about how he has let down so many believers who tried to warn him. He also realizes how he has compromised his ministry by taking the vow in Jerusalem and offering a sacrifice before the multitudes. In this situation, he asks God to forgive him and Jesus appears to him in the prison. Paul will now get his eyes back on the Lord.

Discouragement comes when we get our eyes off the Lord and on to ourselves or others around us (Hebrews 12:3–4). This is a great hazard in ministry. The Lord is telling Paul to get his eyes back on Him. Jesus told Paul that he has stood in Jerusalem but will speak in Rome. God's will from the beginning was for Paul to preach in Rome, but Paul's desire was to preach in Jerusalem. Jerusalem hates Paul. Believers had an all night prayer meeting for Peter in prison (12:5), but not one prayer is going up for Paul while in Jerusalem. He is hated by the saints in Jerusalem.

He will now go to Rome and will speak and write to the churches of Ephesus, Colosse, and Philippi. Paul is in doubt at this point about his future in the ministry. In this verse, Paul's colossal mistakes have come to a head and he is in maximum discouragement. The Lord tells him to be encouraged. At this point, when Paul is at his weakest, God is at his strongest.

B. Jews Are Determined to Kill Paul

23:12 ¶ And when it was day, some of the Jews banded together and bound themselves under an oath, saying that they would neither eat nor drink till they had killed Paul.

These Jews are taking a vow. Either they gave up on their vow after many days or they died of starvation because Paul lived for many more years. These were religious unbelievers. Paul has been encouraged during the night, and Satan is out to destroy him through these men. The Jews have taken a vow to kill Paul in order to make a name for themselves. Again, Paul's greatest opposition came from religion. Legalism always persecutes grace. These men made this vow out of emotion like many Christians do today who "present their bodies," or "surrender to full-time service." Unless God deals with you, you will either break the vow or live outside God's will for a long time.

23:13–14 Now there were more than forty who had formed this conspiracy. 14 They came to the chief priests and elders, and said, "We have bound ourselves under a great oath that we will eat nothing until we have killed Paul.

This is a new, young, and zealous crowd going to the old religious leaders.

23:15 Now you, therefore, together with the council, suggest to the commander that he be brought down to you tomorrow, as though you were going to make further inquiries concerning him; but we are ready to kill him before he comes near."

Now therefore ye with the council (Sanhedrin) signify to the chief captain that he bring him (Paul) down unto you to morrow, as though ye would enquire something more perfectly (accurately) concerning him: and we, or ever (if) he come near, are ready to kill him.

They are asking the Sanhedrin to act as if they need Paul for further questioning and clarification of his testimony. When he is brought down by the Romans this group of young Jews plans to kill him. This is a trap being set for Paul.

C. Paul Is Informed of a Conspiracy

23:16 ¶ So when Paul's sister's son heard of their ambush, he went and entered the barracks and told Paul.

Apparently Paul's nephew was at the meeting or had connections through someone who was born again where he learned of the conspiracy against Paul. Many times Paul has known of danger in his own spirit (9:24, 20:3), but this time God uses natural circumstances.

III. Paul's Nephew Is Taken to the Chief Captain (17–22)

Paul calls one of the guards and asks him to take his nephew to the chief captain. Paul's nephew is taken before the chief captain and reveals the plot of the Jews to kill Paul.

> **23:17 Then Paul called one of the centurions to *him* and said, "Take this young man to the commander, for he has something to tell him."**

Then Paul called one of the centurions (a guard) unto him, and said, Bring this young man unto the chief captain (*chiliarcho*: commander of a thousand soldiers [21:31]): for he hath a certain thing to tell him.

> **23:18 So he took him and brought *him* to the commander and said, "Paul the prisoner called me to *him* and asked *me* to bring this young man to you. He has something to say to you."**

Paul's nephew tells the chief captain of the assassination plot. The captain represents all that is great in Rome. He handles this by law and order, not personal ambition.

> **23:19–22 ¶ Then the commander took him by the hand, went aside, and asked privately, "What is it that you have to tell me?" 20 ¶ And he said, "The Jews have agreed to ask that you bring Paul down to the council tomorrow, as though they were going to inquire more fully about him. 21 But do not yield to them, for more than forty of them lie in wait for him, men who have bound themselves by an oath that they will neither eat nor drink till they have killed him; and now they are ready, waiting for the promise from you." 22 ¶ So the commander let the young man depart, and commanded *him*, "Tell no one that you have revealed these things to me."**

The guard kept the whole event secret for Paul's protection because Paul was a Roman citizen.

IV. The Captain's Plan (23–24)

The captain calls two centurions and instructs them to gather 470 military men ready to protect Paul as they deliver him to Caesarea to stand before Felix, the governor.

> **23:23 ¶ And he called for two centurions, saying, "Prepare two hundred soldiers, seventy horsemen, and two hundred spearmen to go to Caesarea at the third hour of the night;**

The captain's plan to take Paul safely to Caesarea included 200 infantry, 70 cavalry, and 200 armed guards (470 total for Paul's protection). They will escort Paul at the third hour of the night (9:00 p.m.). Two centurions are sent, one for the infantry and one for the cavalry and armed guards. The armed guards and infantry lead Paul past the point of greatest danger. The cavalry takes Paul the rest of the way into Caesarea (v. 31, 32).

> **23:24 and provide mounts to set Paul on, and bring *him* safely to Felix the governor."**

They provide an animal for Paul to ride to arrive safely to meet Felix, the governor. This is only a sixty-mile ride, but Paul must be bound safely for trials because he is innocent until proven guilty.

At this time, Caesarea is run by Felix. At one time, he had been a slave, and though he rose in the Roman government, Felix still thought like a slave and corrupts the government throughout the reign of Claudius and Nero. He is money-mad and would take a bribe from Paul to free him, but Paul will appeal to Caesar.

V. A Letter to Felix (25–35)

The chief captain writes a letter to Felix explaining the events surrounding Paul's arrest and his reason for delivering Paul to him. Both the letter and Paul are safely delivered to Felix.

> **23:25–31 He wrote a letter in the following manner: 26 ¶ Claudius Lysias, ¶ To the most excellent governor Felix: ¶ Greetings. 27 This man was seized by the Jews and was about to be killed by**

them. Coming with the troops I rescued him, having learned that he was a Roman. 28 And when I wanted to know the reason they accused him, I brought him before their council. 29 I found out that he was accused concerning questions of their law, but had nothing charged against him deserving of death or chains. 30 And when it was told me that the Jews lay in wait for the man, I sent him immediately to you, and also commanded his accusers to state before you the charges against him. ¶ Farewell. 31 ¶ Then the soldiers, as they were commanded, took Paul and brought *him* by night to Antipatris.

Paul and the troops spend the first night in Antipatris, a city named for Herod's father Antipater.

23:32–34 The next day they left the horsemen to go on with him, and returned to the barracks. 33 When they came to Caesarea and had delivered the letter to the governor, they also presented Paul to him. 34 And when the governor had read *it*, he asked what province he was from. And when he understood that *he was* from Cilicia,

When Felix first meets Paul, he asks him where he is from. This is an attempt at getting a bribe. If Paul comes from a rich area, he will have the ability to pay a large sum of money to Felix for his freedom. When Felix learns of Paul's aristocratic background, he mentions bringing the accusers to incite fear in Paul to possibly get even more money from him.

23:35 he said, "I will hear you when your accusers also have come." And he commanded him to be kept in Herod's Praetorium.

24:1–27 Paul Before Felix

The Challenge of Chapter Twenty-Four

Even while Paul's fate is in the hands of his captors, he is not intimidated and shares his faith with any who will listen. Our responsibility is not to force people to accept Jesus Christ as Lord and Savior, but to preach the gospel whenever the opportunity presents itself. In a world where there are no absolute "rights" and "wrongs," where acceptable lifestyles contrary to God's Word are promoted, we must not shrink back from sharing the gospel message.

I. Persecution and the Players

Satan and religion will always bring persecution against those who study and live the Word of God in their daily lives. Paul recounts some of the opposition he has encountered in his walk with God.

Moses had the greatest message of the Old Testament, and just as he is the standard of the law and prophets, Paul is the standard of the New Testament. Both of these men had opposition from religion. Moses had opposition from two magicians in Pharaoh's court, leaders of the Egyptian religion. Paul is also withstood by two religious believers, Phygellus and Hermogenus (2 Timothy 1:15).

A. Resistance of Religion

> 7 always learning and never able to come to the knowledge of the truth. 8 Now as Jannes and Jambres resisted Moses, so do these also resist the truth: men of corrupt minds, disapproved concerning the faith; 9 but they will progress no further, for their folly will be manifest to all, as theirs also was. The Man of God and the Word of God 10 But you have carefully followed my doctrine, manner of life, purpose, faith, longsuffering, love, perseverance, 11 persecutions, afflictions, which happened to me at Antioch, at Iconium, at Lystra—what persecutions I endured. And out of them all the Lord delivered me. 12 Yes, and all who desire to live godly in Christ Jesus will suffer persecution. —2 Timothy 3:7–12

v. 7 Ever learning, and never able to come to the knowledge (*epignosis*) of the truth. . .

This passage from 2 Timothy gives a good description of religious people. They continually learn but never discover the truth.

v. 8 Now as Jannes and Jambres withstood (opposed) Moses, so do these also resist the truth: men of corrupt minds, reprobate concerning the faith (the Word). . . .

The story of Jannes and Jambres is recorded in Exodus 7 and 8. Their names are not given, but the Holy Spirit reveals them here. Religion always opposes grace. These people do not resist the person, but the truth, the Word of God. They came to a point where they could not and would not receive the truth. This is the point the Jews have come to in Jerusalem. Paul is being held by those whose minds have reached corruption and attitudes are reprobate. They can tell others what to do, but cannot do it themselves (1 Corinthians 9:27, 2 Corinthians 13:5, Galatians 6:13).

v. 9 But they shall proceed (advance) no further: for their folly (*anoia*: madness, insanity) shall be manifest (evident) unto all men, as theirs (Jannes and Jambres) also was.

Jerusalem's religious opposition will be brought into the light before believers and unbelievers alike. Their madness will be displayed, just as the opposition of Pharaoh's court was displayed to the whole world at the Red Sea. His madness is part of recorded history. Paul will list seven areas in verses 10 and 11, which Timothy has followed in Paul's ministry.

vv. 10–11; But thou hast fully known (*parakoloutheo*: followed closely, have understanding) my doctrine (teaching), manner of life (instruction by example), purpose (goals in the ministry), faith (lifestyle of faith), longsuffering (endurance), charity (*agape*: love, this is what makes everything else work in the Christian life), patience (steadfast during trials), ¹¹ Persecutions (*diagmos*: opposition by religion), afflictions (sufferings, beatings, attempted assassinations, stoning), which came unto me at Antioch, at Iconium, at Lystra; what persecutions I endured (stood up under): but out of them all the Lord delivered me. . . .

God is faithful to deliver us from all opposition (Psalm 34:19).

v. 12; Yea (furthermore), and all that will live godly in Christ Jesus shall suffer persecution.

You cannot study and live the Word of God without opposition coming from Satan. When you live the Word and become a doer of each promise, you become a primary target for Satan. Sickness, disease, and poverty are not mentioned. This opposition is from religious, legalistic people who oppose grace. Trouble comes from those who judge your food, clothes, personal life and actions.

B. Main Characters

In Acts 24 through 26, Paul will appear before several of the most prominent government figures in the Roman Empire: Felix, Festus, and Agrippa. These three chapters form one trial before three judges during two years in prison in Caesarea.

The ruler of Rome at this time is Claudius. He does not trust the aristocracy or senate of Rome and puts three former slaves in power, Felix, Narcissus, and Pallas. Felix and Pallas are brothers. Narcissus is running much of Rome with Pallas who is the lover of Claudius' wife. Claudius had two wives, Messalina was the first. She was famous for her promiscuity. She had a son by Claudius named Britannicus who never came to power. Because of her unfaithfulness, Claudius ordered her execution. He then married Agrippina who had a son by a previous marriage named Lucius Domitius Ahenobarbus, nicknamed Nero. Nero was named heir over Britannicus. At that time Agrippina poisoned Claudius putting Nero in power. Pallas was having an affair with Agrippina.

When Felix came to power in Palestine, he met Herod's granddaughter, Drusilla, and fell in love with her. He persuaded her to run away with him and leave her husband. This offended the Jews and Arabs of Palestine because she was Jewish and Idumaean.

Drusilla had a sister, Bernice, of whom she ws jealous. Bernice was one of the most beautiful women in the ancient world. Drusilla and her son, Antonius Agrippa, died in the eruption of Mount Vesuvius in Pompeii.

Herod Agrippa I, the grandson of Herod, the brother of Drusilla and Bernice, is now in power and will also hear Paul. Paul will give the gospel to all of these rulers and their wives.

II. Paul Brought Before Tertullus (1)

Five days after being brought to Caesarea, a Roman lawyer named Tertullus informs the governor against Paul.

24:1 ¶Now after five days Ananias the high priest came down with the elders and a certain orator *named* Tertullus. These gave evidence to the governor against Paul.

And after five days Ananias the high priest descended (Jerusalem to Caesarea) with the elders (leaders of the Sanhedrin), and with a certain orator
named Tertullus (an eloquent lawyer), who informed the governor against
Paul.

The Sanhedrin is attempting to find some way to release the forty men
from their starvation vow and now hires a famous lawyer in an attempt to
have Paul turned back over to the Jews. Tertullus is a Roman attorney. Even
though the Jews hate the Romans, they will hire one to get to Paul. Religion
hates grace even more than dictatorships. The Sanhedrin only sends Sadducees to bring Paul back because of the resurrection question Paul used in
Acts 23, verses 6 through 9. Paul will again mention the resurrection while
he stands before Felix, in verses 15 and 21.

All of this is accomplished by the Sanhedrin during the five days after Paul
has been delivered to Caesarea. Ananias has been appointed high priest
by the former procurator of Judea, Titus. He does not believe in God, but
is strongly influential with the Romans. The Jews are upset with Titus for
doing this, but now find it to their advantage. Felix is put in a position over
this third class province for stealing from the Romans. He loves money and
will later try to take a bribe from Paul for his freedom (v. 26).

III. Tertullus Accuses Paul (2–9)

Tertullus accuses Paul of disturbing the peace by leading a faction against
the Jews that would come against Rome. He accuses Paul of dividing a nation that supports Rome. However, Paul is not the leader of a subversive
organization. The evil organization is the one trying to get rid of him. The
last act will be profaning the temple. Tertullus is also commending Felix for
performing worthy deeds. This is not the truth because during this time
Felix is extorting money from the people to add to his own fortune. He did
this in Rome and is doing the same thing in Judea.

> 24:2-3 ¶ And when he was called upon, Tertullus began his
> accusation, saying: "Seeing that through you we enjoy great
> peace, and prosperity is being brought to this nation by your
> foresight, ³ we accept *it* always and in all places, most noble
> Felix, with all thankfulness.

This is all flattery and lies.

24:4 Nevertheless, not to be tedious to you any further, I beg you to hear, by your courtesy, a few words from us.

In other words, "I could go on and on about your greatness, but give me just enough time for a few words."

24:5 For we have found this man a plague, a creator of dissension among all the Jews throughout the world, and a ringleader of the sect of the Nazarenes.

For we have found this man (Paul) a pestilent fellow (a plague), and a mover of sedition (causer of riots) among all the Jews throughout the world, and a ringleader of the sect of the Nazarenes:

Paul is being called subversive and a ringleader of a group to overthrow the Jewish government. He is also accused of causing race riots. Felix does not know what a Nazarene is, but the lawyer is making this as full of intrigue as possible.

24:6 He even tried to profane the temple, and we seized him, and wanted to judge him according to our law.

By profaning the temple, he broke both Jewish and Roman law. Rome protected the temple. If the Jews thought it was holy, then it was important to Roman peace to protect it. Profaning the temple meant Paul was stealing from it. This is designed to anger Felix because he too is stealing from the Jewish treasuries and does not need competition.

The remainder of verse 6 and all of verse 7 is not found in the original, but does add to the story. Felix is sitting before the man who holds the answer to his personal problems and those of the Roman Empire. Rome is on the verge of civil war and Paul has the answers: the gospel, the new birth, and the Word of God.

24:7–8 But the commander Lysias came by and with great violence took *him* out of our hands, 8 commanding his accusers to come to you. By examining him yourself you may ascertain all these things of which we accuse him."

In other words, "If you examine Paul yourself, you will see we are correct."

24:9 And the Jews also assented, maintaining that these things were so.

IV. Paul's Defense to Felix (10–21)

According to Roman law, it is legal for Paul to answer the charges against him. Paul argues that he has been in prison for six of the twelve days since he arrived in Jerusalem. His point is that it would have been impossible for him to arrange a riot in that time frame. Paul claims his innocence, and God's Word will prove him to be truthful. There is no evidence against Paul. Paul states that the only valid accusation against him is his belief in the resurrection.

24:10 ¶ Then Paul, after the governor had nodded to him to speak, answered: "Inasmuch as I know that you have been for many years a judge of this nation, I do the more cheerfully answer for myself,

Tertullus has made a brilliant accusation with no evidence, and Paul will now depend on the Holy Spirit for his words (Luke 12:11–12). Felix still follows Roman law, which allows the defendant to answer. This law had not been implemented with Paul at Philippi (16:19–24). Paul will stay with the facts. He is familiar with Roman law and will not accuse the Jews without facts. He does not flatter with proof and will deny the charges and demand proof. Paul will not attack Felix's weak point (as Tertullus has), but his strong point of Roman justice.

24:11 because you may ascertain that it is no more than twelve days since I went up to Jerusalem to worship.

Felix will never understand spiritually what Paul did, but he understands legally. It has only been twelve days since Paul arrived in Jerusalem and now stands before Felix. He has been in prison for six of those twelve days. It is impossible to organize a riot, lead a revolt, and profane the temple in such a short time. Paul also came to worship and was worshiping when he was attacked by the Jews. You cannot worship and simultaneously profane the temple

24:12 And they neither found me in the temple disputing with anyone nor inciting the crowd, either in the synagogues or in the city.

There are two ways to profane the temple: either to rob it or argue inside of it. Paul states he has not done either one.

24:13 Nor can they prove the things of which they now accuse me.

Paul lays the burden of proof back on the Jews. They had put the burden on Paul in the beginning, now Paul gives it back according to the law. Those who began the entire process were the Jews from Ephesus (21:27–28) who would have been arrested had they shown their faces before the Romans for their lack of legal cause. The witnesses the Jews need have not yet shown up. Paul gives a perfect defense, but will still be detained for two years. He mentions "money" (17), and Felix will keep Paul in an attempt to get a ransom from him (26).

24:14 But this I confess to you, that according to the Way which they call a sect, so I worship the God of my fathers, believing all things which are written in the Law and in the Prophets.

But this I confess (*homologeo*: promise) unto thee, that after the way which they call heresy (*hairesis*: discord, sect), so worship I the God of my fathers, believing all things which are written in the law and in the prophets:

In the early days, Christianity was called "the Way," according to the title Jesus used of Himself (John 14:6). Paul will now show that the Jews are the heretics and are guilty of their own accusations against Paul.

24:15 I have hope in God, which they themselves also accept, that there will be a resurrection of *the* dead, both of *the* just and *the* unjust.

These Jews also accept the scriptures as final authority.

24:16 This *being* so, I myself always strive to have a conscience without offense toward God and men.

Paul says he is innocent and will now prove it. God's Word will vindicate him.

24:17 ¶ "Now after many years I came to bring alms and offerings to my nation,

Paul is not stealing money in Jerusalem as he has been accused of doing; he is bringing money, the Macedonian offering (Romans 15:24–28). Paul states his mission in Jerusalem is to bring money sent from the Macedonian believers to the saints.

When Paul reveals his innocence to Felix, he puts himself in a tough situation. He becomes a "hot potato." If Felix frees him, he will be in trouble with the Jews. If Felix condemns him, he will be in trouble with Rome. There is no evidence to convict Paul. Felix will decide to send Paul through a series of trials simply so someone else will accept the responsibility for Paul. This reveals the weakness of Felix's leadership.

24:18 in the midst of which some Jews from Asia found me purified in the temple, neither with a mob nor with tumult.

Paul is saying, "Not even you, Felix, are over Asia." Paul is keeping Jewish law, not breaking the law. Paul is not in the presence of a large crowd, just four elders (21:23), so he can not have stirred a mob to incite a riot. Paul handles himself in a peaceful manner. In fact, it is the Jews who start the tumult.

24:19 They ought to have been here before you to object if they had anything against me.

Paul asserts, "My accusers who attacked me aren't even here to clarify the case. None of these men were part of the original crime. This is all hearsay." Under Roman law, Paul must have an eyewitness. Because there is no eyewitness to the accusations against Paul, there is no alternative. Paul must be found innocent under the law.

24:20 Or else let those who are *here* themselves say if they found any wrongdoing in me while I stood before the council,

Or else let these (Jewish accusers) same here say, if they have found any evil doing in me, while I stood before the council (Sanhedrin),

These men will not produce a record of the previous trial. They have nothing but accusations against Paul; no evidence, only hatred for him. In the previous trial, the judges ended up arguing among themselves over the resurrection (25:6–7). Claudius Lysias, a Roman, was present and a witness of the entire beating.

24:21 unless *it is* for this one statement which I cried out, standing among them, 'Concerning the resurrection of the dead I am being judged by you this day.'"

Paul is saying, "I am guilty of only one thing. I might be held in contempt of court in defending the resurrection of the dead." Roman law has nothing to say about the resurrection, and, at this point, Felix should have thrown the case out of court.

V. Paul's Trial Comes to an End (22–23)

After Felix hears Paul's defense, Felix places Paul under house arrest and forbids any of Paul's friends or family to visit him. He is held in prison for the next two years.

24:22 ¶ But when Felix heard these things, having more accurate knowledge of *the* Way, he adjourned the proceedings and said, "When Lysias the commander comes down, I will make a decision on your case."

And when Felix heard these things, having more perfect (accurate) knowledge of that way (Christianity), he deferred them (adjourned), and said, When Lysias the chief captain shall come down, I will know the uttermost (full extent) of your matter.

This is what the Jews did not want. Lysias would prove Paul's innocence. However, there is no record of Felix ever sending for Lysias. Felix sees an opportunity to get money from Paul or his friends, and so he illegally holds him for two years on technicalities. This trial ends in a stalemate for Paul, and God will have to work around Felix. Paul continues appealing to higher positions of authority before Roman magistrates.

24:23 So he commanded the centurion to keep Paul and to let him have liberty, and told *him* not to forbid any of his friends to provide for or visit him.

And he commanded a centurion to keep (*tereo*: to guard something which belongs to you, hold fast) Paul, and let him have liberty (minimum confinement under house arrest), and that he should forbid none of his acquaintance to minister or come unto him.

Felix thinks Paul is a good opportunity to get money and bolster his own political career, so he has Paul carefully guarded. Felix put Paul under house arrest with just one guard at the door. Felix allowed Paul's friends and relatives to visit him in hopes they would bring money to bribe Felix for Paul's release. During these two years, Paul will write Ephesians, Philippians, Colossians, and Philemon, his most concentrated doctrinal epistles.

Nero Claudius Drusus, maternal great-grandfather of the Emperor Nero, came from two tribes producing Caesars. One was Claudius; the other tribe was Julius. Nero Claudius Drusus was the younger brother of Tiberius. He married Antonia, the sister of Mark Antony and had three children, Germanicus, Claudius, and a daughter. Germanicus was poisoned. Claudius was considered dumb, but was quiet and studious. Claudius married Messalina, and later, after having Messalina executed, he married Agrippina. Agrippina's son by a previous marriage, Nero, was adopted and became the heir under Claudius.

During his reign, Claudius freed three slaves, one of whom was Felix, who became procurator of Judea. At a party, Felix met Drusilla who was the wife of an Arabian king. She had a sister, Bernice, who was the wife of Herod Agrippa. These two sisters hated each other. (Later, at the time of this story, Bernice is living in incest with her son, Herod Agrippa II.) Felix persuaded Drusilla to run away and marry him. He threatened her husband, who is against Rome, and took Drusilla. Nero became emperor when Agrippa poisoned Claudius and he also lived in incest with her.

VII. Felix Calls for Paul (24–27)

Felix comes to Caesarea with his wife, Drusilla, and asks to see Paul and hear him speak about his faith. Paul answers all of his questions, but in the end, Felix does not accept the Lord. Felix is eventually replaced by Festus, who calls another trial.

24:24 ¶ And after some days, when Felix came with his wife Drusilla, who was Jewish, he sent for Paul and heard him concerning the faith in Christ.

Felix is having a social gathering and invites Paul to speak of his faith.

24:25 Now as he reasoned about righteousness, self-control, and the judgment to come, Felix was afraid and answered, "Go away for now; when I have a convenient time I will call for you."

And as he reasoned (*dialegomai*: discussed) of righteousness (new birth), temperance (holiness), and judgment to come, Felix trembled (was terrified), and answered, Go thy way (get out) for this time: when I have a convenient season, I will call for thee.

Paul answers the many questions Felix has for him, and gives him straight answers about the plan of God. Paul spends the day with Felix and Drusilla, and they are both convicted. Felix is full of fear over Paul's message but does not want to accept the Lord. This is all an excuse to procrastinate by getting Paul out of the house.

24:26 Meanwhile he also hoped that money would be given him by Paul, that he might release him. Therefore he sent for him more often and conversed with him.

Felix brought Paul in for occasional talks strictly to see if money had come. He had already made up his mind to reject the gospel.

24:27 ¶ But after two years Porcius Festus succeeded Felix; and Felix, wanting to do the Jews a favor, left Paul bound.

Nero replaced Felix with Festus as the new procurator of Judea. He will not treat Paul as leniently as Felix did, but will put him in a dungeon and call for another trial. Felix, Drusilla, and her son move to Pompeii and die in the eruption of Mount Vesuvius in 79 AD. All of them had been presented an opportunity to accept the Lord, but rejected it.

25:1–27 Paul Before Festus

The Challenge of Chapter Twenty-Five

After being held unlawfully for two years in prison, Paul does not waver in his trust and confidence in God.

To God, one day is as a thousand years and a thousand years as one day. However, from our human perspective, the passage of time sometimes seems like an enemy. Like Paul, we must not be moved from standing on God's promises to us. If God has spoken a promise to your heart, it will surely come to pass.

I. Jewish Leaders Appeal to Festus (1–9)

Once again, the Jews look for a way to get rid of Paul. They appeal to Festus to send Paul to Jerusalem. They think they can ambush and kill Paul on his journey. Instead, Festus determines that Paul should remain in Caesarea and states he will travel to Caesarea and reopen the case. After arriving in Caesarea, Festus orders Paul to be brought to him. The Jews present bring complaints against Paul, but he defends himself against their accusations.

Paul is confronted by Festus in Caesarea (Chapter 24) and then by Agrippa (Chapter 26). In Chapter 27, Paul travels to Rome, and in Chapter 28, he arrives. Festus will be used by the Jewish mob and change the decision of Felix. Everyone will try to kill Paul, but God will deliver him and send him to Rome.

25:1 ¶ Now when Festus had come to the province, after three days he went up from Caesarea to Jerusalem.

Festus is described by Josephus as a pleasant and fair ruler. But in this chapter, we see him swayed in to breaking Roman laws when entertained by the Jews of Jerusalem.

25:2 Then the high priest and the chief men of the Jews informed him against Paul; and they petitioned him,

For two years, the Jews have been festering over Paul, and they are furious. They look for any way to destroy him. Festus's plan to travel to Jerusalem represents their new hope. They have now built up a monumental case against Paul in their imaginations and accuse him of heresy. They also fabricate stories that are grossly exaggerated.

25:3 asking a favor against him, that he would summon him to Jerusalem—while *they* lay in ambush along the road to kill him.

And desired favour against him (Paul), that he (Festus) would send for him to (come to) Jerusalem, laying wait in (along) the way to kill him.

They ask that the case be reopened in Jerusalem, not to try Paul but to kill him. They are going to ambush Paul. Religion sponsors violence and murder to get its desired end. In verses 4 and 5, Festus demonstrates his wisdom.

25:4 But Festus answered that Paul should be kept at Caesarea, and that he himself was going *there* shortly.

Paul has undergone a trial by legal steps, and Caesarea is the proper place to be, but Festus now promises he will personally look into the situation when he gets there.

25:5 "Therefore," he said, "let those who have authority among you go down with *me* and accuse this man, to see if there is any fault in him."

Festus says, "If any irregularities exist, I will reopen the case." In the opening verses, he refuses to bring Paul to Jerusalem, but in verse 9 he will reverse himself, which causes Paul to take his case to Caesar. Paul sticks with Roman law. He knows that he will not receive a fair trial in Jerusalem with the Jews.

25:6 And when he had remained among them more than ten days, he went down to Caesarea. And the next day, sitting on the judgment seat, he commanded Paul to be brought.

And when he had tarried (*diatribe*: to wear down, remain, abide, continue) among them more than ten days, he went down unto Caesarea; and the next day sitting on the judgment seat commanded Paul to be brought.

The Jews "wined and dined" Festus for more than ten days to influence him to turn Paul over to them.

25:7 When he had come, the Jews who had come down from Jerusalem stood about and laid many serious complaints against Paul, which they could not prove,

These accusations have previously been made in Chapter 24. They are the same now, except more vicious after two years. They are still unfounded and cannot be proven.

25:8 while he answered for himself, "Neither against the law of the Jews, nor against the temple, nor against Caesar have I offended in anything at all."

While he answered for (defended) Himself, Neither against the law of the Jews (disturbing the peace, causing a riot), neither against (profaning) the temple, nor yet against Caesar (a revolt against Rome), have I offended any thing at all.

25:9 ¶ But Festus, wanting to do the Jews a favor, answered Paul and said, "Are you willing to go up to Jerusalem and there be judged before me concerning these things?"

Festus feels obligated to give the Jews a break in this case. He will now even break the law to please them.

II. Paul Requests an Audience with Caesar (10–12)

Paul states he is a Roman citizen, therefore, under Roman law. He continues by declaring that if he has committed a crime worthy of death, so be it. Festus' response to Paul is to ask him if he has appealed to Caesar.

25:10 ¶ So Paul said, "I stand at Caesar's judgment seat, where I ought to be judged. To the Jews I have done no wrong, as you very well know.

Paul says, "I am under Roman law. Roman law found me innocent of Jewish accusations, and the charges have not changed. I will stick with Roman law until released or sentenced." Festus knows Paul has done no wrong, even though he would not admit it.

25:11 For if I am an offender, or have committed anything deserving of death, I do not object to dying; but if there is nothing in these things of which these men accuse me, no one can deliver me to them. I appeal to Caesar."

For if I be an offender, or have committed any thing worthy of death (under Roman law), I refuse not to die: but if there be none of these things whereof these accuse me, no man may deliver me unto them. I appeal (*apikaleomai*: call on, appellate) unto Caesar.

Paul believes in capital punishment even for himself if he is guilty. Now under Roman law, he has removed himself from Festus and desires to go to the authority above Festus. Paul cannot go lower (back to Jewish court), but only higher, all the way to Caesar in Rome.

> **25:12 ⸀ Then Festus, when he had conferred with the council, answered, "You have appealed to Caesar? To Caesar you shall go!"**

Festus finds himself in a tough situation. He has refused to acquit a Roman citizen who has no legal ground for indictment. Paul has now appealed to go higher and Festus will have to write a letter that makes sense and justifies Paul's two years in prison and his stand in refusing to acquit Paul. Paul has played a trump card and called Festus's hand. Festus puts on his poker face and informs Paul he will let him go. Paul knows Roman law and uses it.

III. King Agrippa and Bernice in Caesarea (13–21)

King Agrippa and Bernice travel to Caesarea to greet Festus. After being in Caesarea for many days, Festus explains Paul's situation to Agrippa.

> **25:13 ⸀ And after some days King Agrippa and Bernice came to Caesarea to greet Festus.**

Herod Agrippa II, grandson of Herod the Great, nephew to Herod the Tetrarch (who beheaded John the Baptist) and son of Agrippa I (who killed James in chapter 12) is one of the most handsome men in the ancient world and the ruler of Rome. His sister Bernice is said to be the most beautiful woman of the ancient world. She is the sister of Drusilla. These two sisters continually fight to outdo each other. Bernice has left her husband and is living in incest with her brother Agrippa II. Later she will become the mistress of Vespasian who is ruling Jerusalem. She then becomes the mistress of the son of Vespasian, Titus.

Caesarea is the hometown of Agrippa and Bernice. It was built by their grandfather, and they want to visit this beautiful seaport city. For a long time they would not visit because Drusilla lived there with Felix. But now that Felix was gone, they don't have to be concerned about seeing Drusilla.

25:14 When they had been there many days, Festus laid Paul's case before the king, saying: "There is a certain man left a prisoner by Felix,

Festus wants Agrippa's opinion. They are at a party and apparently everyone is having a good time except Festus. He is bothered about what he has done with Paul and the letter he has to write. He knows how he should have released him, but did not. Now Paul has appealed to Caesar, and Festus is bothered. He brought up Felix's name because he knew how much Agrippa and Bernice hated him and Drusilla. He is basically telling them, "This is all Felix's fault."

25:15 about whom the chief priests and the elders of the Jews informed *me*, when I was in Jerusalem, asking for a judgment against him.

For ten days Festus has been informing them about the situation. He has entertained and catered to both of them during this time and has given them a little bit of information.

25:16 To them I answered, 'It is not the custom of the Romans to deliver any man to destruction before the accused meets the accusers face to face, and has opportunity to answer for himself concerning the charge against him.'

Festus is trying to place himself in a good light. He is telling them of the greatness of Roman law, "You are innocent until proven guilty in a fair trial." Festus is being self-righteous. He is putting himself in a favorable light by twisting the facts of what happened. Festus has failed. Instead of admitting his failure, he is covering it with self-righteousness. It was God's will for Paul, before he sinned, to go to Rome and then on to Spain. Regardless of Paul's failure and repentance, God's will has not changed, only His means of getting Paul to Rome. He will use the excellent means of Roman law to get Paul there.

The weakness in leadership does not stop God. He uses it. God uses failures of others as stepping stones for His plans and His people. God uses any situation for His glory, as we should (Romans 8:28, 1 Corinthians 7:20–21). If

Festus or Felix had used Roman law correctly, they would have allowed Paul to leave much sooner. If they had, Paul would have proceeded to Rome. Regardless of the motives of Felix and Festus in detaining Paul, God will still get Paul to Rome at Rome's expense. On the way, Paul will write some of his greatest epistles. He will also be protected from religious Jews by the Roman military.

25:17 Therefore when they had come together, without any delay, the next day I sat on the judgment seat and commanded the man to be brought in.

He is bragging on his efficiency to minimize his own mistakes. He is saying, "I did not waste any time." Roman law knew the importance of quick justice; no delays for weeks and months causing people to forget the importance of the act of the facts surrounding the crime.

25:18 When the accusers stood up, they brought no accusation against him of such things as I supposed,

During his stay in Jerusalem he had been convinced by the Jews of Paul's guilt. He is now admitting that he has presupposed Paul's guilt but has found out otherwise during the trials because the Jews are actually upset over religious doctrine. Festus knows Agrippa has an understanding of the Jewish religion and can help him straighten out this matter.

25:19 but had some questions against him about their own religion and about a certain Jesus, who had died, whom Paul affirmed to be alive.

But had certain questions against him of their own superstition (*deisidaimonia*: to fear a demon), and of one Jesus, which was dead, whom Paul affirmed to be alive.

We now find out what the trials were like. Festus heard the gospel preached by Paul. He heard of Jesus and the resurrection. The resurrection is the point of contention with the Jews and the point of salvation for Festus (Romans 10:9, 10). "Affirmed" means Paul is dogmatic about Jesus being alive.

25:20 And because I was uncertain of such questions, I asked whether he was willing to go to Jerusalem and there be judged concerning these matters.

And because I doubted (was perplexed) of such manner of questions (the controversy), I asked him whether (if) he would go to Jerusalem, and there be judged of these matters.

This is a lie. Festus felt obligated to the Jews (v. 9) and tried to get Paul to Jerusalem because of his promise to them.

25:21 But when Paul appealed to be reserved for the decision of Augustus, I commanded him to be kept till I could send him to Caesar."

In other words, he is saying "I need help."

IV. Agrippa Requests Paul To Be Brought Before Him (22–27)

After hearing of Paul's case from Festus, Agrippa requests to hear Paul for himself. Paul is then brought before Festus, Agrippa, and Bernice.

25:22 ¶ Then Agrippa said to Festus, "I also would like to hear the man myself." ¶ "Tomorrow," he said, "you shall hear him."

This is exactly what Festus wants to hear. Agrippa is pleased to straighten out something Felix has started.

25:23 ¶ So the next day, when Agrippa and Bernice had come with great pomp, and had entered the auditorium with the commanders and the prominent men of the city, at Festus' command Paul was brought in.

And on the morrow (next morning), when Agrippa was come, and Bernice, with great pomp (*phantasia*: glamour, vain show), and was entered into the place of hearing, with chief captains (high-ranking Roman generals), and principal men (officials) of the city, at Festus' commandment Paul was brought forth.

Agrippa and Bernice represent the fourth generation of Herods who have rejected the gospel. They are also the last of the Herodian line.

Herod the Great had rejected the gospel when he slaughtered the children in an effort to get rid of Jesus shortly after his birth. Herod's son, Antipas, (named after his grandfather Antipater), murdered John the Baptist. The third generation, Herod Agrippa I, had James killed and Peter thrown in prison. Herod Agrippa II is now presented with an opportunity to accept the Lord as Paul ministers to Him. However he and Bernice reject Jesus Christ and die, effectively ending the Herodian line.

When word spread that Agrippa and Bernice were in town and this brilliant man was going to officiate the law, he drew a crowd of dignitaries from Roman and local government circles. Paul will now be brought into this very glamorous occasion before the highest of dignitaries to present his case and the gospel. Paul will hear an introduction to his own case, which will include hypocrisy. Festus will whitewash the case to protect his own image.

25:24 And Festus said: "King Agrippa and all the men who are here present with us, you see this man about whom the whole assembly of the Jews petitioned me, both at Jerusalem and here, crying out that he was not fit to live any longer.

And Festus said, King Agrippa, and all men which are here present with us, ye see this man (Paul), about whom all the multitude of the Jews (Sanhedrin) have dealt with me, both at Jerusalem, and also here (at Caesarea), crying (screaming) that he ought not live any longer.

In other words, "This man has come to me from many people. Apparently, this man must be evil because all these Jews scream to have him killed."

25:25 But when I found that he had committed nothing deserving of death, and that he himself had appealed to Augustus, I decided to send him.

Festus is saying, "When I carefully examined him by the law, I could find nothing wrong with this man. He personally appealed to Caesar and I have given Paul my permission to appeal to him."

25:26 I have nothing certain to write to my lord concerning him. Therefore I have brought him out before you, and especially before you, King Agrippa, so that after the examination has taken place I may have something to write.

Of whom I have no certain (exact) thing to write unto my lord (Caesar). Wherefore I have brought him forth before you, and specially before thee, O king Agrippa, that, after examination had, I might have somewhat to write.

Festus is telling the courtroom of his dilemma. His letter at this point will have no concrete case to present, and his weakness and mishandling of the case will eventually come out through investigation. He could also lose his job.

25:27 For it seems to me unreasonable to send a prisoner and not to specify the charges against him."

For it seemeth to me unreasonable (useless) to send a prisoner, and not withal (clearly) to signify (explain) the crimes laid against him.

Paul now stands before this great Roman assembly. There is Festus, Agrippa, and Bernice along with city and state officials from the area. Paul will now share the gospel with this powerful group of unbelievers.

26:1–32 Paul Before Agrippa

The Challenge of Chapter Twenty-Six

Paul, who could have been intimidated by the political leaders he stands before, does not back down from boldly sharing his conversion experience and call to ministry, even when accused of being a madman. We must not be moved by the opinions others have of our faith in the Lord Jesus Christ. God may bring those across our path who are at the point of almost being persuaded to receive Jesus Christ as Lord and Savior. Perhaps the Lord will use us to plant the final seed so the one standing on the brink of his or her decision to receive Jesus Christ as Lord and Savior will finally be persuaded to enter into His kingdom.

I. Agrippa Permits Paul to Speak (1–11)

When Paul is permitted to address Agrippa, he uses the Roman style of oratory. He explains how he was trained to be a Pharisee. Paul continues by explaining how he was not much different from those now persecuting him because he once also persecuted Christians.

A. Paul Addresses Agrippa

26:1 ¶ Then Agrippa said to Paul, "You are permitted to speak for yourself." ¶ So Paul stretched out his hand and answered for himself:

Paul is completely poised and uses the Roman style in addressing these men. The stretched forth hand is to draw attention in respect to a speaker. There was probably a lot of small talk going on in the room. Paul has a message for them to hear.

26:2 "I think myself happy, King Agrippa, because today I shall answer for myself before you concerning all the things of which I am accused by the Jews,

I think (conclude) myself happy (*makarios*: blessed), king Agrippa, because I shall answer for (defend) myself this day before thee touching (concerning) all the things whereof I am accused of the Jews:

Paul is happy in bonds. These men are unhappy in freedom.

26:3 especially because you are expert in all customs and questions which have to do with the Jews. Therefore I beg you to
hear me patiently.

Paul knows Agrippa's past, that he is a fourth-generation Herod and ruler of
the Jews in Palestine. In truth, Paul is not on trial here; this group is on trial
with God. Paul is God's representative in court.

B. Paul Speaks of Early Life

26:4 ¶ "My manner of life from my youth, which was spent
from the beginning among my own nation at Jerusalem, all
the Jews know.

Paul's life will be divided into his youth (v. 4–5) and his present life as a minister of the gospel (v. 6). Paul is telling them that everything he is about to
say can be confirmed by the Jews who are accusing him.

26:5 They knew me from the first, if they were willing to testify, that according to the strictest sect of our religion I lived
a Pharisee.

Which knew me from the beginning, if they would testify, that after (according to) the most straitest (strictest) sect of our religion I lived a Pharisee.

Paul is saying the Jews will not testify against him on legal grounds in a
court of law. They will accuse him from outside based on accusations and
hearsay. Paul's testimony before salvation is not only taught in Acts 9, but
in Galatians 1:13 and 14, and Philippians 3:4 through 6.

C. Paul Speaks of Present Life as a Minister

26:6 And now I stand and am judged for the hope of the promise
made by God to our fathers.

Paul is saying, "The same ones who knew me then condemn me now." The
"hope of the promise" is the sending of their Messiah, Jesus Christ. Every
author and book of the Old Testament prophesied of His coming. Many of
these promises are covenants.

There are four unconditional covenants given to Israel and are now for
those who are born again. The foundation of each covenant is personal

faith in Jesus Christ, the promised One of the Old Testament. This is what Paul came to preach.

26:7 To this *promise* our twelve tribes, earnestly serving *God* night and day, hope to attain. For this hope's sake, King Agrippa, I am accused by the Jews.

Unto which promise our twelve tribes (all Israel), instantly (earnestly) serving God day and night, hope to come (arrive). For which hope's sake, king Agrippa, I am accused of the Jews.

All the rituals still being observed by Israel still look forward to the coming of Messiah. Their rituals in the temple and court go on day and night at the very time Paul is speaking. Yet Jesus has already come, been crucified, and resurrected, they are expressing their rejection of Jesus by offering animal sacrifices. They do this in hope of a coming, yet the coming has already occurred. The Jews accuse Paul of preaching something they are looking forward to themselves.

26:8 Why should it be thought incredible by you that God raises the dead?

Even those in the courtroom who are not Christians should be able to believe that God could raise someone from the dead.

D. Paul's Persecution of the Church

26:9 ⁋ "Indeed, I myself thought I must do many things contrary to the name of Jesus of Nazareth.

I verily thought (assumed) with myself, that I ought to do (*prasso*: policy, practice) many things contrary (in opposition) to the name of Jesus of Nazareth.

Paul explains he was also like the Jews who persecute him because he himself persecuted the Lord. He was a zealous religious man coming against the church.

The name of Jesus holds the power (Mark 16:17–18) and causes opposition to come. It was the supernatural that Paul (before conversion) had a difficult time with, as do all other religious people.

26:10 This I also did in Jerusalem, and many of the saints I shut up in prison, having received authority from the chief priests; and when they were put to death, I cast my vote against *them.*

Which thing I also did (*poieo*: carried out the policies) in Jerusalem: and many of the saints did I shut up in prison, having received authority from the chief priests; and when they were put to death, I gave my voice against them.

Not only was Paul told to throw Christians in prison and kill them, he also was in favor of and consented with the decision of those in authority over him in regard to Christians.

26:11 And I punished them often in every synagogue and compelled *them* to blaspheme; and being exceedingly enraged against them, I persecuted *them* even to foreign cities.

And I punished them oft in every synagogue, and compelled them to blaspheme; and being exceedingly mad (*emmainomai*: maniac, rage at) against them, I persecuted them even unto strange (foreign) cities.

Paul traveled outside Jerusalem on special trips to persecute and jail believers. If they would renounce Jesus, they would be allowed to live. Paul became as an insane man in his zeal against the Lord. He was driven by a demonic madness to many cities outside of Israel to persecute the church of Jesus.

II. Paul's Conversion Recounted (12–18)

Paul now begins recounting his experience on the road to Damascus. He testifies about hearing a voice from heaven and explains being called to be a minister, especially to the heathen.

26:12 ¶ "While thus occupied, as I journeyed to Damascus with authority and commission from the chief priests,

Whereupon (in madness) as I went to Damascus with authority and commission from the chief priests,

26:13 at midday, O king, along the road I saw a light from heaven, brighter than the sun, shining around me and those who journeyed with me.

Only one type of light is brighter than the sun; the glory of God.

26:14 And when we all had fallen to the ground, I heard a voice speaking to me and saying in the Hebrew language, 'Saul, Saul, why are you persecuting Me? *It is* **hard for you to kick against the goads.'**

Falling to the ground is a natural reaction to coming in contact with God's glory (2 Chronicles 5:13–14). Although Paul was the only one who heard the voice (22:9), everyone saw the light. By persecuting people, Paul was persecuting the Lord Jesus (Matthew 25:40) and was one step away from the point of no return. Like Pharaoh, his heart had become hardened by resisting the gospel. The "prick" is an ox goad, a hard instrument to train a horse or ox. It is much like our spurs today. Saul was so hardened through hearing Stephen and other ministers, the Lord had to do something drastic to reach him.

26:15 So I said, 'Who are You, Lord?' And He said, 'I am Jesus, whom you are persecuting.

Saul understood the Lord was talking to him, but as most religious people, he did not know who the Lord was. He found out Jesus is Jehovah and Messiah.

26:16 But rise and stand on your feet; for I have appeared to you for this purpose, to make you a minister and a witness both of the things which you have seen and of the things which I will yet reveal to you.

But rise, and stand upon thy feet: for I have appeared unto thee for this purpose, to make thee a minister (*huperetes*: under rower, servant, subordinate [13:5]) and a witness both of these things which thou hast seen, and of those things in the which I will appear unto thee;

Paul had no more answers for Jesus. He quietly believed and rose up a new man. Paul also had a new purpose (a new commission): to be an under rower, a beginning minister in the kingdom of God.

Paul could not minister until he first learned as a servant, a "helps" minister (Galatians 1:15–16). When Paul began to preach, it consisted of his vision on the road to Damascus and the Word revealed to him (Galatians 1:16). The revelation of the Word is just as dramatic as a vision of Jesus in His glory. And God promised Paul there would be more visions and revelations to come.

26:17 I will deliver you from the *Jewish* people, as well as *from* the Gentiles, to whom I now send you,

Paul will be supernaturally delivered from religious Jews and Gentile heathen. Paul is called to preach to the Gentiles (Galatians 2:8), but always has a place in his heart for the Jewish people (Romans 9:1–3, 10:1).

26:18 to open their eyes, *in order* to turn *them* from darkness to light, and *from* the power of Satan to God, that they may receive forgiveness of sins and an inheritance among those who are sanctified by faith in Me.'

To open their eyes, and to turn them from darkness to light, and from the power (*exousia*: authority) of Satan unto God, that they may receive forgiveness (remission) of sins, and inheritance among them; which are sanctified (positional) by faith that is in (deposited in) me.

Unbelievers have been blinded by sin and Satan (2 Corinthians 4:4), but the Word of God brings light (Ephesians 1:17–18). With the entrance of the gospel and repentance, their eyes are opened, and they can see the Word (light) and walk toward it. Sinners receive forgiveness because everything has been provided (2 Peter 1:3). Man's part is to simply accept the free gift as an act of his will.

III. Paul Recounts His Life After Conversion (19–23)

Paul then testifies about obeying the "heavenly vision" in taking the gospel to the Gentiles. He explains how the Jews tried to kill him. Paul continues by testifying that he had witnessed and continues witnessing about Jesus' suffering, dying, and being the first raised from the dead for both Jews and Gentiles.

26:19 ¶ "Therefore, King Agrippa, I was not disobedient to the heavenly vision,

Whereupon (God visiting and instructing me), O king Agrippa, I was not disobedient unto the heavenly vision:

Paul received Jesus when he saw the vision and also accepted the call to minister to the Gentiles.

26:20 but declared first to those in Damascus and in Jerusalem, and throughout all the region of Judea, and *then* to the Gentiles, that they should repent, turn to God, and do works befitting repentance.

Paul declared the gospel first at Damascus. He announces what he has seen. This verse also covers the first three missionary journeys (Judea to the Gentiles). Good works is also a part of the gospel message. When a person accepts Jesus as Lord and Savior, they should also begin to step out into good works which speak of their conversion.

26:21 For these reasons the Jews seized me in the temple and tried to kill *me*.

Paul was taken and beaten by the Jews for preaching about Jesus Christ being the Messiah of Israel and the Savior of mankind. This may not be how the Romans believe or the Jews, but it is not the issue. Paul is free to preach his own beliefs without being taken to jail. The Jews want to kill Paul over preaching his own beliefs about Jesus Christ.

26:22 Therefore, having obtained help from God, to this day I stand, witnessing both to small and great, saying no other things than those which the prophets and Moses said would come—

Having therefore obtained help (acquired assistance) of God (Roman intervention), I continue (perfect tense—remain standing) unto this day, witnessing both to small (citizens) and great (government leaders), saying none other things than those which the prophets (major and minor) and Moses (Genesis to Deuteronomy) did say should come (to pass):

Paul is saying, "The God they say they serve helped me to escape from them."

26:23 that the Christ would suffer, that He would be the first to rise from the dead, and would proclaim light to the *Jewish* people and to the Gentiles."

That Christ should suffer, and that he should be the first that should rise from the dead, and should shew (*kataggello*: announce, declare, teach) light unto the people (Jewish), and to the Gentiles.

The Old Testament is filled with prophecy showing that Jesus would suffer, be resurrected, and proclaim salvation to Jews and Gentiles (Psalm 22, Isaiah 42:6, 53:1–12, 60:1). Even though Agrippa is presiding over the meeting, Festus interrupts Paul. Paul will use this occasion to answer Festus and hit Agrippa with Old Testament scriptures.

IV. Paul Continues His Defense Under Pressure (24–32)

Festus interrupts Paul's testimony accusing him of being mad. Paul refutes his accusation. After hearing Paul, Agrippa recognizes he is innocent and is in jail because of a religious dispute between Paul and the Jews. However, King Agrippa also does not release Paul and uses Paul's appeal to Caesar as the excuse.

26:24 ¶ Now as he thus made his defense, Festus said with a loud voice, "Paul, you are beside yourself! Much learning is driving you mad!"

And as he thus spake for (defended) himself, Festus said (interrupted) with a loud voice, Paul, thou art beside thyself (*mainomai*: maniac, mad); much learning doth make thee mad (*mania*: mania, crazy).

Festus calls Paul insane, raving mad. Festus has heard of Paul's study even while in prison and attacks his knowledge of the Word.

26:25 ¶ But he said, "I am not mad, most noble Festus, but speak the words of truth and reason.

Even under great pressure, Paul keeps his composure. Paul is speaking the Old Testament scriptures which Festus knows nothing of. Paul now makes him look bad before the Jews and Agrippa.

26:26 For the king, before whom I also speak freely, knows these things; for I am convinced that none of these things escapes his attention, since this thing was not done in a corner.

For the king (Agrippa) knoweth of these things, before whom also I speak freely (Agrippa would never interrupt me): for I am persuaded that one of these things are hidden from him; for this thing (death, burial, resurrection) was not done in a corner.

Coming from the Herodian line, Agrippa was well versed in the Old Testament scriptures. If Paul is angry, Agrippa is also angry. Agrippa has seen the rituals, heard the prophesies, and knows of the injustices done to Jesus.

26:27 King Agrippa, do you believe the prophets? I know that you do believe."

Paul has known for some time that Agrippa believed the Old Testament scriptures. Agrippa figures out quickly where Paul is heading. He knows Paul will tie Jesus into the Old Testament verses and stops short of believing in Jesus as his own Savior.

26:28 ¶ Then Agrippa said to Paul, "You almost persuade me to become a Christian."

And Agrippa [replied] to Paul, "In a short time you will persuade me to become a Christian" (NIV).

This is a sarcastic remark made by Agrippa to cut Paul off. He saw the close coming and did not want to have to make the decision for or against Jesus. He is simply saying, "If I allow you to speak any longer, I might accept Jesus."

26:29 ¶ And Paul said, "I would to God that not only you, but also all who hear me today, might become both almost and altogether such as I am, except for these chains."

And Paul said, I would (wish) to God, that not only thou, but also all that hear me this day (the full crowd in the court), were (*ginomai*: would become) both almost, and altogether (by my few or many words) such as I am, except these bonds.

Paul wishes they will become born again through a few or many words from him, in a little amount of time or much. Paul will do or say whatever it takes to make them believers, but he does not wish prison on any of them.

26:30 ❡ When he had said these things, the king stood up, as well as the governor and Bernice and those who sat with them;

And when they had thus spoken, the king rose (jumped) up, and the governor, and Bernice, and they that sat with them:

When the king jumps up, so does everyone else.

26:31 and when they had gone aside, they talked among themselves, saying, "This man is doing nothing deserving of death or chains."

They now all understand Festus' dilemma. They see Paul's innocence and understand he is simply in prison for a religious disagreement with the Jews. They are also angry with Festus for allowing this to continue as long as it has. He should not have kept Paul in prison for political expediency.

28:32 Then Agrippa said to Festus, "This man might have been set free if he had not appealed to Caesar."

This is not true. Why doesn't he just walk in and set Paul free? He is afraid of Paul and of displaying weakness before the people. Paul has been in prison for two years now, and it would be an admission of his own oversight to free Paul. Paul upset him in the courtroom, and it would be a blow to his pride to now set Paul free. He uses Paul's appeal to Caesar as a scapegoat. Like Festus and Felix, he is also a weak leader.

27:1-44 Paul Travels to Rome

The Challenge of Chapter Twenty-Seven

As Paul travels to Rome and is about to be shipwrecked, Paul has a word from God: none would perish who stayed on board. His confidence and trust are in God, even as the storm rages on and circumstances are declining.

When the storms of life rage around you, and it looks like you are headed for shipwreck, where is your focus? Is your attention on the waves of circumstances that appear to be tearing your life apart, or are you looking to the people around you, being influenced by their reactions instead of being an influencer for the kingdom of God? We have God's Word that ensures joy, peace, provision, divine health, and all the benefits of being a child of the King. His Word confirms the authority we have been given in Christ Jesus and through Him, our ability to overcome any storm that may come against us in life.

I. Introduction

Chapter 27 is a description of the first part of Paul's trip to Rome, sailing from Caesarea to Malta.

Paul sails toward Rome by ship. The Romans were the worst sailors of the ancient world. They tried to take the land to sea and made ships as large as a football field, and the ships sank easily. Many of their ships sunk before they even sailed.

The Phoenicians, on the other hand, were the best sailors and were famous for their trade ships and routes in the ancient world. When the Romans went sailing or took over a ship, Roman law applied to the passengers while on board just as if they were on land. Roman ships had one mast in the middle of the ship. Phoenicians ships had many masts. This put all the stress on the middle of the hull and it was not uncommon for their ships to break apart at the center. "Frapping" became common by running ropes around the hull to help hold the ships together ("undergirding" [v. 17]).

Chapter 27 shows the impact of one man who knows and stands on the Word against the attacks of Satan. The entire crew will be saved through the faith of Paul.

II. The First Storm (1–13)

Festus and the court decide to put Paul on a ship to Rome with other prisoners. The day after setting sail they land in Sidon, and Paul is permitted to visit the believers there. They then sail around the tip of Cyprus and come to Lycia. Paul and the other prisoners are then transferred to a ship sailing slowly to Italy, which would normally take many days. A fierce storm moves in and they sail to Crete where they remain for a time. Contrary to the thinking of the captain and owner of the ship, Paul warns them about sailing to Phoenix to remain for the winter.

27:1 ⸿ And when it was decided that we should sail to Italy, they delivered Paul and some other prisoners to *one* named Julius, a centurion of the Augustan Regiment.

And when it was determined (*krino*: judged, ordained) that we should sail into (toward) Italy, they delivered Paul and certain other prisoners unto one named Julius, a centurion of Augustus' band (a famous Roman band).

Festus and the court decide to send Paul to Rome by ship in October, the worst time of the year for traveling by sea, But Festus had a reason for sending Paul at this time. This was not a regular sailing vessel, but an old ship that usually carried cargo along the coast. It was not designed for open-sea sailing. This is why they sailed along the coast for the first part of the trip to Crete (v. 1–3).

Julius was an officer Festus did not like. He planned to get rid of Paul and Julius in one move by sending them away in a worn-out ship at the worst time of the year. To Festus, the other prisoners and crew members were expendable. Festus does not intend for Paul, the letter he has written, Julius, or any of the crew to actually make it to Rome.

However, Festus does not take into account the will of God. Paul cannot be killed because he has a message to deliver and a ministry to fulfill. All the men will be saved because Paul is with them. This is blessing and protection by association (1 Corinthians 7:14).

27:2 So, entering a ship of Adramyttium, we put to sea, meaning to sail along the coasts of Asia. Aristarchus, a Macedonian of Thessalonica, was with us.

The "we" in this verse includes Luke and the rest of Paul's team. The ship will not make it to the Asian coast, but will be deserted in Myra (vv. 5–6). Aristarchus, who is accompanying Paul, is accustomed to danger (19:29, 20:4).

27:3 And the next *day* we landed at Sidon. And Julius treated Paul kindly and gave *him* liberty to go to his friends and receive care.

And the next day we touched at Sidon. And Julius courteously (*philanthropos*: humanely) entreated Paul, and gave him liberty (freedom) to go unto his friends (21:3–5) to refresh himself.

This is a kind and gracious officer. He allows Paul to disembark from the ship to visit with believers in Sidon.

27:4 When we had put to sea from there, we sailed under *the shelter of* Cyprus, because the winds were contrary.

There was no other direction the ship could sail. It would have been less distance to sail to the western side of Cyprus, but the winds forced this sailing ship along the eastern side of Cyprus.

27:5 And when we had sailed over the sea which is off Cilicia and Pamphylia, we came to Myra, *a city* of Lycia.

Paul sees his home for the last time.

27:6 There the centurion found an Alexandrian ship sailing to Italy, and he put us on board.

This ship is also blown off course by the northwest winds into Myra. It was headed toward Crete (port of Fair Havens) and onto Puteoli, filled with grain from Egypt (v. 38). This ship would hold 276 people (v. 37).

27:7 ¶ When we had sailed slowly many days, and arrived with difficulty off Cnidus, the wind not permitting us to proceed, we sailed under *the shelter of* Crete off Salmone.

And when we had sailed slowly many days, and scarce were come over against Cnidus (ka-ni-tus), the wind not suffering (allowing) us, we sailed under (around the tip of) Crete, over against (around) Salmone;

After ditching the other ship, this one is more secure but is being slowed down by one of the worst sea storms in history. They are headed into the wind and are now in the last safe port before entering open sea to Crete.

27:8 Passing it with difficulty, we came to a place called Fair Havens, near the city *of* Lasea.

After passing Salmone, they are protected from the harsh winds.

27:9 ¶ Now when much time had been spent, and sailing was now dangerous because the Fast was already over, Paul advised them,

Now when much time was spent (had elapsed), and when sailing was not dangerous, because the fast was now already past (Atonement [October 10]; Leviticus 23:27, Numbers 29:7), Paul admonished (warned) them,

From October until March, ships usually remain in their home harbor because the weather is too unpredictable. Paul will advise them not to sail, but remain in Crete for the winter. He will sense in his spirit the extreme danger of the voyage to the ship, its cargo, and the passengers.

27:10 saying, "Men, I perceive that this voyage will end with disaster and much loss, not only of the cargo and ship, but also our lives."

Paul waits for his spirit to bear witness because of the natural danger of this time of year. He perceives that the danger will be too great. Some believers would want to go on "in faith" and trust God. If something is not directly told you in God's Word, you can only act in faith on what your spirit perceives by the direction of the Holy Spirit. In this case, the Holy Spirit is telling Paul not to go. The crew is tired of Lasea and wants to go on to Rome where times are more exciting. Paul will be overruled by the captain and majority opinion. The will of the majority is not always correct.

Paul went through three shipwrecks during his lifetime (2 Corinthians 11:25).

27:11 Nevertheless the centurion was more persuaded by the helmsman and the owner of the ship than by the things spoken by Paul.

Once a Roman officer steps on board a ship, he is the final authority. Roman law is in effect. However, this officer takes the word of the ship's owner over Paul. The owner wants to get his money for the grain, and he wants it quickly. The crew and passengers want to travel to Rome because they are bored.

27:12 And because the harbor was not suitable to winter in, the majority advised to set sail from there also, if by any means they could reach Phoenix, a harbor of Crete opening toward the southwest and northwest, *and* winter *there*.

And because the haven was not commodious (accommodating) to winter in, the more part (crew and passengers) advised to depart thence (from there) also, if by any means they might attain (make it) to Phenice (Phoenix), and there to winter; which is an haven of Crete, and lieth toward the south west and north west (navigational directions).

Phoenix is around the island and a more popular resort city in which to spend the winter. Yet when it is not God's will to move at all, even a small move is a play into the devil's hands.

27:13 ¶ When the south wind blew softly, supposing that they had obtained *their* desire, putting out to sea, they sailed close by Crete.

The weather looked calm and perfect to sail into Phoenix. The men are so confident in making this short journey, they do not pull up the lifeboats or frap the ship for high winds.

III. The Worst Storm (14–32)

While on their journey, they sail into a fierce storm. The winds of the storm push the ship toward the island of Clauda. They strengthen the hull against the storm. For the next two weeks, they are blown nearly 500 miles across an open sea. They throw cargo overboard to lighten the ship. Next, the ship's machinery is thrown overboard in an attempt to keep the ship afloat. The storm continues many more days, and all aboard are without food during this time. Paul then encourages the crew explaining that an angel has appeared to him telling him all who remain on board will live.

27:14 But not long after, a tempestuous head wind arose, called Euroclydon.

But not long after there arose (*ballo*: throw, thrust) against it a tempestuous (*tuphonikos*: typhoon) wind, called Euroclydon (*euro*: east, Europe;
clydon: north, a northeasterly wind) .

This wind pushes the ship away from the shores of Crete, not along them.
They are being pushed toward the island of Clauda and the ship and crew
are unprepared for this violent storm. There are two long sandbars off the
coast (v. 17) of North Africa, and the ship was now in danger of becoming
stuck and battered to pieces by the wind.

> **27:15 So when the ship was caught, and could not head into
> the wind, we let *her* drive.**

There would be a danger of the ship breaking in half because it was not
undergirded (frapped) for violent weather.

> **27:16 And running under *the shelter of* an island called Clauda,
> we secured the skiff with difficulty.**

And running under (around the tip of) a certain island which is called Clauda, we had much work to come by (hoist up) the boat:

This is the shore boat that has been sitting in water and is now being pulled
on board the ship. The shore boat will be very important later (v. 30).

> **27:17 When they had taken it on board, they used cables to
> undergird the ship; and fearing lest they should run aground
> on the Syrtis *Sands*, they struck sail and so were driven.**

Which (boat) when they had taken (pulled) up, they used helps (hoists),
under girding the ship; and, fearing lest they should fall (stick) into the
quicksand (sandbar), strake sail (exchanged sails), and so were driven.

The crew use ropes and hoists to strengthen the hull of the ship so it will
not drift apart if broken. When this is completed, they take down the main-
sails and put up a small storm sail allowing the ship to be taken by the wind.
They will hold on for their lives for the next two weeks as the ship is blown
over 480 miles across open sea from Crete to Miletas. The wind will now
blow them parallel to the sandbars directly west toward Italy.

27:18–19 And because we were exceedingly tempest-tossed, the next _day_ they lightened the ship. ¹⁹ On the third _day_ we threw the ship's tackle overboard with our own hands.

Now the passengers are unloading the ship. This is the machinery on deck for the functioning of the ship. Apparently, the ship is leaking from the pressure on the mainsail and the frapping equipment was no longer needed. The captain's objective is just to remain afloat.

27:20 Now when neither sun nor stars appeared for many days, and no small tempest beat on _us_, all hope that we would be saved was finally given up.

Because of the storm, the passengers and crew have not seen the sun for almost eleven days and have become despondent. This storm is not only furious, it continues for many days beyond any normal storm known in the Mediterranean. All hope is gone, and everyone resigns themselves to die. Also, the food supply has been depleted which adds to the misery.

27:21 ¶ But after long abstinence from food, then Paul stood in the midst of them and said, "Men, you should have listened to me, and not have sailed from Crete and incurred this disaster and loss.

But after long abstinence (no food) Paul stood forth (up) in the midst of them (crew, passengers, captain/owner), and said, Sirs (_anhr_: noblemen), ye should have hearkened (taken my advice) unto me, and not have loosed (set sail) from Crete, and to have gained this harm (to passengers) and loss (to cargo).

Paul is establishing his credibility as a prophet. The captain will listen to him from this time forward. He is not saying "I told you so," but letting him know if he had been right before, he would be right again. Paul's commands will be responsible for the saving of the people though the ship will be destroyed.

27:22 And now I urge you to take heart, for there will be no loss of life among you, but only of the ship.

And now I exhort (advise) you to be of good cheer (be encouraged): for there shall be no loss of any man's life among you, but of the ship.

Paul encourages everyone to "be of good cheer." These are the same words the Lord spoke to Paul when he was discouraged in the Roman prison (23:11). Paul will give them a word from the Lord to once again restore hope (v. 20).

27:23 For there stood by me this night an angel of the God to whom I belong and whom I serve,

Paul states an angel stood by him. He wants to establish his office and God's confirmation of it so these men will listen to his commands. God will preserve Paul and all those around him. These people are being blessed by being in Paul's presence. Paul makes a distinction between the new birth in his life and service to God. The new birth is not service.

27:24 saying, 'Do not be afraid, Paul; you must be brought before Caesar; and indeed God has granted you all those who sail with you.'

Saying, Fear not, Paul; thou must (it is necessary) be brought before Caesar (Nero): and, lo, God hath given thee all them that sail with thee.

Even Paul had begun to worry. Paul is the one on this ship who is predominantly under attack by Satan. His faith is keeping the ship afloat. If fear is permitted to enter, Paul's faith will not work, and the ship will be lost. An angel appears to Paul to bolster his confidence, and the other passengers benefit.

Paul is "salt" on this voyage and preserving the entire crew. Paul's ministry is not yet completed. His faith is active again. He will stand before Caesar, and he has complete confidence knowing no devil or storm will destroy him.

27:25 Therefore take heart, men, for I believe God that it will be just as it was told me.

This encouragement comes directly from God. Even though Paul speaks the words, he is delivering God's word to these men. This word will be received and acted upon and come to pass. God's Word never fails and is always fulfilled.

27:26 However, we must run aground on a certain island."

This certain island was Miletas (Acts 28:1).

God has a plan for Paul, the people with him, and the inhabitants of the island. They will be evangelized by the healing and saving power of God.

27:27 ¶ Now when the fourteenth night had come, as we were driven up and down in the Adriatic *Sea*, about midnight the sailors sensed that they were drawing near some land.

But when the fourteenth night was come, as we were driven up and down in Adria, about midnight the shipmen (crew) deemed (suspicioned) that they drew near to some country (land);

At this time, Paul and those on board the ship are completely at the mercy of the wind and waves. Adria is a port on the Mediterranean between Italy and Macedonia, which crosses the path of Paul's ship. This area is near the island of Miletas.

27:28 And they took soundings and found *it* to be twenty fathoms; and when they had gone a little farther, they took soundings again and found it to be fifteen fathoms.

And sounded, and found it twenty fathoms (120 feet): and when they had gone a little further, they sounded again, and found it fifteen fathoms (90 feet).

A weight on the end of a rope is dropped to determine the depth of the water. By knowing the water is becoming shallower, they know they are moving toward shore.

27:29 Then, fearing lest we should run aground on the rocks, they dropped four anchors from the stern, and prayed for day to come.

Being near a shore is no indicator of safety. The coastline is unknown and the crew waits for daylight to see what conditions await them. They throw out the anchors located at the rear of the ship to keep it from being torn apart.

27:30 And as the sailors were seeking to escape from the ship, when they had let down the skiff into the sea, under pretense of putting out anchors from the prow,

And as the shipmen (seamen) were about to flee out of (desert) the ship, when they had let down the boat into the sea, under colour (pretense, look like) as though they would have cast anchors (anchored) out of the foreship (front),

The lifeboat looks like a good means of escape, and the crew decides to make a run for their lives under the pretense of anchoring the front of the ship. However, they are caught because Paul is observing the entire scene.

27:31 Paul said to the centurion and the soldiers, "Unless these men stay in the ship, you cannot be saved."

Paul says, "All must remain on board the ship for God's promise of their lives being spared to come to pass."

27:32 Then the soldiers cut away the ropes of the skiff and let it fall off.

Then the soldiers cut off the ropes of the boat, and let her fall off.

IV. The Shipwreck at Miletas (33–44)

Paul encourages everyone to take a little meat and bread. They then throw the wheat overboard. They see a shoreline and decide to head the ship toward the shore. The ship becomes grounded in a sandbar. Two currents come together ripping the ship apart. The soldiers decide to kill all the prisoners, including Paul, but the centurion stops them. Some swim to shore and others float on the wreckage from the ship.

27:33 ¶ And as day was about to dawn, Paul implored *them* all to take food, saying, "Today is the fourteenth day you have waited and continued without food, and eaten nothing.

They hav not thrown all of the food overboard; they saved a small amount. Paul now asks them to eat the food for strength to make it to shore. Paul has taken command. In fear, no one has eaten and they have lost track of time. Fear of death has kept them from eating. When people are in fear, they need a leader to instruct them in doing the simplest of things.

27:34 Therefore I urge you to take nourishment, for this is for your survival, since not a hair will fall from the head of any of you."

Paul is using common sense along with the discernment of the Holy Spirit.

27:35 And when he had said these things, he took bread and gave thanks to God in the presence of them all; and when he had broken *it* he began to eat.

We are not told that Paul witnessed to these people, although he probably does. When Paul takes food, he prays and blesses it in front of them all (1 Timothy 4:3, 4).

27:36 Then they were all encouraged, and also took food themselves.

They followed Paul's leadership and also ate the food available.

27:37–38 And in all we were two hundred and seventy-six persons on the ship. 38 So when they had eaten enough, they lightened the ship and threw out the wheat into the sea.

After eating they all went to work, both the crew and the passengers. Since wet wheat is heavy, they throw out the wheat so the ship will not sit low in the water and become stuck before reaching shore.

27:39 ¶ When it was day, they did not recognize the land; but they observed a bay with a beach, onto which they planned to run the ship if possible.

They see the shore, but this is an uncharted island. They have no map of where to land.

27:40 And they let go the anchors and left *them* in the sea, meanwhile loosing the rudder ropes; and they hoisted the mainsail to the wind and made for shore.

And when they had taken up (cut off) the anchors, they committed themselves unto the sea, and loosed the rudder bands (which held the rudder fast), and hoisted up the mainsail (storm sail) to the wind, and made (moved) toward shore (the beach).

27:41 But striking a place where two seas met, they ran the ship aground; and the prow stuck fast and remained immovable, but the stern was being broken up by the violence of the waves.

And falling into a place where two seas met (strong currents), they ran the ship aground; and the forepart (bow) stuck fast, and remained unmovable, but the hinder part (stern) was broken with the violence of the waves.

The ship gets stuck on a sandbar that has been formed by the two currents coming together. The waves are splitting the ship in half.

27:42 ¶ And the soldiers' plan was to kill the prisoners, lest any of them should swim away and escape.

Now that the ship is stuck outside the harbor, the soldiers want to kill the prisoners, including Paul. Paul has already prophesied this would not happen, but they don't care. Now that they appear to be safe, the centurion will again assume command.

27:43 But the centurion, wanting to save Paul, kept them from *their* purpose, and commanded that those who could swim should jump *overboard* first and get to land,

Paul is now responsible again for sparing lives. This time it is the prisoners. Those who can swim are commanded to dive in and head toward shore first.

27:44 and the rest, some on boards and some on *parts* of the ship. And so it was that they all escaped safely to land.

The centurion takes command, and they all make it to shore safely.

28:1–32 Paul Arrives in Rome

The Challenge of Chapter Twenty-Eight

Paul has experienced the same shipwreck as the other passengers. He is cold, tired, wet, and hungry, yet he is the only one mentioned as gathering sticks with the natives of the island to help build the fire so the other survivors can be warmed in the heat of the flames. While doing something that will benefit others, he is bitten by a venomous snake. Most would focus on the poison of the situation, but Paul doesn't even give one thought to the attack, and it has no affect on him.

When we walk with the Lord for any length of time, while doing good for others, we will eventually be unexpectedly attacked by another. The attack may come from the world outside or from someone in the family of God. Our response should be to shake off the offense, and not allow ourselves to be poisoned by the venom of unforgiveness. When we respond in this way, we will be free to bless those around us who may be weary and worn out by the storms of life.

I. Paul's Ministry on the Island of Miletas (1–11)

All passengers, in fulfillment of Paul's prophecy, make it to the shore alive, and the natives of the island build a fire for those shipwrecked to warm themselves. Paul gathers sticks to lie on the fire. When he is bitten by a venomous snake, Paul shakes the snake off his hand into the fire. The natives observe that no harm has come to Paul. The governor of the island, Publius, invites Paul to stay on his estate. Publius's father is sick, Paul prays for him, and he is healed. Others suffering from diseases then come to Paul for prayer and are healed. The people of the island bless Paul and the others from the ship who have lost everything.

> **28:1 ¶ Now when they had escaped, they then found out that the island was called Malta.**

Swimmers and nonswimmers all make it to shore and fulfilled Paul's prophecy (27:22).

> **28:2 And the natives showed us unusual kindness; for they kindled a fire and made us all welcome, because of the rain that was falling and because of the cold.**

These are unbelievers with great manners and concern for others. They do not prey on shipwrecks and kill people for their possessions. They prepare a fire for them because the survivors are wet, and it is was a very cold time of the year.

> **28:3 But when Paul had gathered a bundle of sticks and laid *them* on the fire, a viper came out because of the heat, and fastened on his hand.**

Paul is not laying on the shore with the rest of the people who are recovering from the shipwreck. He is helping start the fire. He is gathering sticks because this has always been his ministry as an under rower. Snakes become dormant in the cold. This snake has been sleeping among the sticks, and Paul does not distinguish the snake from the wood. The fire causes the snake to jump out at Paul and fasten to his hand. Its fangs are buried deep into Paul's hand.

> **28:4 So when the natives saw the creature hanging from his hand, they said to one another, "No doubt this man is a murderer, whom, though he has escaped the sea, yet justice does not allow to live."**

And when the barbarians saw the venomous beast (snake) hang on his hand, they said among themselves, No doubt this man is a murderer, whom, though he hath escaped the sea, yet vengeance (an act of the gods) suffereth not to live.

The snake keeps hanging onto Paul's hand in plain sight of everyone while they questioned and reasoned among themselves. These sinners assume the same thing many Christians do, "God is punishing him." They do not understand the tactics of Satan, therefore, they blame God for everything in life. These natives assume the god of vengeance is after Paul because he must be a murderer. They have assigned to him a sin and already judged him. Their venom is worse than that of the snake.

> **28:5 But he shook off the creature into the fire and suffered no harm.**

The snake holds fast to Paul's hand. Paul has to take authority over it (Luke 10:19, Mark 16:18) for the grip to loosen. Paul does not pry its mouth open with his other hand; God breaks the grip, and Paul suffers no harm. Paul is not too concerned about ecology. He drops the snake into the fire to be burned up! He does not release it back into its natural habitat.

28:6 However, they were expecting that he would swell up or suddenly fall down dead. But after they had looked for a long time and saw no harm come to him, they changed their minds and said that he was a god.

There are two reactions caused by this snake: An instant death or the body swelling up, causing a slow death. As these men continue to stare at Paul, neither reaction occurs. Paul is miraculously spared. Because of this, one minute Paul is a murderer in their thinking, and the next, he is a god. Because of this miracle, many people receive Jesus as savior. Because of the healing of the father of the Roman governor of the island, many more will believe and be born again. There will be a church started on Malta. Many of the Maltese believers will also be healed and taught the Word during the next three winter months Paul is with them.

28:7 ¶ In that region there was an estate of the leading citizen of the island, whose name was Publius, who received us and entertained us courteously for three days.

In the same quarters (neighborhood, area) were possessions (estates, castles) of the chief man (*protos*: governor, ruler) of the island, whose name was Publius; who received us, and lodged us three days courteously.

This is a Roman man. He officiates over this island as a Roman possession. He is rich and has a large estate. Paul's team spends three days on the estate in the castle. This is a good leader over a good island of people. He and all of his people are courteous.

28:8 And it happened that the father of Publius lay sick of a fever and dysentery. Paul went in to him and prayed, and he laid his hands on him and healed him.

And it came to pass, that the father of Publius lay sick ("and dying" [Greek]) of a fever (*puretos*: on fire, inflamed) and of a bloody flux (*dusenteria*: dysentery; *dus*: dangerous; *enteria*: intestines): to whom Paul entered in, and prayed, and laid his hands on him, and healed him.

Publius' father is bleeding from the rectum. Paul does not pray "for him," he just prays. He hears the Holy Spirit, then lays hands on him, and the man is healed by God through Paul. This opens the entire island to the gospel.

28:9 So when this was done, the rest of those on the island who had diseases also came and were healed.

So when this was done (*ginomai*: came to pass, came into being), others also, which had diseases (*astheneia*: all kinds of diseases, infirmity, sickness, weakness) in the island, came, and were healed:

The healing power of the Lord is demonstrated to show that God is no respecter of persons. Many probably think God will heal the governor's father, but not them. Paul shows God's mercy is toward all.

28:10 They also honored us in many ways; and when we departed, they provided such things as were necessary.

Who also honoured us with many honours; and when we departed, they laded (laid heavy upon) us with such things as were necessary.

They give many materialistic things to Paul and those on the ship who have lost everything. This includes food and clothing. Paul has been on the island for three months and has been treated well by these people. He has been on a three month vacation after many years of work and imprisonment.

II. Heading Toward Rome (12–16)

After three months on the island, Paul is put on a ship heading toward Rome. He finds great favor and is permitted to stay with believers in Puteoli for seven days. Once arriving in Rome, rather than being delivered to the captain of the guard, he is allowed to remain with a soldier, a private guard.

28:11 ¶ After three months we sailed in an Alexandrian ship whose figurehead was the Twin Brothers, which had wintered at the island.

The captain of this ship decides not to attempt sailing any further and remains in Malta for the winter. Castor and Pollux are the twin sons of Zeus and Lida. One was a famous horse tamer, the other a boxer. The two together are believed to be "good luck" for sailors against storms. The image of these two sons is carved on the front of this grain ship sailing from Alexandria to Rome.

28:12 And landing at Syracuse, we stayed three days.

Syracuse is a southeast port of the island of Sicily. Syracuse is a famous Greek military stronghold that is eventually conquered by Rome.

28:13 From there we circled round and reached Rhegium. And after one day the south wind blew; and the next day we came to Puteoli,

And from thence we fetched a compass (*perierchomai*: went around, wandering about), and came to Rhegium: and after one day (Paul probably prayed) the south wind blew, and we came the next day to Puteoli:

They are headed toward the straits of Messina, and the winds are unfavorable to pass through. They then sail around to Rhegium to wait for a south wind. This is the only way a ship can safely pass through and not be smashed on the rocks or drowned by the whirlpool formed by the currents. They continue on to Puteoli, a resort city in the bay of Naples. At this time, it is a very wealthy city, the home of many millionaires.

28:14 where we found brethren, and were invited to stay with them seven days. And so we went toward Rome.

Where we found brethren (believers), and were desired (asked permission) to tarry with them seven days: and so we went toward Rome.

Paul's influence on the ship is now so great he is granted permission to stay a week with the believers in Puteoli.

28:15 And from there, when the brethren heard about us, they came to meet us as far as Appii Forum and Three Inns. When Paul saw them, he thanked God and took courage.

Appii forum is ninety miles up the coast from Puteoli. Word has spread of Paul's presence and believers come to the docks to meet him. Three Taverns is the next city, famous for its taverns. Many travelers stop there. Two groups of believers travel from Rome to see Paul. One group goes forty miles and meet him at Appii forum. The others travel thirty miles and meet him at the Three Taverns. Paul takes courage at their presence. He has probably become discouraged about his mission to Rome and thinks he will be the only believer in the city. He now finds others who probably tell him of the many churches praying for him and for his visit. Paul is overjoyed and encouraged to find the gospel has been spread throughout Italy despite his own disobedience.

We may be stopped, but the gospel can never be stopped.

> **28:16 ❡ Now when we came to Rome, the centurion delivered the prisoners to the captain of the guard; but Paul was permitted to dwell by himself with the soldier who guarded him.**

Paul has so impressed the centurion that he is put in a private cell with a private guard. Paul stays here for two years before taking his fourth missionary journey. The remainder of this chapter deals with Paul's stay in prison.

III. Paul's First Meeting with the Roman Jews (17–32)

Paul is permitted to address the Roman Jews, preaching that the Messiah has already come. The hearts of the Jews in Rome are open to hearing the gospel. Paul remains in this place for two years, preaching the kingdom of God.

> **28:17 ❡ And it came to pass after three days that Paul called the leaders of the Jews together. So when they had come together, he said to them: "Men *and* brethren, though I have done nothing against our people or the customs of our fathers, yet I was delivered as a prisoner from Jerusalem into the hands of the Romans,**

Paul is now meeting with the most prominent Jews in the city. He thinks either these Jews or the Jews from Jerusalem have written ahead to the Roman government and told them Paul was coming and all the trouble he had caused him. This is probably one reason he is becoming discouraged as he comes nearer to Rome (v. 15).

> **28:18 who, when they had examined me, wanted to let *me* go, because there was no cause for putting me to death.**

The Romans could find no fault with Paul.

28:19 But when the Jews spoke against *it*, I was compelled to appeal to Caesar, not that I had anything of which to accuse my nation.

Paul is saying, "I am not here to accuse Israel before Rome."

28:20 For this reason therefore I have called for you, to see *you* and speak with *you*, because for the hope of Israel I am bound with this chain."

Paul is preaching the Jewish message, but instead of the Messiah coming, Paul preaches He has come.

28:21 ¶ Then they said to him, "We neither received letters from Judea concerning you, nor have any of the brethren who came reported or spoken any evil of you.

The Jews of Jerusalem think Paul is dead. When he was put on the first ship from Adramyttium, they believed he would never make it to Rome. They forgot about Paul, and never told the Roman Jews what they had done.

28:22 But we desire to hear from you what you think; for concerning this sect, we know that it is spoken against everywhere."

But we desire to hear of (from) thee what thou thinkest: for as concerning this sect (faction, heresy [24: 5, 24]), we know that every where it is spoken against.

They want to hear and be objective about Christianity. This is probably a great revelation to Paul. He had such a great desire to go to Jerusalem that he was willing to miss the will of God entirely. He did what he wanted to do and met opposition to the gospel, and not one Jew received Jesus because Paul never had an opportunity to preach. God's intention was for Paul to preach in Rome and He had to work a miracle to get Paul there safely. Now Paul sees the open hearts of the Jews in Rome and realizes God knew the condition of their hearts the entire time. God sends us to places where hearts are open and people will listen.

28:23 ¶ So when they had appointed him a day, many came to him at *his* lodging, to whom he explained and solemnly testified

of the kingdom of God, persuading them concerning Jesus from both the Law of Moses and the Prophets, from morning till evening.

Paul uses the Old Testament to persuade them of Jesus as Messiah of Israel.

28:24 And some were persuaded by the things which were spoken, and some disbelieved.

This is the usual response to the gospel. Yet, this is a better response to the gospel than Paul received at Jerusalem.

28:25–27 So when they did not agree among themselves, they departed after Paul had said one word: "The Holy Spirit spoke rightly through Isaiah the prophet to our fathers, 26 saying,

> *Go to this people and say:*
> *"Hearing you will hear, and shall not understand;*
> *And seeing you will see, and not perceive;*

> *27 For the hearts of this people have grown dull.*
> *Their ears are hard of hearing,*
> *And their eyes they have closed,*
> *Lest they should see with their eyes and hear with*
> *   their ears,*
> *Lest they should understand with their hearts*
> *   and turn,*
> *So that I should heal them." '*

Paul is quoting Isaiah 6:9 and 10 here. Because of their negative attitude toward the Lord, they may hear and see physically, but never have their spiritual eyes and ears been opened (cf. Proverbs 4:20–22, Matthew 13:13–17).

28:28 ¶ "Therefore let it be known to you that the salvation of God has been sent to the Gentiles, and they will hear it!"

Paul explains, "You are no longer under the age of Israel, the Jewish dispensation, but the Church age, the age of the Gentiles."

28:29 And when he had said these words, the Jews departed and had a great dispute among themselves.

This verse is not found in the original text.

28:30 ¶ Then Paul dwelt two whole years in his own rented house, and received all who came to him,

These are Gentiles who want to grow in the Word and those who need salvation.

28:31 preaching the kingdom of God and teaching the things which concern the Lord Jesus Christ with all confidence, no one forbidding him.

"Preaching" is to unbelievers and "teaching" is to believers. Paul ministers in peace for two years under Roman protection.

Reference Book List

Barclay, William, 1976. *New Testament Words*. Westminster: John Knox Press.

Jamison, Robert; Brown, David & Fausset, A.R., 1997. *A Commentary on the Old and New Testaments* (3 Volume Set). Peabody, MA: Hendrickson Publishers.

Strong, James H., 1980. 15th Edition. *Strong's Exhaustive Concordance of the Bible*. Nashville, TN: Abingdon Press.

Strong, James & Thayer, Joseph, 1995. *Thayers Greek-English Lexicon of the New Testament: Coded with Strong's Concordance Numbers*. Peabody, MA: Hendrickson Publishers.

Unger, Merrill, 1996. *Vine's Complete Expository Dictionary of Old and New Testament Words: With Topical Index*. Nashville, TN: Thomas Nelson.

Vincent, Marvin R., 1985. *Vincent Word Studies in the New Testament* (4 Volume Set). Peabody, MA: Hendrickson Publishers.

Wuest, Kenneth, 1980, Second Edition. *Word Studies from the Greek New Testament* (4 Volume Set). Grand Rapids: MI: William B. Eerdmans Publishing Company.

Zodhiates, Spiros, 1991. *The Complete Word Study New Testatment* (Word Study Series). Chatanooga, TN: AMG Publishers.

The writings of Arthur W. Pink.

The writings and audio recordings of Donald Grey Barnhouse.

Meet Bob Yandian

From 1980 to 2013, Bob Yandian was the pastor of Grace Church in his hometown of Tulsa, Oklahoma. After 33 years, he left the church to his son, Robb, with a strong and vibrant congregation. During those years, he raised up and sent out hundreds of ministers to churches and missions organizations in the United States and around the world. He has authored over thirty books and established a worldwide ministry to pastors and ministers.

He is widely acknowledged as one of the most knowledgeable Bible teachers of this generation. His practical insight and wisdom into the Word of God has helped countless people around the world to live successfully in every area of the daily Christian life.

Bob attended Southwestern College and is also a graduate of Trinity Bible College. He has served as both instructor and Dean of Instructors at Rhema Bible Training Center in Broken Arrow, Oklahoma.

Bob has traveled extensively throughout the United States and internationally, taking his powerful and easy to apply teachings that bring stability and hope to hungry hearts everywhere. He is called "a pastor to pastors."

Bob and his wife, Loretta, have been married for over forty years, are parents of two married children, and have five grandchildren. Bob and Loretta Yandian reside in Tulsa, Oklahoma.

Contact Bob Yandian Ministries

Email: bym@bobyandian.com
Phone:
(918) 250-2207
Mailing Address:
Bob Yandian Ministries
PO Box 55236
Tulsa, OK 74155
www.bobyandian.com

Other Books by Bob Yandian

Calling and Separation
Decently and in Order
Faith's Destination
From Just Enough to Overflowing
God's Word to Pastors
How Deep Are the Stripes?
Leadership Secrets of David the King
Morning Moments
One Flesh
Proverbs
Spirit Controlled Life
The Bible and National Defense
Understanding End Times
Unlimited Partnership
What If the Best Is Yet to Come?
When God Is Silent
From *A New Testament Commentary* Series (sold individually or as a set):

> *Acts*
> *Colossians*
> *Ephesians*
> *Galatians*
> *James*
> *Philippians*
> *Romans*

PRAYER OF SALVATION

God loves you— no matter who you are, no matter what your past. God loves you so much that he gave his one and only begotten Son for you. The Bible tells us that "…whoever believes in him shall not perish but have eternal life" (John 3:16 NIV). Jesus laid down His life and rose again so that we could spend eternity with Him and experience His absolute best on earth. If you would like to receive Jesus into your life, say the following prayer out loud and mean it in your heart.

Heavenly Father, I come to you admitting that I am a sinner. Right now, I choose to turn away from sin, and I ask you to cleanse me of all unrighteousness. I believe that Your son, Jesus, died on the cross to take away my sins. I also believe that he rose again from the dead so that I might be forgiven of my sins and made righteous through faith in him. I call upon the name of Jesus Christ to be the Savior and Lord of my life. Jesus, I choose to follow You and ask that You fill me with the power of the Holy Spirit. I declare that, right now, I am a child of God. I am free from sin and full of the righteousness of God. I am saved in Jesus' name. Amen.

If you prayed this prayer to receive Jesus Christ as your Savior for the first time, please contact us to receive a free book:

www.harrisonhouse.com
Harrison House
PO Box 35035
Tulsa, Oklahoma 74153

Fast. Easy.
Convenient.

For the latest Harrison House product information and author news, look no further than your computer. All the details on our powerful, life-changing products are just a click away. New releases, email subscriptions, testimonies, monthly specials — find them all in one place. Visit harrisonhouse.com today!

harrisonhouse.com

Prayer Journal

Say with your lips, I am Ruled

I commel — to &!